HOW TO BE AN EVEN BETTER MANAGER

THIRD EDITION

MICHAEL ARMSTRONG

KOGAN PAGE

First published in Great Britain in 1983 by
Kogan Page Limited, 120 Pentonville Road,
London N1 9JN, entitled *How To Be a Better Manager.*
Second edition, 1988, *How To Be an Even Better Manager.*
Third edition 1990.

British Library Cataloguing in Publication Data
A CIP record for this book is available from the British Library.

ISBN 0–7494–0000–0
ISBN 0–7494–0293–8 Pbk

Typeset by DP Photosetting, Aylesbury, Bucks
Printed and bound in Great Britain by
Biddles Limited, Guildford

Contents

Foreword to the Third Edition

This substantially revised edition is designed to reflect the new demands which are being made on managers in the 1990s. They have arisen because of the phenomenon of change and its impact on attitudes and firms.

The phenomenon of change

The economics and business environment has become much more turbulent, uncertain and demanding. Tom Peters (41)* in *Thriving on Chaos* has referred to 'an era of unprecedented change' and suggested that 'predictability is a thing of the past'.

Environmental change has taken place in a number of ways as described below:

- Economic and political change has seen the rise in recent years of the enterprise culture and its associated phenomenon, the market economy. However, in the late 1980s in the light of Wall Street and City scandals people were beginning to question whether an approach to management based purely on greed was appropriate. Hence the increasing importance attached to mission and value statements, which are dealt with in this edition.
- In the 1980s social change produced a trend towards individualism and away from collectivism, although it is now realized that the flatter, decentralized and flexible firm of the 1990s will have to rely more on commitment and teamwork.
- Consumer expectations are higher than ever before. Consumers want

---

* The numbers in brackets after authors' names refer to the General Bibliography; see page 330.

value for money, as always, but they are now demanding, quite rightly, higher standards of quality and service.
- The business environment is changing significantly with an emphasis on growth, a rash of takeovers and acquisitions and increased competition from Europe, Japan and from multinational firms.
- Product life cycles are shorter and firms must innovate to sustain their competitive advantage and to establish and maintain their position in increasingly segmented markets.
- New technology is playing a much greater part in the management process in so far as process is largely concerned with information flows.

The impact of change on attitudes

A new managerial revolution has taken place over the last decade. Attitudes have changed in the following directions:

- *The market place.* It is at last recognized that organizations are market driven and that management must be market-orientated.
- *Customers.* Customer care and service has become a major feature in marketing strategies.
- *Excellence.* Peters and Waterman (42) in *In Search of Excellence* initiated what has become almost a cult of excellence. ICL, for example, in its message to all employees has stated that 'ICL's sights are now set on world success. That demands excellence in everything we undertake. And excellence will be achieved only by adopting "can do" attitudes and the highest levels of cooperation and commitment throughout the organization.'
- *Turbulence.* Managements are beginning to accept turbulence as a way of life. Tom Peters (41) has redefined his original definition of excellence to read:

> Excellent firms don't believe in excellence – only in constant improvement and constant change. That is, excellent firms of tomorrow will cherish impermanence and thrive on chaos.

The impact of change on the firm

Environmental and technological developments have resulted in fundamental changes to the ways in which firms are structured and managed.
We now have:

- *The responsive firm* which has to react quickly to changes in the marketplace and in customer needs and preferences.
- *The proactive firm* which has to make markets as well as adapt itself to them.
- *The flexible firm* which has to adjust its structure, its product range, its marketing strategies and manufacturing facilities quickly to respond to and, more important, anticipate change.
- *The information-based firm* which will be knowledge-orientated and composed largely of specialists who direct and discipline their own performance through organized feedback from colleagues, customers, and the strategic business units into which the organization is divided in accordance with the markets it serves. Peter Drucker (13) in an article in the *Harvard Business Review* has suggested that: 'Information is data endowed with meaning and purpose.' And it is on this basis that many organizations are rethinking the ways in which they are managed.
- *The compact firm* which has a flatter organization structure because superfluous layers of management have been stripped away. Peter Drucker followed up his remarks about new technology quoted above with the comment that many organizations have not rethought their structures in the light of its availability: 'Whole new layers of management neither make decisions nor lead. Instead their main, if not their only function, is to serve as 'relays' – human boosters for the faint unfocused signals that pass for communications in the traditional pre-information organization.'
- *The decentralized firm* which consists of strategic business units placed firmly in their market niches and capable of responding quickly to opportunities. These units are tightly managed to achieve well-defined goals with the minimum of interference from above.
- *The global firm* which is operating across many international boundaries.

The impact on managers

Managers have to learn to exist with change, like the organizations in which they work. They have to be more flexible and more responsive to new and challenging demands.

In the decentralized organization of today they must be able to operate independently – the very essence of effective managers is that they achieve the goals they set themselves. But in the flatter organization they also have to be good team workers able to deploy a wider range of skills in working with others across organizational boundaries.

These demands can result in role conflict and role ambiguity, which can produce stress, and stress management is a new topic included in this edition. People generally prefer to work in an orderly structure which provides a framework within which they have a fair degree of autonomy. They prefer to know where they stand and where they are going. They like a certain amount of predictability and, although they welcome variety, it has to be within reasonable bounds. But life in organizations is not like that. Change, uncertainty and ambiguity are ever present. Organizations are supposed to behave rationally, progressing steadily from A to B. But they don't. They consist of webs of power and politics and proceed by fits and starts.

The balancing act practised by all managers is between the need for order and continuity and the demands of the situation, which involve flexibility and discontinuity. Organizations suffer too. As Rosabeth Moss Kanter points out in *When Giants Learn to Dance* (28), businesses and managers are continually being bombarded with conflicting advice on these and many other matters.

This edition addresses these matters by re-examining the role of management in the introductory chapter and the concept of organizational effectiveness in a new chapter (36). Another new chapter (46) has been included describing strategic management as a means of increasing the ability of organizations to define the direction they are going in in conditions of turbulence. The chapters on change management (5) and power and politics (40) have also been expanded. The need for managers to pay even more attention to developing their careers in the new organizations of the 1990s has been responded to by extending the chapter concerned with getting on (21). In other chapters changes have been made to reflect new approaches to management, many of them based on the writer's recent experience as a consultant specializing in strategic management issues.

Introduction:
On being a better manager

However good you are – or think you are – you can always get better.
That's the theme of this book. It is about self-development and as Peter
Drucker wrote in *The Effective Executive* (15):

> Self-development of the effective executive is central to the development of
> the organization.

You may already be a good manager, but to be an even better one it is
worth spending some time increasing your understanding of:

- What management is about
- The aims of management
- The processes of management
- Managerial roles
- Managerial qualities
- The role of experience
- The role of personality
- What you can do.

This introductory chapter reviews each of these overall requirements as a
lead to the 50 specific areas of management covered by this book.

What is management?

Essentially, management is about deciding what to do and then getting it
done through people. This definition emphasizes that people are the most
important resource available to managers. It is through this resource that
all the other resources – knowledge, finance, materials, plant, equipment,
etc – will be managed.

However, managers are there to achieve results. To do this they have to
deal with events and eventualities. They may do this primarily through
people, but an over-emphasis on the people content of management diverts

15

attention from the fact that in managing events managers have to be personally involved. They manage themselves as well as other people. They cannot delegate everything. They frequently have to rely on their own resources to get things done. These resources consist of experience, know-how, skill and, most important, time – all of which have to be deployed not only in directing and motivating people but also in understanding situations and issues, problem analysis and definition, decision-making and taking direct action themselves as well as through other people. They will get support, advice and assistance from their staff, but in the last analysis they are on their own. They have to make the decisions and they have to initiate and sometimes take the action. A chairman fighting a takeover bid will get lots of advice but he will personally manage the crisis, talking directly to the financial institutions, merchant banks, financial analysts, City editors and the mass of shareholders.

The basic definition of management should therefore be extended to read 'deciding what to do and then getting it done through the effective use of resources'. The most important part of management will indeed be getting things done through people, but managers will be concerned directly or indirectly with all other resources, including their own.

The aims of management

Management is a process which exists to get results by making the best use of the human, financial and material resources available to the organization and to individual managers. It is very much concerned with adding value to these resources, and this added value depends on the expertise and commitment of the people who are responsible for managing the business.

The processes of management

The overall process of management is subdivided into a number of individual processes which are methods of operation specially designed to assist in the achievement of objectives. Their purpose is to bring as much system, order, predictability, logic and consistency to the task of management as possible in the ever-changing, varied and turbulent environment in which managers work. The main processes of management were defined by the classical theorists of management as:

1. *Planning* – deciding on a course of action to achieve a desired result and focusing attention on objectives and standards and the programmes required to achieve the objectives.

2. *Organizing* – setting up and staffing the most appropriate organization to achieve the aim.
3. *Motivating* – exercising leadership to motivate people to work together smoothly and to the best of their ability as part of a team.
4. *Controlling* – measuring and monitoring the progress of work in relation to the plan and taking corrective action when required.

But this classical view has been challenged by the empiricists, such as Rosemary Stewart (48) and Henry Minzberg (37), who studied how managers actually spend their time. They observed that the work of managers is fragmented, varied, subjected to continual adjustment and governed to a large degree by events over which the manager has little control and by a dynamic network of interrelationships with other people. Managers exist to control their environment but sometimes it controls them. They may consciously or unconsciously seek to plan, organize, direct and control but their days almost inevitably become a jumbled sequence of events.

To the empiricists, management is a process involving a mix of rational, logical, problem-solving, decision-making activities and intuitive, judgemental activities. It is therefore both science and art.

Managers carry out their work on a day-to-day basis in conditions of endless variety, turbulence and unpredictability. A single word to describe all these features would be chaos. Tom Peters (41), however, in *Thriving in Chaos* has suggested that it is possible for managers to thrive on chaos.

Managers also have to be specialists in ambiguity, with the ability to cope with conflicting and unclear requirements, as Rosabeth Moss Kanter (28) has demonstrated.

Managerial roles

During the course of a typical day a chief executive may well meet the marketing director to discuss the programme for launching a new product, the personnel director to decide how best to reorganize the distribution department, the production director to ask him why costs per unit of output are going up and what he is going to do about it, and the finance director to review the latest set of management accounts before the next board meeting. These activities could be categorized under the headings of planning, organizing, directing and controlling, but the chief executive would not have attached these labels when deciding how to spend his time (in so far as there was any choice). The fact that these processes took place was imposed by the situation and the need to exercise one or more of the roles inherent in the manager's job. These roles are fundamentally concerned with:

- Getting things done – maintaining momentum and making things happen
- Finding out what is going on
- Reacting to new situations and problems
- Responding to demands and requests.

They involve a great deal of interpersonal relations, data processing and decision-making.

Henry Minzberg (37) in *The Nature of Managerial Work* has suggested that managerial activities can be divided into ten roles within the three groups of interpersonal roles, informational roles and decisional roles.

Managerial qualities

Pedlar, Burgoyne and Boydell (39) in *A Manager's Guide to Self-Development* suggest, on the basis of their extensive research, that there are 11 qualities or attributes which are possessed by successful managers:

1. Command of basic facts.
2. Relevant professional knowledge.
3. Continuing sensitivity to events.
4. Analytical, problem-solving and decision/judgement-making skills.
5. Social skills and abilities.
6. Emotional resilience.
7. Proactivity.
8. Creativity.
9. Mental agility.
10. Balanced learning habits and skills.
11. Self-knowledge.

The role of experience

'How can I develop these qualities?' A familiar answer to this question is to say that 'managers learn to manage by managing under the guidance of a good manager'. But can experience alone be the best teacher? Several writers have expressed their doubts on this score. Tennyson called it 'a dirty nurse'. Oscar Wilde noted that 'experience is the name everyone gives to their mistakes'. And the historian Froude wrote that 'experience teaches slowly and at the cost of mistakes'.

Experience is an essential way of learning to improve but it is an imperfect instrument. We also need guidance – from a good manager *and* from other sources such as this book – which will help us to interpret experience, learn from our mistakes and make better use of our experience in the future.

The role of personality

'Managers are born not made.' This is the discouraging answer which has been given to the manager who seeks a way to improve himself. The implication that neither experience nor study can be beneficial is of course unacceptable, but the statement does contain some truth in that our personality strongly influences the way in which we manage and our effectiveness as a manager.

Studies carried out on the qualities displayed by successful top managers as quoted by Rosemary Stewart (48) in *Managers and Their Jobs* show a number of common characteristics, such as:

- A willingness to work hard
- Perseverance and determination
- A willingness to take risks
- An ability to inspire enthusiasm
- Toughness.

Psychologists claim that personality is formed in the early years of life. Apparently it is in the cradle, or at least in the nursery, that we learn to be ruthless. If this is the case, maybe there is not much we can do about it when we grow up and become managers. Spending ten minutes every morning before a mirror practising being ruthless may not get us very far. Neither will much good come from our boss's exhortations to display different personality characteristics, or from attending lectures, or reading management textbooks. We can, however, modify the way in which we behave – the way in which we use our personalities. And guidance – not exhortations – from outside sources as well as from within should help. If we know what we are looking for we are more likely to find it.

What you can do

Perhaps Francis Bacon provided the best answer to this question when he wrote: 'Studies perfect nature and are perfected by experience.'

19

The art of management – and it is an art – is important enough to be studied. The aim of such studies should be to help us to make better use of our natural attributes – our personality and intelligence – and to ensure that past experience is better interpreted and more fully used, and that future experience is more quickly and purposefully absorbed.

How this book can help you to become an even better manager

This book contains 50 chapters, which are arranged in alphabetical order for ease of reference. No book can contain all the answers, neither can it offer prescriptions to cover every eventuality – ultimately, what you do will be largely determined by the situation in which you find yourself. But this book does provide guidelines which will help you to build your managerial knowledge and skills. These cover the following areas:

- *Personal development*

  - achieving results (Chapter 1)
  - assertiveness (Chapter 2)
  - getting on (Chapter 21)
  - stress management (Chapter 47)

- *Factors contributing to success*

  - cost cutting (Chapter 12)
  - efficiency and effectiveness (Chapter 18)
  - entrepreneurship (Chapter 19)
  - excellence (Chapter 20)
  - how things go wrong (Chapter 22)
  - organizational effectiveness (Chapter 35)
  - productivity improvement (Chapter 43)
  - profit improvement (Chapter 44)
  - trouble shooting (Chapter 50)

- *Management processes*

  - budgeting (Chapter 3)
  - corporate culture (Chapter 11)
  - mission and value statements (Chapter 31)
  - organizing (Chapter 36)
  - policies (Chapter 39)
  - power and politics (Chapter 40)
  - strategic planning (Chapter 46)

- *Management skills and techniques*

  - case presentation (Chapter 4)

- change management (Chapter 5)
- clear thinking (Chapter 6)
- communicating (Chapter 7)
- conflict management (Chapter 8)
- controlling (Chapter 9)
- coordinating (Chapter 10)
- counselling (Chapter 13)
- creative thinking (Chapter 14)
- crisis management (Chapter 15)
- delegation (Chapter 16)
- developing people (Chapter 17)
- innovating (Chapter 23)
- integrating (Chapter 24)
- interviewing (Chapter 25)
- leadership (Chapter 26)
- listening (Chapter 27)
- managerial planning (Chapter 28)
- managing your boss (Chapter 29)
- meetings (Chapter 30)
- motivating (Chapter 32)
- negotiating (Chapter 33)
- objectives and targets (Chapter 34)
- performance management (Chapter 37)
- persuading (Chapter 38)
- presentations (Chapter 41)
- problem-solving and decision-making (Chapter 42)
- report writing (Chapter 45)
- team building (Chapter 48)
- time management (Chapter 49).

Note: Masculine pronouns have been used throughout the book for convenience and conciseness, though feminine pronouns are, in most cases, equally applicable.

Chapter 1
Achieving results

Achieving results, getting things done, making things happen. That is what management is all about.

It can be said that there are three sorts of managers: those who make things happen, those who watch things happening, and those who don't know what is happening. Before finding out how to get into the first category, there are three questions to answer:

- Is getting things done simply a matter of personality – characteristics like drive, decisiveness, leadership, ambition – which some people have and others haven't?
- And if you haven't got the drive, decisiveness and so forth which it takes, is there anything you can do about it?
- To what extent is an ability to make things happen a matter of using techniques which can be learnt and developed?

Personality is important. Unless you have willpower and drive nothing will get done. But remember that your personality is a function of both nature and nurture. You are born with certain characteristics. Upbringing, education, training and, above all, experience, develop you into the person you are.

We may not be able to change our personality which, according to Freud, is formed in the first few years of life. But we can develop and adapt it by consciously learning from our own experience and by observing and analysing other people's behaviour.

Techniques for achieving results, such as planning, organizing, delegating, communicating, motivating and controlling, can be learnt. These are dealt with later in this book. But these techniques are only as effective as the person who uses them. They must be applied in the right way and in the right circumstances. And you still have to use your experience to select the right technique and your personality to make it work.

To become a person who makes things happen you therefore have to develop skills and capacities by a process of understanding, observation, analysis and learning. The four actions you should take are:

1. Understand what makes achievers tick – the personality characteristics they display in getting things done.
2. Observe what achievers do – how they operate, what techniques they use.
3. Analyse your own behaviour (*behaviour*, not personality), compare it with that of high achievers, and think how to improve your effectiveness.
4. Learn as much as you can about the management techniques available.

What makes achievers tick?

David McClelland (34) of Harvard University carried out extensive research into what motivates managers. He interviewed, observed and analysed numbers of managers at their place of work and recorded findings before producing his theory. And before you dismiss anything which comes under the heading of theory, remember what Douglas McGregor (36) of the Massachusetts Institute of Technology, said: 'There is nothing so practical as a good theory.'

McClelland identified three needs which he believes are key factors in motivating managers. These are:

- The need for achievement
- The need for power (having control and influence over people)
- The need for affiliation (to be accepted by others).

All effective managers have these needs to a certain degree, but by far the most important one is achievement.

Achievement is what counts and achievers, according to McClelland, have these characteristics:

- They set themselves realistic but achievable goals with some 'stretch' built in.
- They prefer situations which they themselves can influence rather than those on which chance has a large influence.
- They are more concerned with knowing they have done well than with the rewards that success brings.
- They get their rewards from their accomplishment rather than from money or praise. This does not mean that high achievers reject money, which does in fact motivate them as long as it is seen as a realistic measure of their performance.

23

- High achievers are most effective in situations where they are allowed to get ahead by their own efforts.

What do achievers do?

High achievers do some, if not all, of these things:

1. They define to themselves precisely what they want to do.
2. They set demanding but not unattainable time-scales in which to do it.
3. They convey clearly what they want done and by when.
4. They are prepared to discuss how things should be done and will listen to and take advice. But once the course of action has been agreed they stick to it unless events dictate a change of direction.
5. They are single-minded about getting where they want to go, showing perseverance and determination in the face of adversity.
6. They demand high performance from themselves and are somewhat callous in expecting equally high performance from everyone else.
7. They work hard and work well under pressure; in fact, it brings out the best in them.
8. They tend to be dissatisfied with the status quo.
9. They are never completely satisfied with their own performance and continually question themselves.
10. They will take calculated risks.
11. They snap out of setbacks without being personally shattered and quickly regroup their forces and their ideas.
12. They are enthusiastic about the task and convey their enthusiasm to others.
13. They are decisive in the sense that they are able quickly to sum up situations, define alternative courses of action, determine the preferred course, and convey to their subordinates what needs to be done.
14. They continually monitor their own and their subordinates' performance so that any deviation can be corrected in good time.

How to analyse your own behaviour

It is no good trying to analyse your own behaviour unless you have criteria against which you can measure your performance. You have to set standards for yourself, and if you don't meet them, ask yourself why. The answer should tell you what to do next time.

The basic questions you should ask yourself are:

- What did I set out to do?
- Did I get it done?
- If I did, why and how did I succeed?
- If not, why not?

The aim is to make effective use of your experience.

Use the list of things that high achievers do to check your own behaviour and actions. If your performance has not been up to scratch under any of these headings, ask yourself specifically what went wrong and decide how you are going to overcome this difficulty next time. This is not always easy. It is hard to admit to yourself, for example, that you have not been sufficiently enthusiastic. It may be even harder to decide what to do about it. You don't want to enthuse all over the place, indiscriminately. But you can consider whether there are better ways of displaying and conveying your enthusiasm to others in order to carry them with you.

Learning

There are a number of management techniques that you need to know about. These techniques are discussed in subsequent chapters in this book. The ones you should be particularly interested in are:

- Planning
- Objective and target setting
- Decision-making
- Delegating
- Communicating
- Motivating
- Leadership
- Coordinating
- Controlling.

Conclusion

This process of observation, analysis and learning will help you to become an achiever. But remember, achieving results is ultimately about making promises – to others and to yourself – and keeping them. Robert Townsend (51), in his book *Up the Organization*, has some excellent advice: 'Promises: keep. If asked when you can deliver something ask for time to think. Build in a margin of safety. Name a date. Then deliver it earlier than you promised.'

Chapter 2
Assertiveness

Assertion and aggression

Assertiveness, as defined by Ken and Kate Back (3) in *Assertiveness at Work*, is:

- Standing up for your own rights in such a way that you do not violate another person's rights
- Expressing your needs, wants, opinions, feelings and beliefs in direct, honest and appropriate ways.

When you are being assertive you are not, therefore, being aggressive, which means violating or ignoring other people's rights in order to get your own way or dominate a situation. Aggressive behaviour causes two counter-productive reactions: fight or flight. In other words, aggression either breeds aggression, which gets you nowhere, or it forces people to retreat in a demoralized or dissatisfied way. Inducing this sort of behaviour will not help to achieve your aim of getting them to go along with you.

Assertive behaviour

Behaving assertively puts you into the position of being able to influence people properly and react to them positively. Assertive statements:

- Are brief and to the point
- Indicate clearly that you are not hiding behind something or someone and are speaking for yourself by using words such as: 'I think that . . .', 'I believe that . . .', 'I feel that . . .', – your beliefs and views are important
- Are not overweighted with advice

- Use questions to find out the views of others and to test their reactions to your behaviour
- Distinguish between fact and opinion
- Are expressed positively but not dogmatically
- Indicate that you are aware that the other people have different points of view
- Express, when necessary, negative feelings about the effects of other people's behaviour on you – pointing out in dispassionate and factual terms the feelings aroused in you by the behaviour, and suggesting the behaviour you would prefer
- Point out to people politely but firmly the consequences of their behaviour.

Handling aggression

If you are faced by aggression, take a breath, count up to ten and then:

- Ask calmly for information about what is bugging the aggressors
- State clearly, and again calmly, the position as you see it
- Empathize with the aggressors by making it plain that you can see it from their point of view, but at the same time explaining in a matter-of-fact way how you see the discrepancy between what they believe and what you feel is actually happening
- Indicate, if the aggressive behaviour persists, your different beliefs or feelings, but do not cut aggressors short – people often talk, or even shout, themselves out of being aggressive when they realize that you are not reacting aggressively and that their behaviour is not getting them anywhere
- Suggest, if all else fails, that you leave it for the time being and talk about it again after a cooling-off period.

Influencing skills

Assertiveness is about fighting your own corner. You have to believe in yourself and what you are doing and express these beliefs confidently and without hesitation. It is about using influencing skills.

There are four influencing styles you can use:

1. *Asserting* – making your views clear.
2. *Persuading* – using facts, logic and reason to present your own case, emphasizing its strong points (benefits to the organization or the

individual(s) you are dealing with), anticipating objections to any apparent weaknesses and appealing to reason.

3. *Bridging* – drawing out other people's points of view, demonstrating that you understand what they are getting at, giving credit and praise in response to their good ideas and suggestions, joining your views with theirs.

4. *Attracting* – conveying your enthusiasm for your ideas, getting people to feel that they are all part of an exciting project.

Chapter 3
Budgeting

The need for budgets

Budgets don't win friends but they do influence people. They can be painful to create and agonizing to manage. But they do translate policy into financial terms and, whether we like it or not, that is the way in which plans must be expressed and, ultimately, performance controlled.

Budgets are needed for three reasons:

- To show the financial implications of plans
- To define the resources required to achieve the plans
- To provide a means of measuring, monitoring and controlling results against the plans.

Limitations of budgets

The main problems in budgeting are:

- An inadequate basic budgeting procedure: imprecise guidelines, unsatisfactory background data, cumbersome systems, lack of technical advice and assistance to managers, arbitrary cuts by top management
- An unskilled or cynical approach by managers to budgeting, resulting from inadequate basic procedures, lack of guidance, training or encouragement or a feeling that budgets are simply weapons to be deployed against them, rather than tools for them to use
- Lack of accurate forecasts of future activity levels
- Difficulty in amending the budget in response to changing circumstances
- The fundamental weakness of basing budgets on past levels of

expenditure which are simply 'plussed up' rather than subjecting the whole of the budget to a critical examination

- Weaknesses in reporting or controlling procedures which prevent the budget being used to monitor performance.

Preparing budgets

Most of the problems concerning the preparation of budgets mentioned above can be reduced, if not eliminated, if the following steps are taken:

1. Prepare budget guidelines which set out policies on where you want to go and, broadly, how you want to get there. These could be expressed as targets, for sales production or activity levels, and as an outline of the major marketing and production plans. In addition, the assumptions to be used in budgeting should be given. These could include rates of inflation and increases in costs and prices.
2. Ensure that those responsible for preparing budgets are given advice and encouragement by management accountants. These experts should be there to help, not to prod or threaten.
3. Get people to think hard about their budgets. They should not be allowed just to update last year's actuals. Wherever there is any choice on how much is spent, they should be asked to go back to first principles and justify what they are doing (zero-base budgeting).
4. Do not accept any significant increase or even decrease from last year's budget without an explanation.
5. Probe to ensure that budgets submitted to you are realistic and do not include a 'fudge factor'.
6. Do not slash budgets arbitrarily. Give reasons. If you don't, you will get 'fudge factors' or a couldn't-care-less attitude.
7. Update or 'flex' budgets regularly, especially when activity levels and costs are subject to large variations.

Zero-base budgeting

The traditional approach to budgeting tends to perpetuate the commitments of previous years. For instance, past levels of expenditure are used as a base from which to project increases or decreases. Only part of the budget is analysed, and managers concentrate on justifying increases, rather than challenging the need for any function or activity in its present form.

Zero-base or priority-based budgeting requires budget managers systematically to re-evaluate all their activities and programmes in order to establish their relative priority and decide whether they should be eliminated or funded at a reduced, similar or increased level. Appropriate funding levels will be determined by the priorities established by top management and the overall availability of funds.

Each activity is broken down into defined decision units, and each unit is analysed to establish:

- Its objectives
- The activities carried out
- The present costs of these activities
- The benefits resulting from each activity
- The standards and other performance measures that exist
- Alternative ways of achieving objectives
- Priorities among the objectives
- The advantages and disadvantages of incurring different levels of expenditure.

This is a fairly exhaustive list, and the amount of detail you want to pursue will depend on the importance you attach to a rigorous examination of expenditure. Zero-base budgeting is no panacea and it has often failed because companies have introduced over-elaborate procedures which have sunk almost without trace in a sea of paperwork. But the approach is right: cost control is about challenging and justifying proposed expenditures as well as monitoring what has actually been spent. The most elaborate control system in the world is useless if its foundation is unsound. Zero-base budgeting techniques should be used by managers to develop an attitude of mind in which they examine and control all their activities and attach priorities to them. The techniques should not be used in a threatening way. The emphasis should be on their value in getting priorities right and ensuring that costs and benefits are thoroughly reviewed to the advantage of all concerned.

Flexible budgets

If it is possible, with a reasonable degree of accuracy, to relate changes in income and costs to levels of activity, the use of flexible budgets is worthwhile. Budgets are 'flexed' by recalculating income and costs which vary with activity levels by reference to actual activity levels, thus giving an 'expected' level of income and costs. The difference between the original and expected levels is termed an 'activity variance' and the difference between expected levels and actual levels is termed a 'controllable variance'. It is on the latter figure that you must concentrate if you want a realistic picture of how costs are performing.

If a full system of flexible budgetary control cannot be operated because of the difficulty of relating costs accurately to activity levels, you should consider introducing an updating system. This means that periodically during the year the budget is revised to meet changing conditions. This is sometimes called a rolling budget and, while it is not so effective as the fully flexible system, it is easier to operate.

Budgetary control

A budgetary control procedure is not easy to achieve. You have to work at it. There is no problem in designing a system with elegant forms and lots of information. The difficulty is in maintaining the scheme as a useful instrument once it has been set up. The impetus can only come from the top. The chief executive must insist on a rigorous approach to building budgets and a reporting procedure which is used to make things happen the way he wants them to happen. And he must ensure that everyone concerned knows what is expected of him and is accountable for any failure to perform.

Chapter 4
Case presentation

As a manager, you will frequently have to make out a case for what you think should be done. You have to persuade people to believe in your views and accept your recommendations. To do this, you must have a clear idea of what you want, and you have to show that you believe in it yourself. Above all, the effectiveness of your presentation will depend upon the care with which you have prepared it.

Preparation

Thorough preparation is vital. You must think through not only what should be done and why, but also how people will react. Only then can you decide how to make your case: stressing the benefits without underestimating the costs, and anticipating objections.

You should think of the questions your audience is likely to raise, and answer them in advance, or at least have your answers ready. The most likely questions are:

What – is the proposal?
      – will be the benefit?
      – will it cost?
      – are the facts, figures, forecasts and assumptions upon which the proposal is based?
      – are the alternatives?
Why – should we change what we are doing now?
      – is this proposal or solution better than the alternatives?
How – is the change to be made?
      – are the snags to be overcome?
      – have the alternatives been examined?
      – am I affected by the change?

Who – will be affected by the change and what will be their reaction?
 – is likely to have the strongest views for or against the change, and why?
 – will implement the proposal?
When – should this be done?

To make your case you have to do three things:

1. Show that it is based on a thorough analysis of the facts and that the alternatives were properly evaluated before the conclusion was reached. If you have made assumptions, you must demonstrate that these are reasonable on the basis of relevant experience and justifiable projections, which allow for the unexpected. Bear in mind Robert Heller's words (24) that 'a proposal is only as strong as its weakest assumption'.

2. Spell out the benefits – to the company *and* the individuals to whom the case is being made. Wherever possible, express benefits in financial terms. Abstract benefits, such as customer satisfaction or workers' morale, are difficult to sell. But don't produce 'funny numbers' – financial justifications which will not stand up to examination.

3. Reveal costs. Don't try to disguise them in any way. And be realistic. Your proposition will be destroyed if anyone can show that you have underestimated the costs.

Remember, boards want to know in precise terms what they will get for their money. Most boards are cautious, being unwilling and often unable to take much risk. For this reason, it is difficult to make a case for experiments or pilot schemes unless the board, committee or individual can see what the real benefits and the ultimate bill will be.

Presentation

Your proposal will often be made in two stages: a written report followed by an oral presentation. The quality of the latter will often tip the balance in your favour (or against you). Making presentations and writing reports are dealt with in Chapters 41 and 45 respectively, but it is appropriate to note at this stage some special points you should bear in mind when making a case orally in front of an audience:

1. Your presentation should not just consist of a repetition of the facts in the written report. It should be used to get across the main points of the argument, leaving out the detail.

2. Do not assume that your audience has read the written report or

understood it. While you are talking, try to avoid referring to the report. This may switch people's attention from what you are saying. Use visual aids, preferably a flip chart, to emphasize the main points. But don't overdo them – it is possible to be too slick. The audience will be convinced by you, not by your elegant visual aids.

3. Make sure your opening secures people's attention. They must be immediately interested in your presentation. Begin by outlining your plan, its benefits and costs, and let the audience know how you are going to develop your case.

4. Bring out the disadvantages and the alternative courses of action so that you are not suspected of concealing or missing something.

5. Avoid being drawn into too much detail. Be succinct and to the point.

6. An emphatic summing up is imperative. It should convey with complete clarity what you want the board, committee or individual to do.

The effectiveness of your presentation will be largely dependent on how well you have prepared – not only getting your facts, figures and arguments clearly down on paper but also deciding what you are going to say at the meeting and how you are going to say it. The more important the case, the more carefully you should rehearse the presentation.

Checklist

1. Do you know exactly what you want?
2. Do you really believe in your case?
3. Have you obtained and checked all the facts that support your case?
4. What are the strongest arguments for your case?
5. Why must the present situation be changed?
6. Who else will be affected? Unions, other divisions or departments?
7. What are the arguments against your plan?
8. What alternatives are there to your plan?
9. To whom are you presenting your plan? Have you done any lobbying?
10. Have you discussed the finances with the experts?
11. Do you know who are your probable allies and who are likely to be your opponents?
12. Have you prepared handouts of any complicated figures?
13. Have you discussed the best time to present your case?
14. Your ideas were good when you first thought of them: are they still as good?

Chapter 5
Change management

Change is the only thing that remains constant in organizations. As A P Sloan (Chief Executive Officer, General Motors) said: 'The circumstances of an ever-changing market and an ever-changing product are capable of breaking any business organization if that organization is unprepared for change.' All organizations are, to a greater or lesser extent, in a perpetual state of change. To survive and thrive, businesses have to grow. They must innovate, develop new products, expand into new markets, reorganize, introduce new technology, and change working methods and practices. Even if this does not happen voluntarily, it may be forced upon them by competition and changes in the business, political and social environment.

Managers have to be able to introduce and to manage change and gain the commitment of their teams. They must become, in the words of Rosabeth Moss Kanter (27) in *The Change Masters*: 'Change masters, helping and guiding the organization, its management and all who work in it to manage and, indeed, to exploit and triumph over change.'

Change is inevitable. How, therefore, should you prepare for it and how should you manage it as it happens? To answer this question, you need to know something about:

- The process of change – the factors and forces that produce change
- The impact of change
- Resistance to change – why and how people resist change
- Change management techniques.

The process of change

Change occurs in an organization because of internal and external factors. Changes in the environment which affect the enterprise are often unpredictable. You can try to predict their size and impact and prepare plans to meet them, but, for example, no model of the economy has yet been made that can reliably forecast the rate of inflation for more than 12 months ahead.

Internally, changes may take place in the company's product or service, the technology it uses, the people it employs, and its structure, which includes ownership as well as organization.

Internal and external factors interact in a complex manner. Corporate planners make lots of noise about analysing external threats and opportunities and internal strengths and weaknesses. But it all boils down to crystal ball gazing in the end. A wise man constantly expects the unexpected.

Organizations and the people in them would like to remain in equilibrium but cannot. Forces acting on them regularly create imbalances which disturb the pattern. This creates a demand for opposing forces to restore equilibrium.

The impact of change

If not properly managed, change can decrease morale, motivation and commitment, and create conditions of conflict within an organization.

Change can create instability and ambiguity, and replace order and predictability with disharmony and surprise. The corporate culture, as discussed in Chapter 11, can produce solidarity and meaning, and can inspire commitment and productivity. But the culture can actively and forcefully work against an organization when change becomes necessary.

Some people welcome change as a challenge and because it brings variety to their lives. But most people resist it to a greater or lesser degree, and therefore we must explore why this resistance exists before we can discuss what can be done about it.

Resistance to change

Resistance to change is natural. It arises because of:

Preference for stability

Human beings generally seek stability. The first reaction of most people affected by change is to try and regain their equilibrium.

Habit

Once a habit has been established it often provides comfort and satisfaction.

Conformity

Most people like to conform to the customary and expected ways of behaving; they are able to work together because each knows what to expect from the other. If anything diverging from the accepted norm is introduced into the environment it will be disruptive.

Threat to economic interests or prestige

This is perhaps the most obvious source of resistance. Joan Woodward (54) made this point forcibly when she wrote in an article in *Management International Review*:

> When we talk about resistance to change we tend to imply that this is an irrational behavioural tendency. There is a general assumption that management is always rational in changing its direction or modifying its objectives to achieve its goals better, and that operators are stupid, emotional or irrational in not responding in the way they should. But if an individual is going to be worse off explicitly or implicitly in any way when the proposed changes have been made, any resistance is entirely rational in terms of his own best interest. The interests of the organization and the individual do not always coincide.

People focus on their own best interests and often think that any change must be for the bad. Consider these two examples:

> The managing director of a rapidly growing organization decided that its size demanded the creation of a new product planning and development department to be headed by a director. This change would eliminate most of the decision-making power that the directors of marketing, engineering and production had over new products. As new products were very important in this organization the change also reduced their much-valued status. During the two months after the managing director announced his idea for a new product director, the existing directors each came up with six or seven reasons why the new arrangement might not work. Their objections grew louder and louder until the managing director shelved the idea.

> A manufacturing company had traditionally employed a large group of personnel people as counsellors and 'father confessors' to its production employees. Morale was high among these counsellors because of the professional satisfaction they received from the 'helping relationships' they had with employees. Then a new performance-appraisal system was

installed. Every six months the counsellors were required to provide each employee's supervisor with a written evaluation of the employee's 'emotional maturity', 'promotional potential', and so forth. The personnel people immediately recognized that the new system would alter their relationship to the employees from peer and helper to boss and evaluator. Predictably, they resisted the change. Arguing that the new system was not as good for the company as the old one, they put on as much pressure as possible until the new system was altered significantly.

Misunderstanding

People may not understand the implications of change and believe that it will cost them much more than they will gain. Such situations often occur when there is a lack of trust between the person initiating the change and the employees. Here is an example:

When the chairman of a small company announced to its managers that the company would implement a flexible working schedule for all employees, it never occurred to him that he might run into resistance. He had been introduced to the concept at a management course and decided to use it to make working conditions more attractive, particularly to clerical and factory personnel.

Shortly after the announcement numerous rumours began to circulate among factory employees, none of whom really knew what flexible working hours meant and many of whom were distrustful of the manufacturing manager. One rumour, for instance, suggested that flexible hours meant that most people would have to work whenever their supervisors asked them to, including evenings and weekends. The union held a quick meeting and then presented the management with a non-negotiable demand that the flexible hours concept be dropped. The chairman, caught completely by surprise, complied.

Different perceptions

Resistance to change also takes place when the expected goals, norms and values of management are in conflict with those of employees. The change is then perceived as a threat to familiar patterns of behaviour. If it is also perceived as a threat to the security, income, status, authority or personal circumstances of an individual it can be regarded with suspicion, fear or even open hostility. These reactions may well occur if people feel in any way that they are going to be worse off, even if their fears are without foundation.

People may assess the situation differently from their managers or those initiating the change and see more costs than benefits resulting from the change, not only for themselves but for their company as well. For example:

The president, of one moderate size US bank was shocked by his staff's analysis of the bank's real estate investment trust (REIT) loans. This complicated analysis suggested that the bank could easily lose up to $10 million, and the possible losses were increasing each month by 10 per cent. Within a week, the president drew up a plan to reorganize the part of the bank that managed REITs. Because of his concern for the bank's stock price, however, he chose not to release the staff report to anyone except the new REIT section manager.

The reorganization immediately ran into massive resistance from the people involved. The group sentiment as articulated by one person was: 'Has he gone mad? Why in God's name is he tearing apart this section of the bank? His actions have already cost us three very good people (who quit) and have crippled a new programme we were implementing (which the president was unaware of) to reduce our loan losses.'

Fear of the unknown

Change often happens in conditions of uncertainty and can itself create feelings of uncertainty. Fear of the unknown is likely to happen when the situation creates ambiguities in:

- Goals – people not being clear about what they are supposed to achieve
- Data – information about the situation and its likely effects is absent, unclear, changing or confused
- Roles – lack of clarity about authority and responsibility and how the individual fits into the new set-up
- Methods – lack of clarity about the means required to achieve the ends
- Criteria – no means of judging whether or not the change has been introduced successfully and the objectives of the change programme have been achieved.

What management in general and individual managers in particular should always remember is that resistance to change is a natural, not an unnatural, process. Change is a threat to familiar patterns of behaviour as well as to security, status and financial rewards.

Managing change

Change management is one of the biggest challenges that executives have to face. Charles Brown, when he was chairman of the board of AT&T, recognized this when he said: 'I think we can do the internal job of changing without fear of failure, once we're given some decent understanding of what is expected of us. But the complexity of trying to change ourselves, when we don't know what the future rules are going to be, injects a degree of uncertainty that creates a lot of anxiety.'

To manage change you need to:

- Understand the basic mechanisms of change
- Develop the change programme
- Analyse the forces affecting change
- Take steps to overcome resistance to change
- Gain commitment to change
- Accelerate the pace of change.

These steps are discussed below.

Basic mechanisms

The basic mechanisms for managing change are:

1. *Unfreezing* – altering the present stable equilibrium which supports existing behaviours and attitudes. This process must take account of the inherent threats that change presents to people and the need to motivate those affected to attain the natural state of equilibrium by accepting change.
2. *Changing* – developing new responses based on new information.
3. *Refreezing* – stabilizing the change by introducing the new responses into the personalities of those concerned.

Programming change

A change programme should incorporate the following processes as suggested by Richard Beckhard (5) in *Organizational Development*:

1. Setting goals and defining the future state or organizational conditions desired after the change.
2. Diagnosing the present condition in relation to these goals.
3. Defining the transition state activities and commitments required to meet the future state.
4. Developing strategies and action plans for managing this transition in the light of an analysis of the factors likely to affect the introduction of change.

Analysing the forces affecting change

Those wanting change should be constant about the ends but they may have to be flexible about the means. This requires them to understand the forces likely to resist change as well as those creating the need for change.

This can be done by analysing the 'helps' and 'hindrances' to change and then exploiting the former and overcoming the latter.

This process is sometimes called field force analysis, and it involves:

1. Analysing the restraining or driving forces which will affect the transition to the future state. These restraining forces will include the reactions of those who see change as unnecessary or constituting a threat.
2. Assessing which of the driving or restraining forces are critical.
3. Taking steps both to increase the critical driving forces and to decrease the critical restraining forces.

When analysing the potential impact of change in one part of the organization, it is necessary to consider not only how it directly affects the people in that area but also to take a helicopter view of how the proposed changes will affect the organization as a whole.

In making this analysis the individual introducing the change, who is often called the 'change agent', should recognize that new ideas are likely to be misunderstood and make ample provision for the discussion of reactions to proposals to ensure complete understanding of them. It is also necessary to try to gain an understanding of the feelings and fears of those affected so that unnecessary worries can be relieved and, so far as possible, ambiguities can be resolved.

Overcoming resistance to change

While people often take an antagonistic or negative attitude to change, it is also true that the desire for new experience underlies much of human behaviour. This fact will help you to overcome resistance to change. People come to accept change in three ways:

- *Compliance*, or 'do it because I say so'. The individual accepts the change because he has to. He does not necessarily believe in what he has to do.
- *Identification*, or 'do it because I do it'. The individual defines his own beliefs and actions in terms of what someone else is or does. Identification is like compliance in that the individual does not agree to change because it is satisfying. It differs from compliance, however, in that the individual actually believes in the opinions and actions he adopts.
- *Intrinsic satisfaction*, or 'do it because it is worth doing'. The individual accepts change because the new situation is intrinsically satisfying or because it is in accordance with his own set of values. He may be influenced by others in forming this view, but ultimately he

accepts the change because he likes it rather than because someone else likes it.

Resistance to change will be less if:

- Those affected by change feel that they can accept the project as their own, not one imposed upon them by outsiders
- The change has the wholehearted support of management
- The change accords with well-established values
- The change is seen as reducing rather than increasing present burdens
- The change offers the kind of new experience which interests participants
- Participants feel that their autonomy and security are not threatened
- Participants have jointly diagnosed the problems
- The change has been agreed by group decisions
- Those advocating change understand the feelings and fears of those affected and take steps to relieve unnecessary fears
- It is recognized that new ideas are likely to be misinterpreted and ample provision is made for discussion of reactions to proposals to ensure complete understanding of them.

Gaining commitment to change

'People support what they help create.' Commitment to change will be greater if those affected by change are allowed to participate as fully as possible in planning and implementing it. The aim should be to get them to 'own' the change as something they want and will be glad to live with.

Getting involvement in the introduction of change will only be effective in gaining commitment when management is prepared to listen and to change its plans if there is a clear message that they are unworkable, or if the plans could be made more acceptable without prejudicing the achievement of the objectives of the change programme.

Accelerating the pace of change

The steps outlined above to gain commitment to change are an essential part of a change management programme. If they are carried out properly the further actions required to accelerate the pace of change are as follows:

1. Agree firm objectives, ie an 'agenda for change'.
2. Determine success criteria and define methods of measuring performance and progress towards achieving the objectives, both short- and long-term.
3. Provide in Rosabeth Moss Kanter's words (27): 'An environment of

support in which recognition of achievements to date will reinforce confidence to do more.'
4. Deliver visionary leadership which encourages people to be bold and innovative and harnesses the ideas and talents of employees in the search for better ways of doing things.
5. Ensure the full collaboration and partnership of all resources in the business.
6. Generate a widespread attitude among all employees that encourages commitment to innovation and change by:

   • conducting personal briefings on the proposed changes cascading down through each level in the organization to cover all employees. This is better than simply issuing pieces of paper which may only generate a 'so what' reaction;
   • conducting workshops in which groups get together to discuss, analyse and interpret the proposed changes. These should be treated as opportunities for employees to become involved in planning change as well as implementing it;
   • introducing educational and training programmes which allow plenty of time to get the various messages across and to discuss their meaning and application fully.

Case studies

Book Club Associates

A customer service department had a large section of about 40 people – mainly women – who dealt with correspondence. A large proportion of the letters contained complaints from customers about how their accounts had been handled.

Unfortunately, the data required to answer letters were not immediately accessible. Some data were held in the computer while the rest were contained in individual customer files which were often split between different locations or products. Consequently, there were delays in answering letters and, because the full picture was not readily available, some replies did not answer the complaint specifically enough and generated additional complaints.

The female clerks in the department had been working this system for a number of years and had got used to it. Staff turnover was very low (less than 10 per cent per year) and there was no pressure from them for any change.

Management, however, wanted to improve the accuracy of replies and speed up their processing. A new computer-linked system could be developed which would achieve both these aims *and* save staff. The work would be no more demanding and could even bring greater job satisfaction because of the facility for dealing comprehensively and quickly with individual customers without leaving any loose ends.

A carefully planned programme of change management was therefore worked out. Preliminary informal meetings were held with small groups of staff to sound out their feelings about the present system and how they would like it to be improved. They were told that there were a number of possible ways of doing this but that no plans would be finalized until their ideas had been taken into account.

When the initial ideas of management were presented to the staff the benefits to the individual were emphasized – less hassle, not so much effort spent in walking about the building getting information, and the satisfaction they could gain from being given greater responsibility. They were not bribed with more money nor was the fact that there would be some staff savings disguised. But it was emphasized that any staff surplus would be taken up by natural wastage. The staff were also told that the scheme would be tested thoroughly using a small team of volunteers who would be consulted continuously about their work. Progress reports to all the staff of the department would also be issued regularly.

The staff accepted this proposal because they recognized that the company clearly stood to gain by the new system, and they themselves would not lose and might even benefit in a number of ways. The pilot test was carried out, consultation took place as planned, and the full scheme was implemented on time and without any fuss.

ICI – John Harvey-Jones

John Harvey-Jones became chairman of ICI in 1982 – a massive but then an ailing business, with profits before tax in 1981 being £325 million. In his words, it was 'growing barnacles'. When he retired in 1987 he left behind a thriving business making £1 billion profit, together with an organization that is less hierarchical, less bureaucratic and is able to respond quickly to change.

How did he achieve this turn-round? His methods can be summarized as follows:

- The organization has to be capable of renewing itself constantly
- Small units are more manageable than big ones
- The individual matters.

Taking the fear out of change

Change percolated through ICI by a cascade effect. The board set the pace and everyone else took up the baton. The aim was to get every individual to see his own place in relation to the rest of the company and from this picture to glean an idea of his part in the changes that were taking place. This would take the fear out of change, and that is the biggest brake on individuals embracing new ideas. Harvey-Jones has made the point that 'people have first to decide that they want to change, then they must be encouraged not to be afraid of change, and finally they must be able to see where change is leading them'.

Organization
The organization had to be continually adaptive. All large organizations have tendencies towards creeping centralization and top-heavy bureaucracy, and this inhibits innovation and change. Harvey-Jones approached this problem by relaxing the grip of the centre and thus giving people 'headroom to grow'. He put the decision-making authority back into the hands of the people who were competent to exercise it. As he said: 'How the hell can I know whether the guy in India should be changing his product, or whether somebody in Australia should be changing his technology? People don't like centralization because it uses them like machines.'

Control
Decentralization did not, however, mean lack of control. 'While we've set businesses free to pursue their own objectives, the controls have actually got more rigid. We only manage on a small number of parameters, but they are pretty ruthless.'

Chapter 6
Clear thinking

Clear thinking is logical thinking. It is a process of reasoning by which one judgement is derived from another and correct conclusions are drawn from the evidence. Clear thinking is analytical: sifting information, selecting what is relevant, establishing and proving relationships.

If you say someone is logical you mean that he draws reasonable inferences – his conclusions can be proved by reference to the facts used to support them. He avoids ill-founded and tendentious arguments, generalizations and irrelevancies. His chain of reasoning is clear, unemotional and based on relevant facts.

Clear thinking – a logical approach to problem-solving, decision-making and case presentation – is an essential attribute of an effective manager. This does not mean that it is the only way to think. Edward de Bono has made out an incontrovertible case for lateral, ie creative, thinking as a necessary process for innovative managers to use alongside the more traditional vertical or logical thinking pattern (see Chapter 14). But a logical approach is still an essential requirement.

A further attribute of a good manager is the ability to argue persuasively and to detect the flaws in other people's arguments. To think clearly and to argue well, you need to understand: first, how to develop a proposition or a case from basic principles; second, how to test your proposition; and third, how to avoid using fallacious arguments and how to expose the fallacies used by others.

Developing a proposition

The first rule is to 'get the facts'. It is the starting point for clear thinking. The facts must be relevant to the issue under consideration. If comparisons are being made, like must be compared with like. Trends must be related to an appropriate base date and, if trends are being compared, the same base should be used. Treat opinions with caution until they are supported by evidence. Avoid a superficial analysis of surface data. Dig deep. Take nothing for granted. Sift the evidence and discard what is irrelevant.

Your inferences should be derived *directly* from the facts. Where possible, the connection between the facts and the conclusion should be shown to be justified on the basis of verifiable and relevant experience or information on similar relationships occurring elsewhere.

If, as is likely, more than one inference can be deduced from the facts, you should test each inference to establish which one most clearly derives from the evidence as supported by experience. But it is no good saying 'it stands to reason' or 'it's common sense'. You have to produce the evidence which proves that the inference is reasonable and you have to pin down the vague concept of common sense to the data and experience upon which it is based. It was Descartes who wrote: 'Common sense is the best distributed commodity in the world, for every man is convinced that he is well supplied with it.'

Testing propositions

Susan Stebbing (47) in *Thinking to Some Purpose* wrote: 'We are content to accept without testing any belief that fits in with our prejudices and whose truth is necessary for the satisfaction of our desires.' Clear thinking must try to avoid this trap.

When we form a proposition or belief we generalize from what is observed – our own analysis or experience – and thence infer to what is not observed. We also refer to testimony – other people's observations and experience.

If your proposition or belief is derived from a generalization based upon particular instances you should test it by answering the following questions:

- Was the scope of the investigation sufficiently comprehensive?
- Are the instances representative or are they selected to support a point of view?
- Are there contradictory instances that have not been looked for?
- Does the proposition or belief in question conflict with other beliefs for which we have equally good grounds?
- If there are any conflicting beliefs or contradictory items of evidence, have they been put to the test against the original proposition?
- Could the evidence or testimony lead to other equally valid conclusions?
- Are there any other factors which have not been taken into account

which may have influenced the evidence and, therefore, the conclusion?

If your belief is based on testimony, you should test the reliability of the testimony, its relevance to the point, and whether or not your belief follows logically from the evidence, ie can reasonably be inferred from the facts.

Fallacious and misleading arguments

A fallacy is an unsound form of argument leading to a mistake in reasoning or a misleading impression. The main fallacies to avoid or to spot in other people's arguments are:

- Sweeping statements
- Potted thinking
- Special pleading
- Over-simplification
- Reaching false conclusions
- Begging the question
- False analogy
- Using words ambiguously
- Chop logic.

These are discussed briefly below.

Sweeping statements

In our desire for certainty and to carry the point we often indulge in sweeping statements. We sometimes then repeat them more and more loudly and angrily in order to convince our opponent. If we do it often enough and forcibly enough we can even deceive ourselves.

It has been said that 'it's never fair, it's never wise, it's never safe to generalize'. But that is a generalization in itself. Scientific method is based on generalizations. They can be valid if they are inferred properly from adequate, relevant and reliable evidence.

Generalizations are invalid when they have been produced by over-simplifying the facts or by selecting instances favourable to a contention while ignoring those that conflict with it. The classic form of a fallacious generalization is the contention that if some A is B then all A must be B. What frequently happens is that people say A is B when all they know is that *some* A is B or, at most, A *tends* to be B. The argument is misleading unless the word 'some' or 'tends' is admitted.

Many of the fallacies considered below are special cases of unsafe generalization, the most common symptom of unsound reasoning.

Potted thinking

Potted thinking happens when we argue using slogans and catch phrases, when we extend an assertion in an unwarrantable fashion.

It is natural to form confident beliefs about complicated matters when we are proposing or taking action. And it is equally natural to compress these beliefs into a single phrase or thought. But it is dangerous to accept compressed statements that save us the trouble of thinking. They are only acceptable if fresh thinking has preceded them.

Special pleading

If anyone says to you: 'everyone knows that', 'it's obvious that' or 'it's indisputably true that', you can be certain that he has taken for granted what he is about to assert.

We indulge in special pleading when we stress our own case and fail to see that there may be other points of view, other ways of looking at the question. Special pleading happens when we cannot detach ourselves from our own circumstances. We often blunder because we forget that what is true of one of us is also true of the other in the same situation.

A safeguard against this mistake is to change *you* into *I*. Thus, *I* feel that you can't see what is straight in front of your nose; *you* feel that I can't see what is on the other side of my blinkers. A rule that appears to be sound when I apply it to you may seem to be unsatisfactory when you ask me to apply it to myself.

Of course, thinking for too long about other points of view is a recipe for indecision. There are not necessarily two sides to every question and even if there are, you eventually – and often quickly – have to come down firmly on one side. But before you do this, check in case the other points of view or the alternative approaches are valid, and take them into account.

Over-simplification

Over-simplification is a special form of potted thinking or special pleading. It often arises in the form of what Susan Stebbing terms 'the fallacy of either black or white', the mistake of demanding that a sharp line should be drawn, when in fact no sharp line can be drawn. For example, we cannot ask for a clear distinction to be drawn between the sane and the insane, or between the intelligent and the unintelligent. Our readiness to make this mistake may be taken advantage of by a dishonest opponent, who insists that we define precisely that which does not admit of such definition.

Reaching false conclusions

One of the most prevalent fallacies is that of forming the view that because *some* are or may be, *all* are. An assertion about several cases is twisted into an assertion about all cases. The conclusion does not follow the premise.

The most common form of this fallacy is what logicians call the 'undistributed middle', which refers to the traditional syllogism consisting of a premise, a middle term and a conclusion.

A valid syllogism takes the following form:

Premise : All cows are quadrupeds.
Middle term : All quadrupeds are vertebrates.
Conclusion : Therefore, all cows are vertebrates.

This may be represented as:

Premise : All A is B.
Middle term : All B is C.
Conclusion : Therefore, all A is C.

This is logical. The middle term is fully distributed. Everything that applies to A also applies to B, everything that applies to B also applies to C, therefore, everything that applies to A must apply to C.

An invalid syllogism would take the following form:

All cows are quadrupeds.
All mules are quadrupeds.
Therefore, all mules are cows.

This may be represented as:

All A is B.
All C is B.
Therefore, all A is C.

This is false because, although everything that applies to A and C also applies to B, there is nothing in their relationship to B which connects A and C together.

The difference between the true and false syllogism may be illustrated as shown in the diagram opposite.

In the false syllogism, A and C could be quite distinct although still contained within B. To link them together goes beyond the original evidence. Because two things A and B are related to another thing, C, it

True syllogism   *False syllogism*

 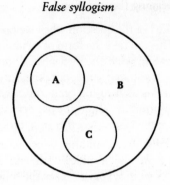

does not *necessarily* mean that they are related together. In forming arguments, we too often jump to the conclusion that *some* means *all*.

Allowing the conclusion to go beyond the evidence can also take the form of assuming that because we are aware of the effect (the *consequent*), we also know the cause (the *antecedent*). But this assumption may be incorrect. An effect can have many different causes. This fallacy of the consequent, as it is termed, can be illustrated by the following example:

> If he came up on the pools, he would go to the West Indies.
> He has gone to the West Indies.
> Therefore he has come up on the pools.
>
> ie If P then Q,
>   Q
> Therefore P.

But there are a number of other reasons why he could have gone to the West Indies besides coming up on the pools. A clear inference can only be drawn if the cause is directly related to the effect, thus:

> If he comes up on the pools he will go to the West Indies.
> He has come up on the pools.
> Therefore he will go to the West Indies.
> ie If P then Q,
>   P
> Therefore Q.

A further danger in drawing conclusions from evidence is to forget that circumstances may alter cases. What has happened in the past will not necessarily happen again unless the circumstances are the same. You may be able to infer something from history but you cannot rely on that inference. Times change.

Begging the question

We beg the question when we take for granted what has yet to be proved. This can take the form of assuming the point in dispute without adequate reason; what the logicians call *petitio principio*.

If you spot someone taking for granted a premise which is not contained in his conclusion you must challenge the assumption and ask for information about the premises upon which the conclusion is based. You can then assess whether or not the conclusion follows logically from those premises.

Challenging assumptions is a necessary part of thinking clearly. You should challenge your own assumptions as well as those made by others.

False analogy

Analogy forms the basis of much of our thinking. We notice that two cases resemble each other in certain respects and then infer an extension of the resemblance. Analogies also aid understanding of an unfamiliar topic.

Analogies can be used falsely as vivid arguments without any real evidence. Just because A is B, where both are familiar matters of fact, does not mean that X is Y, where X and Y are unfamiliar or abstract. When we argue by analogy we claim that if:

x has properties of p1, p2, p3 and f, and
y has properties of p1, p2 and p3, therefore
y also has the property of f.

This could be true unless y has a property incompatible with f, in which case the argument is unsound.

Analogies may be used to suggest a conclusion but they cannot establish it. They can be carried too far. Sometimes their relevance is more apparent than real.

Use argument by analogy to help to support a case but do not rely upon it. Don't allow anyone else to get away with far-fetched analogies. They should be tested and their relevance should be proved.

Using words ambiguously

The Lewis Carroll approach – 'When I use a word it means just what I choose it to mean, neither more nor less' – is a favourite trick of those who aim to deceive. People use words that beg the question, that is, they define a word in a special way that supports their argument. They shift the meaning of words in different contexts. They may choose words which have the same meaning as each other but which show approval or disapproval. There is a well-known saying that the word 'firm' can be declined as follows: 'I am firm, You are obstinate, He is pigheaded.'

Chop logic

'Contrariwise,' continued Tweedledee, 'if it was so, it might be, and if it were so, it would be; but as it isn't, it ain't. That's logic.'

Chop logic is not quite as bad as that, but it can be equally misleading. It includes such debating tricks as:

- Selecting instances favourable to a contention while ignoring those that conflict with it
- Twisting an argument advanced by an opponent to mean something quite different from what was intended – putting words in someone's mouth
- Diverting an opponent by throwing on him the burden of proving something he has not maintained
- Deliberately ignoring the point in dispute
- Introducing irrelevant matter into the argument
- Reiterating what has been denied and ignoring what has been asserted.

Chapter 7
Communicating

People recognize the need to communicate but find it difficult. Like Schopenhauer's hedgehogs, they want to get together, it's only their prickles that keep them apart.

Words may sound or look precise, but they are not. All sorts of barriers exist between the communicator and the receiver. Unless these barriers are overcome the message will be distorted or will not get through.

Barriers to communication

Hearing what we want to hear

What we hear or understand when someone speaks to us is largely based on our own experience and background. Instead of hearing what people have told us, we hear what our minds tell us they have said. We have preconceptions about what people are going to say, and if what they say does not fit into our framework of reference we adjust it until it does. (Advice on how to listen is given in Chapter 27.)

Ignoring conflicting information

We tend to ignore or reject communications that conflict with our own beliefs. If they are not rejected, some way is found of twisting and shaping their meaning to fit our preconceptions. When a message is inconsistent with existing beliefs, the receiver rejects its validity, avoids further exposure to it, easily forgets it and, in his memory, distorts what he has heard.

Perceptions about the communicator

It is difficult to separate what we hear from our feelings about the person who says it. Non-existent motives may be ascribed to the communicator. If we like someone we are more likely to accept what he says – whether it is right or wrong – than if we dislike him.

Influence of the group

The group with which we identify influences our attitudes and feelings. What a group hears depends on its interests. Workers are more likely to listen to their colleagues, who share their experiences, than to outsiders such as managers or union officials.

Words mean different things to different people

Essentially, language is a method of using symbols to represent facts and feelings. Strictly speaking, we can't convey *meaning*, all we can do is to convey *words*. Do not assume that because something has a certain meaning to you, it will convey the same meaning to someone else.

Non-verbal communication

When we try to understand the meaning of what people say we listen to the words but we use other clues which convey meaning. We attend not only to *what* people say but to *how* they say it. We form impressions from what is called body language – eyes, shape of the mouth, the muscles of the face, even posture. We may feel that these tell us more about what someone is really saying than the words he uses. But there is enormous scope for misinterpretation.

Emotions

Our emotions colour our ability to convey or to receive the true message. When we are insecure or worried, what we hear seems more threatening than when we are secure and at peace with the world. When we are angry or depressed, we tend to reject what might otherwise seem like reasonable requests or good ideas. During heated argument, many things that are said may not be understood or may be badly distorted.

Noise

Any interference to communication is 'noise'. It can be literal noise which prevents the message being heard, or figurative in the shape of distracting or confused information which distorts or obscures the meaning.

Size

The larger and more complex the organization, the greater the problem of communication. The more levels of management and supervision through which a message has to pass, the greater the opportunity for distortion or misunderstanding.

Overcoming barriers to communication

Adjust to the world of the receiver

Try to predict the impact of what you are going to write or say on the receiver's feelings and attitudes. Tailor the message to fit the receiver's vocabulary, interests and values. Be aware of how the information might be misinterpreted because of prejudices, the influence of others and the tendency of people to reject what they do not want to hear.

Use feedback

Ensure that you get a message back from the receiver which tells you how much has been understood.

Use face-to-face communication

Whenever possible talk to people rather than write to them. That is how you get feedback. You can adjust or change your message according to reactions. You can also deliver it in a more human and understanding way – this can help to overcome prejudices. Verbal criticism can often be given in a more constructive manner than written reproof which always seems to be harsher.

Use reinforcement

You may have to present your message in a number of different ways to get it across. Re-emphasize the important points and follow up.

Use direct simple language

This seems obvious. But many people clutter up what they say with jargon, long words and elaborate sentences.

Suit the actions to the word

Communications have to be credible to be effective. When you say you are going to do something, do it. Next time you are more likely to be believed.

Use different channels

Some communications have to be in writing to get the message across promptly and without any variations in the way they are delivered. But, wherever possible, supplement written communications with the spoken word. Conversely, an oral briefing should be reinforced in writing.

Reduce problems of size

If you can, reduce the number of levels of management. Encourage a reasonable degree of informality in communications. Ensure that activities are grouped together to ease communication on matters of mutual concern.

Chapter 8
Conflict management

You will not escape conflict in your organization. It is inevitable, because the objectives, values and needs of groups and individuals in the organization do not always coincide.

Conflict may be a sign of a healthy organization. Bland agreement on everything would be unnatural and enervating. There should be clashes of ideas about tasks and projects, and disagreements should not be suppressed. They should come out into the open, because that is the only way in which you can ensure that the issues are explored and conflicts are resolved. There is such a thing as creative conflict. But conflict becomes counter-productive when it is based on personality clashes, or when it is treated as an unseemly mess to be hurriedly cleared away, rather than as a problem to be 'worked through'.

Resolving conflict

There are three principal ways of resolving conflict.

Peaceful co-existence

The aim here is to smooth out differences and emphasize the common ground. People are encouraged to learn to live together; there is a good deal of information, contact and exchange of views, and individuals move freely between groups (eg between headquarters and the field, or between sales and manufacturing).

This is a pleasant ideal, but it may not be practicable in many situations. There is much evidence that conflict is not necessarily resolved by grouping people together. Improved communications and techniques such as briefing groups may appear to be good ideas but are useless if management has nothing to say that people want to hear. There is also the danger that the real issues, submerged for the moment in an atmosphere of superficial bonhomie, will surface again at a later date.

Compromise

The issue is resolved by negotiation or bargaining and neither party wins or loses. This concept of splitting the difference is essentially pessimistic. The hallmark of this approach is that there is no 'right' or 'best' answer. Agreements only accommodate differences. Real issues are not likely to be solved.

Problem-solving

An attempt is made to find a genuine solution to the problem rather than just accommodating different points of view. This is where the apparent paradox of 'creative conflict' comes in. Conflict situations can be used to advantage to create better solutions.

If solutions are to be developed by problem-solving, they have to be generated by those who share the responsibility for seeing that the solutions work. The sequence of actions is: first, those concerned work to define the problem and agree on the objectives to be attained in reaching a solution; second, the group develops alternative solutions and debates their merits; third, agreement is reached on the preferred course of action and how it should be implemented.

Conflict, as has been said, is in itself not to be deplored; it is an inevitable concomitant of progress and change. What is to be deplored is the failure to use conflict constructively. Effective problem-solving both resolves conflicts and opens up channels of discussion and cooperative action.

Over 50 years ago one of the pioneering writers on management, Mary Parker Follett (18), wrote something on managing conflict which is as valid today as it was then: 'Differences can be made to contribute to the common cause if they are resolved by integration rather than domination or compromise.'

Case studies

Who should do market research?

A new market research manager had been engaged. Described by her boss as 'pushy' she quite naturally wanted to establish her position quickly.

Her predecessor had been a quiet fellow who had come to an arrangement with the head of operational research that they should divide the market research activity between them: external field research was conducted by the market research manager and internal research on customer buying habits was conducted within the operational research department.

The new market research manager would have none of this. She believed that her department should handle all research and analysis concerning customer behaviour. Any division would be artificial. The operational research manager strongly disagreed. He could advance the rational argument that the information wanted for internal research was on the computer to which he had immediate access and the skills and resources to use. In any case, he liked to feel that he and his department were in touch with current issues and were not just operating in a small back room divorced from reality.

Both those involved felt equally strongly that they were right. Their divisional head tried to get them to accept a compromise solution which would make the operational research manager responsible for the initial collection and analysis of the internal data while the market research manager would collate and comment on the information for the benefit of the marketing department.

Having failed to impose this compromise, the divisional head called on the help of a management consultant friend of his who specialized in dealing with this sort of situation. The consultant saw each of the parties separately to get a full run-down of facts and opinions. He then persuaded them to sit down together, with the divisional head, and, by the end of the day, to try to come up with an integrated solution about which everyone would be happy – no compromises. The consultant emphasized that the aim was to come up with a solution that would not leave either party with the feeling that they had lost something.

The original discussions which the consultant held with each of the managers helped them to leave their emotions outside the meeting and to concentrate on coming up with a mutually acceptable solution. And, eventually, this is what they did. Each agreed to collect external and internal data separately from their respective sources. They would then jointly analyse and present their findings to marketing management. This solution was implemented and it worked. The rivalry between them largely vanished and a better service was provided to marketing.

The canteen crisis

The union was most unhappy about the decision to increase canteen prices by the amount of inflation without any prior consultation. The new factory manager said that it was generally understood that prices, like wages, had to keep pace with inflation and that there was nothing in the procedural agreement which stated that consultation was necessary before increasing prices.

The union convenor admitted that the agreement contained no specific reference to canteen prices but pointed out that terms and conditions of employment were negotiable and asked: 'If canteen prices aren't terms and conditions of employment, what are they?'

The factory manager, however, would not budge and the union called for a ban on overtime and a work-to-rule which was particularly damaging at that time.

The divisional personnel director was despatched urgently to the factory to sort things out. He wanted to achieve a settlement in which neither side would have to give in completely to the other but which, without compromise, would satisfy all parties. His approach was to call for a joint 'problem-solving' meeting of union and management. There were to be no recriminations, only an analysis of how to get out of the impasse and how to set up an arrangement which would prevent it happening again.

The meeting started by being rowdy, but the personnel director rapidly defused it by insisting that they were there to discuss and solve a problem, not to shout at one another. He provided the union with a full analysis of the canteen accounts and an explanation of why price increases were necessary. He agreed to modify the increases where the union showed that the charges were not absolutely justified. And, most important, he got agreement to a joint arrangement for monitoring the canteen accounts and agreeing on any price increases required before announcements were made. Management got most of the increases they wanted, normal working was resumed and the union felt it was in a stronger position than before. Honour was satisfied on all sides.

Chapter 9
Controlling

Basically, you are seeking to control two things – input and output – and the relationship between them, which is productivity or performance. All managers will know Murphy's two laws: if anything can go wrong, it will; and of the things that can't go wrong, some will.

The aim of good control is to protect your plans from the operation of these laws as far as possible; to detect trouble spots before they erupt; to prevent those accidents which are just waiting to happen. Prevention is better than cure.

Essentials of control

Control is relative. It does not deal with absolutes, only with the difference between good and not-so-good performance.

The basis of control is measurement. It depends on accurate information about what is being achieved. This is then compared with what *should* have been achieved and with what has been achieved in the past. But that is only a starting point. Good control also identifies responsibility and points the way to action.

Effective control

If you want to exercise good control you need to:

1. *Plan* what you aim to achieve
2. *Measure* regularly what has been achieved
3. *Compare* actual achievements with the plan
4. *Take action* to exploit opportunities revealed by this information or to correct deviations from the plan.

Note that control is not only a matter of putting things right. It also has a positive side – getting more or better things done on the basis of information received.

Problems of control

A good control system is not easy to set up. There are two essentials:

- To set appropriate and fair targets, standards and budgets. (This may be difficult where the scope for quantification is limited or if circumstances make forecasts unreliable.)
- To decide what information is crucial for control purposes and design reports which clearly convey that information to the people who need it and can use it to point the way to action. This also produces problems. Too many control systems generate a surfeit of indigestible data which go to the wrong people and are not acted upon. You can have too little information, but there is also such a thing as information overkill. There is, moreover, a tendency for some people to report good results and cover up poor results. In any case, the figures may not tell the whole story.

Overcoming the problem

There are five steps to take if you want to achieve good control:

1. Decide what you want to control
2. Decide how you are going to measure and review performance
3. Use ratio analysis to make comparisons and to identify variations and problems
4. Set up a control system
5. Manage by exception.

Controlling inputs and outputs

In controlling input and output, and hence productivity, an overview is essential. It is no good concentrating on inputs, mainly expressed as costs, unless you look at the benefits arising from these expenditures and the effectiveness with which the costs have been incurred. Cost benefit and cost effectiveness studies are an essential part of the control process.

Input control

When you control inputs you should aim to measure and assess the performance of:

- *Money* – its productivity, flow, liquidity and conservation.

You need to know what return you are getting on investments compared with the return you want.

You should ensure that you have the cash and working capital to run the business. Cash-flow analysis is vital. One of the golden rules of management, as stated by Robert Heller, is 'cash in must exceed cash out'.

You must conserve and provide the money needed to finance future trading and development projects and for capital investment.

Management has to know how effectively its financial resources are being used to produce goods, services and profits and this requires continuous and close attention to the control of direct and indirect costs and overheads generally.

- *People* – the effectiveness of the people you employ in terms of their quality and performance
- *Materials* – their availability, condition, convertibility and waste
- *Equipment* – machine utilization and capability.

Output control

- *Quantitative control measures* – the units produced or sold, the amount of services provided, the sales turnover obtained and the profits achieved. Key performance measures will vary between organizations. You need to determine through analysis which are the crucial indicators of success or failure.
- *Qualitative control measures* – the level of service provided by an organization (eg a public corporation) or by a non-productive department within an organization (eg personnel). It is more difficult to select valid performance measures in these areas, but the attempt should be made.

Productivity control

Productivity is the relationship between input and output. Cost benefit studies are productivity studies in that they assess how much benefit (output) is obtained from a given cost (input).

Productivity is expressed by ratios. A productivity index can be produced as follows:

$$\text{Productivity index} = \frac{\text{Output}}{\text{Input}} = \frac{\text{Performance achieved}}{\text{Resources consumed}} = \frac{\text{Effectiveness}}{\text{Efficiency}}$$

Ratio analysis

Expressing items as percentages or ratios of other items – ratio analysis – is the best way to measure and control inputs, outputs, productivity and the financial resources of the company generally. Ratios should not, however, be used in isolation. You should always take account of trends between present and past performance. And you should compare ratios within the business and between your business and other businesses. Most important, you should compare actual ratios with planned ratios.

It is essential to seek the *key* indicators in the form of ratios for your business. You will not want to collect sheets of ratios from every direction, but you should know when you look at a set of figures which one you have got to divide into the other to tell you what is really happening. It is no good just knowing how much sales have increased over the last period. You also need to know how the number of sales representatives has changed and the volume of sales per representative, this period compared with budget, the last period, and the same period last year.

The most important financial and productivity ratios are described below.

Return on capital employed

This is usually expressed as net profit as a percentage of capital. It tells you the extent to which an investment is paying off. It could apply to the whole business from the point of view of the shareholders, to part of the business, or to the specific return on an investment in capital equipment. When compared with the return you could get if you invested your money elsewhere, this ratio indicates the extent to which the investment is justified.

This can lead into an analysis of opportunity costs which are the costs as compared with the profit or loss expected from an alternative investment or course of action. In other words, if you failed to make a decision or take an opportunity that would have produced a better result than the decision you did make, that lost revenue is an 'opportunity cost'.

When analysing returns on capital employed, be careful to check the basis of the figures to ensure that like is compared with like. A common, but not universal, definition of capital employed includes share capital, reserves (excluding those for taxation), long-term loans and bank overdraft. The return figure is usually defined as net profit, excluding tax and interest on capital.

Tax is excluded because its varying nature makes it difficult to compare data from year to year. Interest on capital is omitted because its inclusion would mean that the return on capital would be measured *after* a return

67

had been obtained on investment. Bear in mind that comparisons can be distorted when there are few fixed assets, for example, when plant is rented or leased by the company.

Profit to sales ratio

This is the fundamental measure of the profitability of the company as a trading concern. It is expressed as a ratio:

$$\frac{\text{Net trading profit (ie the difference between expenses and income from sales)}}{\text{Sales revenue}}$$

Solvency ratios

These measure the company's short-term financial liabilities – its ability to pay its current liabilities as they fall due.

The 'current' ratio is calculated as follows:

$$\frac{\text{Current assets (stock, debtors and cash)}}{\text{Current liabilities (creditors and accrued charges)}}$$

If the current ratio is more than 1:1, the company has more current assets than current liabilities and, if it were forced to pay out all its current liabilities, would have sufficient current assets to do so.

If a really strict appraisal of a company's solvency is required, however, it is best to leave stock out of the current assets, and to take only the liquid assets into consideration. This is because if a company were forced to realize its stock quickly, it is doubtful if it would even recover its cost value. The ratio then becomes:

$$\frac{\text{Current assets excluding stock}}{\text{Current liabilities}}$$

This is sometimes called the 'acid test'. Ideally, the ratio should be at least 1:1 but there are cases where a ratio of somewhat less than 1:1 is acceptable. Too high a ratio, on the other hand, would mean that the company is not making sufficient use of its finances – cash by itself does not generate much profit.

Stock ratios

If the company holds too much stock it will be wasting its financial resources in an unused asset. If it holds too little stock it will lose sales revenue through not being able to service its customers.

To measure how much is being tied up in stock use the ratio:

$$\frac{\text{Stock}}{\text{Current assets}}$$

To measure how quickly the stock is turned over (stock turn) the ratio is:

$$\frac{\text{Sales}}{\text{Stock}}$$

The greater the stock turnover figure the better for the company. If the goods are being sold at a profit, the more that are sold the better the profit at the year end.

Other financial ratios

There are a number of other financial ratios you can use. Perhaps the most important are:

$$\frac{\text{Debtors}}{\text{Average daily sales}}$$

This measures how well management is speeding the flow of cash through the business, ie how many days' credit is being allowed to customers.

$$\frac{\text{Debtors}}{\text{Creditors}}$$

If creditors begin to outweigh debtors this may be a sign that the company is over-trading. The bad debt ratio (bad debts/sales) is also revealing.

$$\frac{\text{Current liabilities} - (\text{current assets minus stock})}{\text{Profit before tax and interest}} \times 365$$

This is the current liquidity ratio. It shows how many days it would take at current profit levels to pay off the deficit between current liabilities and liquid assets.

Productivity ratios

The most useful productivity ratio is:

$$\frac{\text{Results}}{\text{Resources}} \text{ ie } \frac{\text{Sales}}{\text{Employees}}$$

The other main ratios are:

$$\frac{\text{Units produced or processed}}{\text{Number of employees}}$$

$$\frac{\text{Added value (ie sales revenue minus cost of sales)}}{\text{Number of employees}}$$

$$\frac{\text{Profit after tax}}{\text{Number of employees}}$$

Cost ratios

The best way to look at costs is to express them as a percentage of sales. Thus the fundamental measure is:

$$\frac{\text{Overheads}}{\text{Sales}} \times 100$$

Other measures include:

$$\frac{\text{Payroll costs}}{\text{Sales}} \times 100$$

$$\frac{\text{Cost of materials and bought in parts}}{\text{Sales}} \times 100$$

$$\frac{\text{Selling costs}}{\text{Sales}} \times 100$$

Use of ratios

Use ratios as you would use any other figures. They are no more than indicators. In themselves, they will not tell the whole story. You have to dig. A ratio is no more than a symptom. You need to find out the real cause of a variation or problem.

Control systems

What you need from a control system

Your basic requirement is reports that clearly identify areas of good and bad performance so that appropriate action can be taken.

At higher levels 'exception reporting' should be adopted so that significant deviations, on which action should be taken, can be highlighted. Overall summaries of performance against plan and of trends will also be necessary at this level, but these may disguise significant underlying deviations which would be pointed out in an exception report.

The reports themselves should:

- Contain measurements which are accurate, valid and reliable. Permit a direct and easy comparison between planned and actual performance
- Analyse trends, comparing one period's performance with that of the previous period or of the same period the previous year and, where appropriate, summarizing the year to date position
- Be given to the person who is responsible for the activity concerned

- Arrive promptly, in time to allow the necessary action to be taken
- Provide succinct explanations of any deviations from plan.

Measurements

Measurement is a good thing, but all figures need to be treated with caution. They may conceal more than they reveal. The weaknesses to look for are:

- *Non-representative reporting* – data selected which do not cover the key issues, disguise unfavourable results or over-emphasize favourable performance.
- *Not comparing like with like* – the 'apples and pears syndrome'. For example, a trend or projection which does not take account of changing or new factors which have altered or will alter the situation since the base data were collected.
- *Not starting from a common base.* This is a variant on the 'like with like' problem. Trend comparisons should be related to a common base in terms both of the period and the elements covered by the information.
- *Misleading averages.* Averages do not always tell you the whole story. They may conceal extremes in performance, which are significant.
- *Unintentional errors* – simple mistakes in calculation, presentation or observation.
- *Measurements out of context.* Almost any single measure is influenced by, or inseparable from, other measures. Figures in isolation may not mean very much. You have to know about relationships and underlying influences.

Management by exception

Management by exception is a system which rings alarm bells only when the manager's attention is needed. The principle was invented by the father of scientific management, Frederick Taylor (50). In 1911 he wrote in *Principles of Scientific Management*:

> Under the exception principle the manager should receive only condensed, summarized and invariably comparative reports covering, however, all of the elements entering into the management and even these summaries should all be carefully gone over by an assistant before they reach the manager, and have all the exceptions to the past averages or standards pointed out, both the especially good and the especially bad exceptions, thus giving him in a few minutes a full view of progress which is being

made, or the reverse, and leaving him free to consider the broader lines of policy and to study the character and fitness of the important men under him.

Management by exception frees the boss to concentrate on the things that matter. It gives the subordinate more scope to get on with his work while knowing that events out of the ordinary will be reported upwards.

Deciding what constitutes an exception is a useful exercise in itself. It means selecting the key events and measures which will show up good, bad or indifferent results and indicate whether or not performance is going according to plan.

The chosen indicators or ratios can be studied so that the significance of changes or trends is readily understood. More important, the possible causes of deviations can be analysed and kept in mind. Investigations will then be quickly launched in the right direction and swift remedial action can be taken.

Most of us have come across the boss or manager who seems to have the almost magic facility for studying a mass of figures and immediately spotting the one really important deviation or the item that does not ring true. It sometimes seems to be pure instinct, but of course it is not. Such managers are practising the art of management by exception, even if they never call it by that name. Their experience and analytical powers have told them what constitutes normal performance. But they can spot something out of the ordinary at a thousand paces. They *know* what the key indicators are and they look for them, hard. This is a skill that anyone can develop. And the effort of acquiring it is well worthwhile.

Chapter 10
Coordinating

Coordinating – 'achieving unity of effort' – is not a separate function of a manager. The concept of coordination does not describe a *particular* set of operations but *all* operations which lead to a certain result.

Coordination is required because individual actions need to be synchronized. Some activities must follow one another in sequence. Others must go on at the same time and in the same direction in order to finish together.

How to coordinate

Obviously, you can get good coordination if you get people to work well together. This means integrating their activities, communicating well, exercising leadership, and team building (all subjects covered in individual chapters). But you should also pay attention to the specific techniques discussed below.

Planning

Coordination should take place before the event rather than after it. Planning is the first step. This means deciding what should be done and when. It is a process of dividing the total task into a number of sequenced or related sub-tasks. Then you work out priorities and time-scales.

Organizing

You know what should be done. You then decide who does it. When you divide work between people you should avoid breaking apart those tasks which are linked together and which you cannot separate cleanly from each other.

Your biggest problem will be deciding where the boundaries between distinct but related activities should be. If the boundary is either too rigid or insufficiently well defined, you may have coordination problems. Don't rely too much upon the formal organization as defined in job descriptions, charts and manuals. If you do, you will induce inflexibility and set up communication barriers, and these are fatal to coordination.

The informal organization which exists in all companies can help coordination. When people work together they develop a system of social relationships which cut across formal organizational boundaries. They create a network of informal groups which tend to discipline themselves. This frees management from detailed supervision and control and leaves it more time for planning, problem-solving and the overall monitoring of performance.

Delegating

The informal organization can help, but you still need to delegate work to individuals in a way that ensures they know what is expected of them *and* are aware of the need to liaise with others to achieve a coordinated result.

The art is to make everyone concerned understand the points on which they must link up with other people and the time in which such actions have to be completed. You should not have to *tell* people to coordinate; they should coordinate almost automatically. This they will do if you delegate not only specific tasks but also the job of working with others.

Communicating

You should not only communicate clearly what you want done, you should also encourage people to communicate with one another.

Avoid situations in which people can say: 'Why didn't someone tell me about this? If they had, I could have told them how to get out of the difficulty.' Nobody should be allowed to resort to James Forsyte's excuse that 'no one tells me anything'. It is up to people to find out what they need to know and not wait to be told.

Controlling

If you use the processes described above, and they work, theoretically you will not have to worry any more about coordination. But of course, life is not like that. You must monitor actions and results, spot problems and take swift corrective action when necessary. Coordination doesn't just happen. It has to be worked at, but avoid getting too involved. Allow people as much freedom as possible to develop horizontal relationships. These can facilitate coordination far more effectively than rigid and authoritarian control from above.

A case study

There is no one right way of coordinating a number of activities. It all depends on the nature of those activities and the circumstances in which they are carried out; for example, the present organization structure, the existence of coordinating committees and the facility with which communication can take place between those involved. Ultimately, good coordination depends upon the will of everyone concerned – to coordinate or be coordinated. Mechanical devices such as committees will not necessarily do the trick.

An example of good coordination took place in a company which was developing a new product in a new market. Neither the product nor the market fitted conveniently into the existing divisional structure and it was therefore decided to appoint one man as project manager to get the product launched. He would have a staff of two – a brand manager and a secretary. The work of development, production, marketing, selling and customer servicing would be carried out by the relevant departments in various divisions of the company.

The project manager had the status and authority to get things done by each department. The board was right behind the project and had allocated the priorities and resources required. But the different activities had to be coordinated and only the project manager could do it.

The easy way out would have been to set up a massive coordinating committee and leave it at that. This would have failed. Projects of this complexity cannot be coordinated just by creating a committee.

The project manager developed a different approach which proved to be highly successful. His first objective was to make everyone concerned enthusiastic about the project. He wanted them to believe in its importance so that they would be committed to working closely with the other departments involved.

His next step was to hold separate discussions with each departmental head so that he completely understood the programme of work required in each area. With the help of a project planner he then drew up a chart showing the key events and activities, and the relationships between them and the sequence in which they needed to take place in order to complete the project. This chart was distributed to all the departmental heads supplemented by an explanatory brief on the work required at each stage of the programme. Only then did he call a meeting to iron out difficulties and to ensure that everyone knew what had to be done and when.

He set up a system of progress reports and held progress meetings with departmental heads. But these were only held as necessary and he did not rely upon them to achieve coordination. He depended much more on personal contacts with individual managers, reviewing problems, noting where adjustments to the programme were needed, and stimulating the managers to even greater efforts when required. It was time consuming, but it kept him closely in touch so that he could anticipate any likely delays, setbacks or failures in communication, and be in a position to take action. He used the chart as his main instrument for checking that the critical events took place as planned.

The successful coordination and completion of the project were not achieved by one method but by the judicious use of a combination of techniques relevant to the situation: motivating, team building, planning, integrating, monitoring and controlling.

Chapter 11
Corporate culture and how to manage it

Definition

Corporate culture is the pattern of shared attitudes, beliefs, assumptions and expectations which will probably not have been recorded, but will shape the way in which people act and interact in an organization and underpin the way things get done. It will encompass the organization's dominant ideologies and may be expressed through its myths, heroes, stories, jargon, rites and legends.

The importance of culture

Corporate culture is a key component of the achievement of an organization's mission and strategies, the improvement of organizational effectiveness and the management of change. It is important because it is rooted in deeply held beliefs. It reflects what has worked in the past, being composed of responses which have been accepted because they have met with success.

Corporate culture can work for an organization by creating an environment which is conducive to performance improvement and the management of change. It can work against an organization by erecting barriers which prevent the achievement of strategic goals. These barriers include resistance to change and lack of commitment.

The significance of corporate culture to managers

Managers have to learn to live with the corporate culture, although they can play their part in changing it if that is necessary. To a large extent, whether they like it or not, there will be established norms and values governing their behaviour. In a bureaucratic, highly structured organization these norms are likely to be strong and difficult to ignore. In a more loosely formed 'organic' organization the norms will be flexible, but they will still exist. After all, if the norm is to behave informally it takes courage and strength of character to deviate from it to any great extent.

Corporate culture is important because it affects much of what you do. If you do not fit the culture or the culture does not fit you, then you may well have problems. If you are not aware of what your corporate culture is and how it manifests itself, or if you ignore the culture, then your ideas, your contributions and your decisions may be seen as irrelevant. Equally, if you do not appreciate that a change or a threat to the existing culture may cause alarm and despondency, you may blunder into situations which rapidly get out of control. To be a better manager you need to know all about corporate culture.

How corporate culture manifests itself

Corporate culture manifests itself in organizational behaviour – how managers and individual employees or groups behave in the context of the organization. In other words, it becomes 'the way things are done around here'. The culture is expressed by behaviour in five areas:

1. *Norms* – the unwritten rules of behaviour which strongly influence how things get done and how people act.
2. *Corporate values* – beliefs in what is best or good for the organization and what should or ought to happen, ie what is felt to be important. They are expressed by reference to both ends (goals) and means (action plans for achieving goals).
3. *Organization climate* – the working atmosphere of the organization as perceived and experienced by its members. This will encompass how people feel about and react to the characteristics and quality of the corporate culture and its values.
4. *Management style* – the way in which managers behave and exercise authority. They may be autocratic or democratic, tough or easy-going, formal or informal.

   The style managers adopt will be affected by the organization's culture and values. It depends to a degree on the individual's attitudes, but will also be affected by the leadership situations in which people are placed and, most important, by the example of more senior managers, especially the person at the top. The chief executive by his own behaviour can exert a great influence on the management style throughout the organization.

A management style that is more likely to encourage commitment and cooperation will lean in the direction of being democratic, relaxed, friendly, informal and open. But this does not mean that it should not be tough and direct when the occasion demands it. And it should always be decisive.

5. *Structure and systems* – including such aspects as the degree of flexibility in the structure and the extent to which a bureaucratic approach to administration is adopted.

The relevance of corporate culture

Corporate cultures can have significant effects on behaviour. These can be fundamental if incorrect assumptions about the market and the company's position in it lead to an unsuitable strategic plan. Even when the correct strategies have been adopted their implementation may be hindered if the wrong assumptions are made about how to sell the product or service, how to organize the people in the business, or how to manage, motivate, develop, reward and communicate with these people. Cultural change programmes may be required if the wrong assumptions have created an inappropriate culture and this is affecting performance.

Can corporate culture be managed?

Corporate culture is a key factor in achieving success but it is not easy to achieve. And because it has been evolved over the years through a number of learning processes a deeply rooted culture may be difficult to change – old habits die hard. The answer to the question, 'Can it be managed?' is yes, but with difficulty.

However, you also have to answer the question, 'Should it be managed?' because there are a number of alternative approaches to culture management, as Howard Schwartz and Stanley Davies (45) suggested. These are:

- Ignore the culture
- Manage round it
- Attempt to change elements of the culture to fit the strategy
- Change the strategy.

You can also take the culture you have got and do your best to maintain what is good about it while attempting to change counter-productive aspects of behaviour.

As Deal and Kennedy (10) said in *Corporate Cultures*, there are only five reasons to justify large-scale cultural change:

1. If your company has strong values that do not fit a changing environment
2. If the industry is very competitive and moves with lightning speed
3. If your company is mediocre or worse
4. If your company is about to join the ranks of the very largest companies
5. If your company is small but growing rapidly.

Deal and Kennedy say that if none of these reasons applies, don't do it. His analysis of ten cases of attempted cultural change indicated that it will cost between 5 and 10 per cent of what you already spend on the people whose behaviour is supposed to change, and even then you are likely to get only half the improvement you want. He warns that it costs a lot (in time, effort and money) and will take a long time.

How should corporate culture be managed?

A culture management programme involves the following steps, which are described in more detail later in this chapter:

1. Identify basic assumptions and beliefs and challenge them if necessary.
2. Define or redefine the core values – stated or unstated.
3. Analyse the organizational climate.
4. Analyse management style.
5. Plan and implement on the basis of steps 1 to 4 what aspects of the culture as defined by assumptions, values, climate and management style need to be changed and what aspects should be maintained or reinforced.

A key part is played in this process by the chief executive who, with the support of his team, achieves excellence by defining the organization's mission, getting his vision of what needs to be done across to everyone, defining and promulgating what he believes to be the right organizational values, exercising leadership in order to motivate the members of the organization, and ensuring that they are involved in and committed to achieving its objectives.

Analysing assumptions

The questions you should ask about cultural assumptions are:

80

1. What business are we in?
2. What is the nature of our marketplace?
   where do we do business?
   who are our customers or clients?
3. Is our business style:
   aggressive or laid-back?
   opportunistic or reactive?
   dynamic or static?
   with the emphasis on personal or professional skills?
   to take the competition head on or seek gaps in the market?
   market or production/technology-orientated?
4. How should work be organized?
   structured (mechanistic) or fluid (organic)?
   bureaucratic or informal?
   multi-level or flat structure?
5. What sort of people do we need in the organization in terms of quality, expertise and professional qualifications?
6. How do we treat people in the organization?
   as partners or servants?
   in close contact or at arm's length?
   openly (trusted with information) or closely (kept in the dark)?
   as able not only to accept but also to seek responsibility (Douglas McGregor's theory Y) or as requiring coercion, control, direction and the threat of punishment to get them to put forth adequate effort towards the achievement of organizational objectives (McGregor's theory X)?
   as needing the carrot more than the stick or vice versa?

The assumptions could be invalid, in which case they need to be challenged, or they could be valid and not acted upon, in which case they need to be reinforced.

Analysing values

The questions you should ask about values are:

1. Are employees proud of the company and its products or services?
2. Does the company truly believe in producing high quality products and providing a good service to its customers?
3. Is the company innovative?
4. Are managers and employees really interested in increasing productivity?
5. Do managers truly believe in the importance of the people who work there? And are they committed to improving the quality of working

life, providing opportunities for growth and development, giving individual attention to the needs of employees, keeping them informed on matters that affect them and involved in decision-making, and maintaining a fair pay system which rewards staff according to their responsibilities and contribution?

A belief in these values and in the organization as a whole will be developed if something that is worth doing is being done well. Pride in the product and pride in the company may exist because of a long tradition of achievement and quality.

But identification and loyalty are not inevitable – they have to be fostered.

Values will only be got across if they are believed in, acted upon and pursued relentlessly. The responsibility for presenting them should start at the top, but it should be shared by all managers and supervisors. You may not wish to go quite as far as the Japanese (in Japan, at 8am every morning 87,000 Matsushita employees are singing the company song and reciting the company's code of values), but it has to be accepted that their belief in getting the total identification of employees with their company has paid off.

Analysing the organizational climate

The questions you should ask about organization climate are:

1. Do people feel they are given enough responsibility?
2. Do people know what is expected of them in the shape of objectives and standards of performance?
3. Is there adequate feedback to people on their performance, whether it is good, bad or indifferent?
4. Is there sufficient challenge in the jobs given to people and sufficient emphasis on doing a good job (eg a strong drive for professionalism among managers)?
5. Are people given enough support by their managers or supervisors in the shape of guidance or help?
6. Is the emphasis in the organization on hard, dedicated work, or is it fairly relaxed?
7. Do people feel they are fairly rewarded for the work they do?
8. Do people feel that promotion policies are fair?
9. Is there an emphasis on positive rewards rather than punishments?
10. Is there a lot of bureaucracy and red tape around the organization or is the approach to work reasonably flexible and informal?
11. Is there an emphasis on taking calculated risks in the organization, or is playing it safe the general rule?

12. Is management open about what the company is doing?
13. Is there a general feeling of warmth and good fellowship in the atmosphere?
14. Do managers and other employees *want* to hear different opinions?
15. Is the emphasis on getting problems out into the open rather than smoothing them over or ignoring them?
16. Do people feel that they belong to a worthwhile company and are valuable members of working teams?

Analysing management style

The questions you should ask about management style are:

1. Does it tend to be autocratic, ie using authority to compel people to do what they are told, or democratic, ie encouraging people to participate and involve themselves in decision-making?
2. Does it tend to be task-centred or people-centred?
3. Do managers tend to be distant and cold or approachable and friendly?
4. Do managers tend to be hard or soft on people?

The culture change or reinforcement programme

The analysis of assumptions, values, climate and management style should indicate any areas where changes need to be made or the existing situation reinforced. The first thing to remember about culture change is that it can be difficult, painful and prolonged. Don't expect quick results. Fundamental changes can take years. And anticipate resistance to change. Cultural assumptions and values may be deeply entrenched and people will not give them up easily.

You cannot simply issue a new charter of corporate values and expect people to act on them wholeheartedly and at once. They have to be convinced that they are relevant and valid and will not prove detrimental to their own position in the organization.

There are two ways of tackling change. The first is to deal with the various manifestations of culture in a general way, allowing particular programmes to emerge. The second is to go straight for one or more specific areas, having first defined your objectives – what change you want to bring about and why. Be general when you have to explore in greater depth what needs to be done. Be specific when you are quite clear about where you are going. But don't try to do too much at once.

General approaches to cultural change

The general approaches to cultural change will examine:

1. *Assumptions.* Get people to challenge them whenever they emerge specifically in discussions, meetings or memoranda, or appear to underlie opinions expressed orally or on paper. Use the checklist given earlier in this section and re-examine the items in discussion. No dramatic changes will be achieved by this means alone, but at least people will become more aware of what they have previously taken for granted and may be more willing to change their behaviour as a result of other aspects of the programme.

2. *Values.* Consciously and deliberately set out the core values of the organization and get them discussed – at board level and throughout the organization. Restate them formally on the basis of these discussions but ensure also that these values are reinforced and acted upon by other cultural change activities as described below.

3. *Organization climate.* Ask people what they think is good and bad about the climate. This can be done comprehensively by an attitude survey or by using focus groups – special semi-structured discussion groups of employees set up to elicit shared attitudes and beliefs about the organization.

4. *Management style.* A change in management style is best achieved by example from above, starting at the top of the organization. Management style will also be strongly influenced by restatements and examinations of values and climate.

   When managers are appraised, their management style should be a subject for discussion and agreement should be reached between the people concerned on where changes are desirable. Appraisals should be both downwards – from management to subordinate – and upwards, ie the subordinate should be given the chance to appraise his manager. Self-appraisal should also be encouraged.

Specific approaches to cultural change

The specific approaches you can use to achieve cultural change are:

1. *Reorganization* to facilitate integration, to create departments or jobs which are responsible for new activities or to eliminate unnecessary layers of management.

2. *Organization development* to improve the effectiveness with which an organization functions and responds to change. OD programmes are concerned with achieving better coordination, teamwork and commitment, and with the management of change and conflict.

3. *Communications* to get the message across about the values and to

achieve the objectives for a communications change programme, such as the one set up in Book Club Associates in 1987, which were to:

- increase the identification of staff with the firm and therefore to enhance their commitment;
- provide the opportunity for all levels of staff to become more involved in the firm's affairs;
- generate ideas from staff to develop the business, improve the levels of customer service and increase productivity.

4. *Training* to help to form new attitudes to such matters as customer service, quality, managing and motivating people or productivity; to increase commitment to the firm and its value; to review and challenge assumptions; and to improve skills or teach new skills.

5. *Recruitment* to change deliberately the type of people recruited to fit the desired culture or to reinforce the existing culture by drawing up related job specifications and finding candidates who meet those specifications.

6. *Management by objectives* to ensure that managers know what they are expected to do.

7. *Performance management* to ensure that managers, supervisors and staff are assessed on the basis of the results they achieve and that performance improvement programmes consisting of self-development, coaching, counselling and training are used to capitalize on strengths or overcome weaknesses.

8. *Reward management* to enhance the cultural assumption that rewards should be related to achievement by introducing performance-related bonus schemes and remuneration systems.

Examples of cultural change programmes

British Airways

To quote what Dr Nicholas Georgiadis, formerly Director of Human Resources British Airways, said at the Management Centre Europe conference in Lisbon in 1987: 'British Airways has changed. Five years ago it was sick. It is now much healthier. At the root of that recovery (from losses of £11 million in 1981/82 to cumulative profits of £536 million over the last three years) is customer service.'

The dominant culture in British Airways, according to Georgiadis, had been militaristic and bureaucratic. And his comment on this was that: 'You cannot determine human behaviour by referring to paragraph 3(9)x. You cannot provide quality customer service by administrative fiat. What you have to have is an empowered workforce – a workforce which knows it has the power to take action and that its decisions will be backed by the bosses.'

The British Airways management decided that the main area for cultural change was customer service and that the key to successful customer service lies in ensuring that your people feel good about themselves and their company. In short, customer care demands caring, skilful management to support the caring skills for which British Airways managers were 'untrained, uninformed and unrewarded'.

The culture change programme was divided into three parts:

1. *Putting people first* – a two-day intensive workshop aimed at all customer contact staff, encouraging them to think about the importance of customer service. The workshop looked at issues such as the importance of helping other people to give good customer service, who owns a customer's problem, and the importance of body language in all human interaction. All 40,000 employees went through this programme.
2. *A day in the life* – a one-day event designed to help all staff to understand their mutual interdependence. Some 30,000 staff enjoyed this day.
3. *Managing people first* – a five-and-a-half-day event for managers which dealt with five themes:

   Urgency which should come from the leader, not from events – this means that managers must be pro-active rather than running just to stand still as they simply react to events.

   Vision which is 'having the image of a cathedral as we mix the cement' – managers must be able to work both in the here and now, as they mix the cement, and focus on the future as they plan the cathedral.

   Motivation which is management by expectation – expect the best and catch them doing it right – because people who feel good about themselves and their manager produce good results.

   Trust which gives confidence to the individual to act alone – and spirit to the group to act together – freeing people to own the problem and use their own judgement without fear.

   Above all, *responsibility*, believing that I am in charge of my own behaviour which means that I can change the way I do things.

In addition to these courses, a new performance appraisal scheme was introduced, based on the mentor system, which focused on managerial behaviour, especially team management and the management of subordinates. Having been told how to do it in the 'managing people first' programme, appraisal tells them how they are doing, and 'pay for performance' rewards them for doing it.

ICL

The background to ICL's cultural change programme was provided by the new managing director who said:

> I gradually realized that I lacked the levers to transfer my strategic insight into the hearts and minds of the organization so that they shared the imperative. They had to know *why*, not just *what*. An impressive programme of communication was not enough. I got immensely frustrated – thousands of bright people all working hard but not buying into the direction.

He is also reported as having used the well-worn Second World War saying of a US general: 'I have seen the enemy, and he is us.'

Mission statement

The approach was based on a new mission for the company implying significant changes in direction. This was defined as: ICL is an international company dedicated to applying information technology to provide profitable high-value customer solutions for operational and management effectiveness.

Key strategies

Objectives were set which were designed to build strength as a major European player in information technology, to focus on specific markets, and to be known as a systems integrator with a reputation for quality.

The key strategies were to be built around:

- High-value solutions to defined markets
- Commitment to open systems – providing customers with greater flexibility in the choice of manufacturer and with confidence for the future
- Collaborations – to gain market or technical leverage
- Organizational responsiveness – to react to the fast-changing market
- Focus on systems and solutions for customers and on providing real added value for them in running their business
- Changing the way that people thought, made their decisions and conducted their lives in the company. These can be summarized as follows:

From	*To*
technology-led	marketing-led
tactical, short-term	strategic, long-term
internal focus	external focus
try and do everything	specialized target markets
parochial	company commitment
procedure-bound	innovative and open-minded
UK expert	global competitor

Chapter 12
Cost cutting

Costs always require to be controlled. You should start with the assumption that costs are too high and that they can be reduced. This assumption is based on the knowledge that some companies have not only survived but have flourished after drastic cost-cutting exercises. When you remove the fat that always exists, you get a leaner and more powerful organization.

Cost cutting requires these basic approaches:

- Decide where and what to cut
- Plan to cut
- Conduct the cost-reduction exercise.

What to cut

Your attack on costs should concentrate on these six areas:

- *Labour costs.* In labour-intensive companies manpower costs may exceed 50 per cent of income. Overmanning, especially in service and staff departments, is a major contributory cause of excessively high costs. Labour costs will include the direct costs of salaries, wages and benefits and the indirect cost of the personnel and training functions.
- *Manufacturing costs.* These are the actual costs incurred in making products; they reflect labour, material and operating costs but also, most important, the way in which the product has been designed.
- *Selling costs.* These may be largely accounted for by the sales force which is covered under labour costs. But the figure will also include advertising, promotions, public relations, packaging and display material.
- *Development costs.* These are the costs of developing new products, markets, processes and materials, and of acquiring new businesses.

- *Material and inventory costs.* The cost of buying materials and bought in parts and of maintaining optimum stock levels.
- *Operating costs.* All the other costs incurred in operating the business. This will include space, computers, the provision of plant and equipment, paperwork systems and all the services required to keep the organization going.

Waste

Any examination of costs should aim to identify wasteful practices. The areas where they can occur need to be identified before conducting a cost-reduction exercise so that attention can be directed to likely trouble spots. Concentrate both on company practices or procedures which lead to waste or pointless costs and on areas where staff can waste time or incur unnecessary expenditure.

The company can be wasteful in any or all of the following ways:

- Unnecessary forms or over-complex paperwork procedures
- Too much checking and verifying of work
- Too many and/or too large committees
- To many layers of management
- Bottlenecks and inefficient work flows or procurement procedures
- Delays in decision-making because authority is not delegated down the line
- Over-rigid adherence to rules and regulations
- Too much commitment to paper.

Time-wasting practices by staff include lateness or leaving early, prolonged tea or meal breaks, unnecessary breaks for any other reason, and dealing with personal matters in company time.

Cost-creating practices include absenteeism and frequent absence through illness (which may or may not be justified). Other wasteful practices include extravagant use of the company's facilities and equipment, such as photocopying machines, telephones and stationery.

Planning to cut costs

First, you build cost effectiveness into your plans, using value analysis techniques when you can. Then you introduce or improve procedures which define what costs you can incur and, at a later stage, control expenditure against budget. Zero-base budgeting, as described in Chapter 3, is a useful technique for taking every expense and 'shaking it' to make sure that it is justified.

Plans

Plans should be based on cost/benefit studies which aim to get the best ratio between expenditure and results, ie to minimize costs and maximize benefits. The emphasis should be on realism. It is good to be forward looking and entrepreneurial. But if you are like that, you are always in danger of becoming euphoric about the future, overestimating the benefits and underestimating the costs. At the planning stage you must be realistic about costs. Don't accept averages and assumed overhead rates. Get actuals. Find out what you are really going to spend and add at least 10 per cent for contingencies. Allow for inflation too.

You should be equally realistic about likely benefits. Do some 'sensitivity analysis' to determine the effects on profits and costs of optimistic, realistic and pessimistic forecasts of performance.

Design

Ensure that when products, systems or services are designed, at every stage the costs of what you are going to do are evaluated. Use value analysis techniques for this purpose.

Value analysis

Value analysis takes each part of the product, service or system, and subjects it to detailed examination to see if there is any way in which its costs could be reduced without affecting quality. You start with the assumption that anything you use or do can be bought, made or operated at less cost.

Value analysis in manufacturing is often carried out by a committee using brainstorming techniques to consider alternative, less costly ways of achieving the functions for which the article is being manufactured. These functions cover the use to which the article is being put and, therefore, consideration has to be given to marketing and pricing considerations as well as manufacturing costs. But, given a definition of use, the main aim of value analysis is to reduce the costs of materials, processing and labour. The following is a checklist of points to be covered.

1. Does its use contribute to value?
2. Is its cost proportionate to its usefulness?
3. Does it need all its features?
4. Is there a better alternative which will meet its intended use?
5. Can a usable part be made by a less costly method?
6. Can a standard and less costly part be used instead?
7. Will another dependable supplier provide it at less cost?
8. Can alternative and cheaper materials or components be used?

9. Can it be manufactured with the use of less skilled labour or less expensive machinery or equipment?
10. Can it be manufactured in a way which will reduce the number of standard labour hours required?
11. Can its design be simplified to reduce manufacturing costs?
12. Can the tolerances specified be modified to ease manufacture and reduce reject rates?

Although value analysis was first developed as a design engineering technique, the approach is equally applicable to the design of any system or service where the component parts can be costed.

The cost-reduction exercise

A cost-reduction exercise is a planned campaign aimed at cutting costs by a specified amount. It requires three steps:

- *Setting targets*, either for immediate cuts in crisis conditions or for specific reductions in the short term (defined in weeks rather than months). Targets may be set in specific areas, eg a 10 per cent cut in staff; or they may be for a more comprehensive overhead reduction or a productivity increase.

   The significant impact of overheads on profits should be emphasized to everyone. It is interesting to note that in a company with a turnover of £200,000 where profits are 10 per cent of sales, a reduction in the ratio of labour costs to sales from 11 to 10 per cent would increase profits by 10 per cent. It all ends up on the bottom line, and that is what counts.

   Productivity targets expressed in financial terms, such as 'reduce costs per unit of output by 3 per cent', may be less immediate but they could usefully be incorporated in a set of cost-reduction targets as longer-term objectives. Increases in productivity can be achieved by reducing costs in relation to output, or by increasing output in relation to costs or, preferably, by both reducing costs and increasing output (see Chapter 43). The message must be got across that unit costs are there to be attacked at all times – after all, they aggregate into total costs. Wherever possible, get down to basics – the shop floor and the general office. That is where the main costs are incurred. Keep it simple. Look at specific items. Use value analysis. Compare and contrast to identify places where costs are excessive.

- *Deciding where to cut*, which will probably be in manpower costs or wasteful practices. It is remarkable how often departmental managers who scream with pain when they are told to cut their staff by 10 per cent cope quite well afterwards. O & M specialists will claim and prove that they can always cut staff numbers by 15 per cent without reducing efficiency.

With regard to wasteful or unnecessary practices, Sir Derek Rayner's campaign in Marks & Spencer illustrated what can be done. A drive on paperwork eliminated 26 million forms in annual use and cut the number of staff by 25 per cent.

- *Deciding how to cut*: allocating responsibilities and then drawing up the programme and implementing it.

Responsibility for the cost-reduction exercise

The most important thing to do is to appoint as senior an executive as possible, preferably a full-time member of the board, to direct the cost-reduction exercise. He should have drive, energy, determination and, most important, the authority and courage to implement measures, however unpleasant some of them may be.

The question of who is to assist this executive then arises. You may consider using management consultants to help and give advice on specific problem areas. But do not ask consultants to carry out the main task. If your organization is not capable of taking action itself, however drastic, it does not deserve to survive.

Neither should you set up a committee to control the exercise. Committees are obstacles to action. You might set up a small (not more than three people) project team of senior executives, but do not let them function as a standing committee with agenda, minutes, and so on. Better still, give complete authority to one director to control the exercise, to use whom he wants when he wants and to call meetings as and when he thinks fit.

The director in charge of the exercise requires terms of reference by which to operate. These should normally take the form of a set of targets for him to achieve by a given date or sequence of dates. If there are any constraints (eg don't sack the chairman's son-in-law) he should be told them now. He should also be told the extent of his authority to make decisions and when and in what circumstances he should report back. He can then proceed to solicit opinions about what needs to be done, get the facts to support or refute the opinions, define the problem areas, decide what to do and draw up a programme for doing it.

Approach to the exercise

The highly successful cost-reduction exercises conducted by Marks & Spencer used the most simple of questioning techniques:

- What is done?
- Why is it done?
- Does it need to be done at all?
- If it needs to be done, can it be simplified or carried out more cheaply?

The basis of the approach, to paraphrase Wittgenstein, was 'if anything needs to be done at all it can be done more simply'.

A number of other principles emerged from the Marks & Spencer experience which are universally applicable. These were summarized by Sir Derek Rayner as follows:

- *Top managers must accept a revision of the administrator's task.* Top management has imposed on administration countless rules and regulations to ensure that the systems and methods used in the business are foolproof. These have apparently been 'written largely on the assumption that all employees fall into two categories: stupid or crooked'. As Sir Derek wrote: 'If you cast the role of the administrator as bureaucrat he will perform it superbly.' The paraphernalia of administrative systems drawn up under this type of regime can only be swept away by top management.
- *The price of perfection is prohibitive: sensible approximation costs less.* Or, in Voltaire's words, 'the best is the enemy of the good'. Aim towards perfection, but don't overstretch yourself in achieving it. Productivity applied to administration means one man trying to achieve 95 per cent efficiency and reaching it, rather than two men trying to achieve 100 per cent and reaching perhaps 90 per cent.
- *Most employees can be trusted.* If this principle is accepted, a wide range of checks and monitoring can be discarded and replaced by managers managing and supervisors supervising. Thorough spot checks can be used to supplement day-to-day management.
- *All staff can help to bring about the desired changes.* Most people, if encouraged, will bring forward ideas to simplify and rationalize their work.
- *Staff can become too specialized.* Too many specialists create unnecessary work and hinder flexibility. 'Specialists exist to serve and ease the running of the business, not to stifle initiative, become barriers to action, and create yet another paper chain.'
- *Never legislate for every eventuality* but instead leave as much as possible to the common sense of those who are trusted in managerial positions.
- *These is no substitute for personal probing into what really happens.* 'You will find your most cherished documents and reports conceal a multitude of inaccuracies and omissions. Do not be afraid of only a

sample first-hand investigation. It is often far more valuable than the all-embracing written one. And do not mistake for personal probing a meeting held in a private office.'

A case study

The policy pursued over a long period by Marks & Spencer is the best example of a company-wide programme for improving productivity by streamlining procedures and eliminating wasteful and unnecessary practices.

The main attack launched by Sir Derek Rayner in Marks & Spencer was on unnecessary paper work, which generates unnecessary work and leads to the employment of superfluous labour.

The purpose was not to achieve economies for economy's sake, but to make more effective use of resources. The campaign eliminated 26 million forms in annual use and progressively reduced the number of staff from 27,000 to 20,000. Yet Marks & Spencer continued to grow rapidly.

An example of the improvements produced by the campaign was a complete change in the method of providing merchandizing information to the stores. There was a detailed system of recording sales, stocks and requirements which was theoretically sound. Unfortunately, it took many people a great deal of time to digest the information and to act upon it. They were tied to paper and could not see the merchandise for the figures. The system was completely swept away and members of the staff were invited to pay more attention to the goods themselves, which, of course, they then had time to do. Very short summaries were now sent to head office and many simple ways of giving the stores a reasonably balanced supply of goods were developed.

Another key change was the reduction in the extent to which staff in the stores had become specialized, largely because of the forms and systems used. For example, there were many stock room specialists and the stock rooms were virtually isolated from the sales floor. Sales personnel had to fill in a form if they required stock for their counters. The stock was sorted out by a stock room specialist and eventually delivered to the counters. This practice was abolished and the stock room was thrown open to all, so that sales staff could simply go and replenish their counters. This not only saved time and paper and speeded up the supply of goods, but also paid an unexpected dividend in that the sales staff quickly became far more interested in their jobs.

Simultaneously with this drive on unnecessary paperwork, Marks & Spencer stopped recruitment. It became apparent in the early stages of the exercise that each stage in simplification meant that the system could work with fewer people. As simplification proceeded, the staff numbers steadily ran down by natural wastage. At the same time, people were redeployed from unproductive to productive work.

To win one battle, however, does not mean that you have won the war. As Sir Derek Rayner wrote:

> Though our management believed it was alert to the dangers of excessive paperwork and over-complication, the familiar signs of trouble began to reappear; for instance, fast-rising administrative expenses and ever-increasing demands for more staff. So . . . we mounted a new campaign known as 'Good Housekeeping'. Again the results were outstanding. Millions of pieces of paper in the shape of reports, forms and returns were eliminated. Thousands of hours spent on needless detail were saved. We reduced the staff from 27,000 people to 26,000 by not hiring replacements as employees left . . . Most important, good housekeeping has freed our managers to spend more time on managing instead of interpreting the written word. It has enabled important staff members to get away more often from their desks and learn first hand what is going on in the stores and in supplier organizations.

This campaign saved 200,000 forms a year by simplifying control of cash in tills. Stock control was simplified and the information needed by headquarters was cut by half a million pages a year. The investigating team dispensed with the 13 million forms used each year to process returned goods before the customer got his or her money back: why not, they asked, meet legitimate claims at once from the till? The campaign reduced staff costs by 5 per cent, *and*, Sir Derek Rayner argues, it gave customers a better service.

Chapter 13
Counselling

People problems

As a manager, you will constantly be faced with people's problems. They come to you with their troubles or you become aware that all is not well and something must be done about it.

Dealing with problems

The four styles that can be adopted to deal with these problems are:

1. *Tell.* You solve the problem for them. You are the expert. You are the person in authority. You pronounce. They listen. Theirs is not to reason why.

   This is the authoritarian approach. The individuals may or may not obey, but even if they do as they are told, they won't know why and they will not know how to cope next time.

2. *Manipulate.* You know best, or think you do. You realize that a 'telling' approach is crude and that more will be achieved if the individuals feel that what they are going to do is what they wanted to do.

   Manipulators steer people in the direction in which they, the manipulators, want them to go. They do not care about the real needs of the individuals concerned; they only offer help and advice which further their own interests and increase their power.

   Manipulators have a poor opinion of the people they are manipulating. They want to change them to the sort of people the manipulator wants them to be. Such men are dangerous, although if they are seen through – and they often are – their efforts will be counter-productive and will only reflect badly on themselves.

3. *Advise.* When you give advice you get the individuals with problems involved in solving them. You are not exactly telling them what to do; instead, you are jointly analysing the situation against the background of their own needs, expectations, hopes and fears.

Advisers can help their clients to learn not only how to solve the current problem but also how to cope with it if it arises again. Good advisers will get their clients involved in discussing alternative solutions to the problem, leaving them to make the final choice. But there is the danger that, as experts, advisers will so weight the pros and cons of each alternative in favour of their preferred solution that their clients are left with little real choice.

This is one of the reasons why good advice is not always taken. What may appear to you as good advice is not perceived as good advice by the recipients. They may agree at the time because of your authority but, deep inside, they see it differently. You may feel that you have passed the problem and its solution over to them but you may well have been in effect saying, 'Which of *my* ideas appeals to you?' They are not truly involved and, because of this, a joint understanding of the roots of the problem will not have been achieved. A superficial solution may well emerge which, on reflection, the individual feels uncomfortable about implementing.

4. *Counsel.* If you adopt a counselling style you are more concerned with the individual than the problem. You genuinely want to get involvement in solving it, not by presenting a choice of solutions from on high, but by getting the individual to decide for himself – with your help – what the best solution would be for him. The strength of the counselling approach over any other is that people will become more truly committed to do something if they can 'own' the problem and its solution. And they do this if they have made up their own minds and personally believe it is the right thing to do. Telling, manipulating, even advising, can each put pressure on people to which they can react negatively.

Why counsel?

As a manager, you may often have to tell people what to do when you want to get them into action and there will be many occasions when you may believe that the right thing to do is to give someone advice because you genuinely feel that you know best.

But advice is often not taken and you should always consider when faced with people problems whether a counselling approach will produce better results. It takes time and trouble, but if someone is really worth saving, your time will have been well spent.

How to counsel

There are two difficulties you have to overcome if you want to counsel effectively. First, you have to help the individuals to identify the real, 'core' problem, and this is hard because they may not be able to do this for themselves, let alone you. Second, you have to get the issue out into the open. This means dealing with feelings that people might not wish to reveal, especially to their boss. Personal problems can be compounded if people cannot talk about them and, somehow, the counsellor has to break through this barrier.

There is no formula for overcoming these difficulties. All you can do is to adopt a flexible approach which can be modified to fit individual circumstances, as described below.

1. *Listen actively.* Active listening means more than simply not talking. The counsellor has to show interest and attention so that the person being counselled thinks that he is the only one that matters. Plenty of eye-contact is needed, coupled with words of encouragement when the individual opens up. People should not be led but can be helped to develop a theme beneficially.

2. *Observe.* Observe as well as listen. Oral communication can be clumsy and full of hidden meanings. Take note of gestures (body language), manner, tone and expression as well as listening to the words. Use imagination to evoke meaning.

3. *Question.* The counsellor helps people to understand and define the problem by asking pertinent, open-ended questions, pertinent in the sense that they emerge from the information which the individual is giving during the session, open-ended in the sense that they are non-directive – they do not suggest the answers you want. Questions are the starting point to get individuals to explore and clarify the problem and their feelings about it so that they can develop possible solutions for themselves.

   The sort of questions you can ask are:

   - What do *you* think is happening?
   - How does this problem affect *you*?
   - When did *you* first become aware of this difficulty?
   - Where have *you* come across this problem?
   - Who else is involved?
   - Why do *you* think the problem has arisen?

- What do *you* feel should be done about it?

Don't tumble out the questions, especially the last one. They should emerge naturally during the course of the session, providing linking points or stepping stones to a further exploration of the problem, its causes and its solution.

4. *Recognize feelings.* The problem, unless it is purely technical, will involve feelings. You have to allow them to be expressed. In fact, by so doing, you may well help individuals by getting them to unburden themselves and release their emotions about the situation. You may be able to help a lot simply by letting these feelings come out and by listening to them sympathetically and without comment. All you need to do from time to time is to 'reflect' feelings. This means feeding back a remark in your own words such as 'so you feel that . . .' which either demonstrates that you understand or gives people a chance to restate their case.

5. *Define the problem.* This is the challenge. Individuals may define their problem in very broad terms, testing the water to find out if you are likely to respond in an understanding way. To get to the root of the matter you have to look for clues and help individuals to explore issues in greater depth, so that they can define the problem for themselves with the aid of sympathetic listening and brief, well-directed questions. A considerable amount of both listening and questioning may be necessary before the point becomes clear, since strong emotions and clarity of expression seldom go together. When you think you understand the individual's viewpoint, it is often helpful to ask a summarizing question such as, 'Is this what you mean?' without passing any moral judgement.

   You should gradually form a hypothesis about the problem as the session continues. Do not reveal it to the individual. Instead, explore views, opinions, reactions and feelings in order to test the hypothesis and adopt, modify or replace it. This hypothesis will be your guide on how to help the individual to come to terms with the problem and deal with it. But you should not prejudge the issue. The hypothesis should emerge from what you hear and see, and you should be prepared to change it if new information becomes available.

   Above all, do not reveal that you think you have the answer. Your hypothesis is just used to indicate the direction that is most likely to lead to a resolution of the problem and your aim is to get the individual to work this out.

6. *Explore solutions.* Start from the hypothesis of why the problem exists – as defined by the individual – who should then be

encouraged to suggest alternative ways of dealing with it. While you should make encouraging noises, you should not specifically approve or disapprove of anything. Simply get the individual to go through the pros and cons and come to a decision, unaided by you, on the best course of action. So long as you are certain that this solution will not harm the individual or anyone else, you can go along with it. But do not get over-enthusiastic. Content yourself with a calm, even a cool statement, to the effect that you believe that the individual will be able to implement it. If you believe the solution is harmful you have to try to get the individual to recognize this. Only suggest that further consideration is required if you know that the solution cannot be implemented because it fundamentally contravenes company policy or because you are convinced that the effect will be detrimental to the individual or others.

7. *Implement.* If you are asked to provide specific help with implementation, you should do so. Otherwise, let the individual carry on, but be ready to provide additional counselling if things look as if they are going wrong.

When to counsel

As a manager, you should be prepared to use the counselling approach if a member of your staff has a personal problem which is affecting his work. You are not there to pry into personal affairs but if you can help someone to get over a hang-up, you thereby achieve a change in behaviour which results in improved performance, the time given to counselling may well prove worthwhile and, of course, the more valuable a member of your staff is, the more time you should be prepared to spend on his problems.

Counselling, however, is not always the appropriate technique. You have to flex your management style to cope with different situations and there will be occasions when to deal with a problem member of staff you have to be more directive. But before taking this route, you should always consider whether in the longer run a counselling approach will be more beneficial, not only for the individuals but also for yourself as their manager.

Chapter 14
Creative thinking

Walter Bagehot wrote: 'It is often said that men are ruled by their imagination; but it would be truer to say that they are governed by the weakness of their imagination.'

Unimaginative management is a sure way to failure. Creative thinking aims to overcome the danger of being governed by this weakness.

Creative and logical thinking

Creative thinking is imaginative thinking. It produces new ideas, new ways of looking at things. It relates things or ideas which were previously unrelated. It is discontinuous and divergent. Edward de Bono (11) invented the phrase 'lateral thinking' for it and this term has stuck; it implies sideways leaps in the imagination rather than a continuous progression down a logical chain of reasoning.

Logical or analytical thinking is a step-by-step process. It is continuous, one step leading to the next until, ideally, you converge on the only possible solution. It is sometimes called 'convergent' thinking; de Bono refers to it as 'vertical thinking' because you go straight down the line from one state of information to another.

De Bono summed up the differences between vertical and lateral thinking as follows:

Vertical thinking	*Lateral thinking*
Chooses	Changes
Looks for what is right	Looks for what is different
One thing must follow directly from another	Makes deliberate jumps
Concentrates on relevance	Welcomes chance intrusions
Moves in the most likely directions	Explores the least likely

Creative thinking is not superior to logical thinking. It's just different. The best managers are both creative and logical. Eventually, however creative they have been, they have to make a decision. And logical thinking is necessary to ensure that it is the right decision.

The process of creativity

In *The Act of Creation*, Arthur Koestler (30) described the process of creativity as one of 'bisociation'; putting together two unconnected facts or ideas to form a single idea. The establishment of the relationship or bisociation is usually accompanied by a release of tension. There is a flash of illumination leading to a shout of 'Eureka!' or at least 'Aha!'. As Koestler remarks, it is like the release of tension after the unexpected punch line of a joke – the 'haha' reaction. Or even the less dramatic release of tension when confronting a work of art.

If we assume that it is desirable to increase our capacity for creative thinking, there are three things to do:

1. Understand the barriers to creative thinking
2. Develop individual capacity for creative thinking
3. Use the collective capacities of groups of people to develop new ideas by 'brainstorming'.

Barriers to creative thinking

The main barriers to creative thinking are:

- Allowing your mind to be conditioned into following a dominant pattern – the mind is a patterning system and this means you can be trapped into a fixed way of looking at things, what de Bono calls a 'concept prison', or a 'tethering factor'
- Restricting the free growth of your ideas within rigidly drawn boundaries which are treated as limiting conditions
- Failure to identify and examine the assumptions you are making to ensure that they are not restricting the development of new ideas
- Polarizing alternatives – reducing every decision to an 'either/or' when there may be other ways of looking at things
- Being conditioned to think sequentially rather than laterally and looking for the 'best' idea, not different ideas. As de Bono says: 'It is better to have enough ideas for some of them to be wrong than always to be right by having no ideas at all.'

- Lack of effort in challenging the obvious – it is tempting to slip into the easy solution
- Evaluating too quickly – jumping to conclusions and not giving yourself enough time to allow your imagination to range freely over other possible ways of looking at things
- A tendency to conform – to give the answer expected
- Fear of looking foolish or being put down.

How to develop your ability to think creatively

If you want to think more creatively, the first thing to do is to analyse yourself. Go through the list of barriers to creativity and ask yourself the question, 'Is this me?' If it is, think about ways in which you can overcome the difficulty, concentrating on:

- Breaking away from any restrictions
- Opening up your mind to generate new ideas
- Delaying judgement until you have thoroughly explored the alternative ideas.

Breaking away

To break away from the constraints on your ability to generate new ideas you should:

- Identify the dominant ideas influencing your thinking
- Define the boundaries (ie past experience, precedents, policies, procedures, rules) within which you are working and try to get outside them by asking questions such as:

    - Are the constraints reasonable?
    - Is past experience reliable?
    - What's new about the present situation?
    - Is there another way?

- Bring your assumptions out into the open and challenge any which restrict your freedom to develop new ideas
- Reject 'either/or' propositions – ask, 'Is there really a simple choice between alternatives?'
- Keep on asking 'Why?' (But bear in mind that if you do this too bluntly to other people you can antagonize them.)

Generating new ideas

To generate new ideas you have to open up your mind. If you have

removed some of the constraints as suggested above you will be in a better
position to:

- Look at the situation differently, exploring all possible angles
- List as many alternative approaches as possible without seeking the
  'one best way' (there is no such thing) and without indulging in
  premature evaluation (which can only lead to partial satisfaction)
- In de Bono's words, 'arrange discontinuity', deliberately set out to
  break the mould. The techniques for triggering off new ideas include:

  - Free thinking, allowing your mind to wander over alternative and
    in many cases apparently irrelevant ways of looking at the
    situation
  - Deliberately exposing yourself to new influences in the form of
    people, articles, books, indeed anything which might give you a
    different insight, even though it might not be immediately
    relevant
  - Switching yourself or other people from problem to problem
  - Arranging for the cross-fertilization of ideas with other people
  - Using analogies to spark off ideas. The analogy should be
    suggested by the problem but should then be allowed to exist in
    its own right to indicate a different way of looking at the
    problem.

Delaying judgement

Your aim in creative thinking should be to separate the evaluation of ideas
from their generation. The worst mistake you can make is to kill off new
ideas too quickly. It is always easy to find ten ways of saying 'no' to
anything. For example:

- It won't work
- We're already doing it
- It's been tried before without success
- It's not practical
- It won't solve the problem
- It's too risky
- It's based on pure theory
- It will cost too much
- It will antagonize the customers/the boss/the union/the workers/
  the shareholders, etc
- It will create more problems than it solves.

Some of these objections may be valid. But they should be held back until you have generated as many ideas as possible. Allow ideas to grow a little. Don't strangle them at birth.

It is too easy to say 'no', too easy to ridicule anything new or different. In creative thinking it is the end result that counts, and if you want it to be original you must not worry too much about the route you follow to get there. It doesn't matter if you stumble sometimes or take the wrong turning, as long as delays are not protracted and you arrive in the right place at the end.

As de Bono (11) says:

> In vertical thinking one has to be right at every step. So, no matter how many steps are taken, the end point (idea, solution, conclusion) is automatically right if all the intervening steps have been right . . . In lateral thinking one does not *have* to be right at each step, but one must be right at the *end*.

Delaying judgement is difficult. It goes against the grain. You have to make a conscious effort to hold back until the right moment arrives, which is when you feel that you have collected as many new ideas as you can in the time available.

Our training, our inhibitions, our reluctance to look foolish or to go out on a limb all work against us. We should certainly try to do it ourselves and persuade other people to go along with us. But we can help the processes of opening up, introducing discontinuity and releasing new ideas by the technique of brainstorming.

Brainstorming

Brainstorming has been defined as a means of getting a large number of ideas from a group of people in a short time. It is essentially a group activity which uses a formal setting to generate as many ideas as possible without pausing to evaluate them.

The main features of a brainstorming session are:

1. A group of between six and twelve people is assembled. Some will be directly involved with the problem, some should be drawn from other areas from which they can bring different ideas and experience to bear on the problem. There is a chairman and a note-taker.

2. The chairman defines the rules, emphasizing that:

   - The aim is to get as many ideas as possible
   - No attempt will be made to evaluate any ideas
   - No one should feel inhibited about coming up with suggestions.

3. If necessary there is a warm-up session to familiarize the group with the procedure. For example, they could be asked to suggest how many uses they can think of for a paper clip.

4. The chairman states the problem, avoiding the trap of defining it too narrowly.

5. The chairman opens the session by a phrase such as 'In how many ways can we . . .?'.

6. The chairman encourages people to contribute and prevents any attempt to evaluate ideas. From time to time he may restate the problem.

7. The note-taker condenses the ideas suggested and lists them on flip charts. He does not attempt to act as an editor or worry about duplications at this stage. The session should not be tape recorded as this may inhibit ideas.

8. The chairman keeps on encouraging the group to contribute, trying to get people to freewheel and produce as many ideas as possible – good, bad, indifferent, sensible or silly. He keeps the pace going and never comments or allows anyone else to comment on a contribution. Every idea is treated as relevant.

9. The chairman closes the meeting after 30 minutes or so – 45 minutes at most. The session must not be allowed to drag on.

10. Evaluation takes place later, possibly with a different group. At this session the aim is to:

   - Select ideas for immediate use
   - Identify ideas for further exploration
   - Review any different approaches which have been revealed by the session.

Brainstorming is a useful technique for releasing ideas, overcoming inhibitions, cross-fertilizing ideas and getting away from patterned thinking. It needs to be planned and executed carefully and proper evaluation is essential.

Use it selectively, where there seems to be ample scope for different ideas. It will not solve all your problems but can help you to crash through the barriers erected by the traditional approaches to decision-making.

Remember that however creative you are, what you finally decide on has to work. Brainstorming and other techniques for increasing creativity will help you to break new ground, but eventually you will have to think clearly and analytically about the pros and cons of the preferred solution before making your final decision.

Chapter 15
Crisis management

What is crisis management?

The phrase 'crisis management' was coined by Robert Macnamara at the time of the Cuban missile crisis when he said: 'There is no longer any such thing as strategy, only crisis management.'

Crisis management is a phrase used most commonly in diplomatic circles but it is something that happens in any organization where the pressure of events – external or internal – forces management into making urgent decisions. These arise because a crisis is a turning-point or a time of danger and suspense, and, in this turbulent age, turning-points and dangerous moments are always with us.

Crisis management can be defined as:

> The process of dealing with a pressurized situation in a way which plans, organizes, directs and controls a number of interrelated operations and guides the decision-making process of those in charge to a rapid but unhurried resolution of the acute problem faced by the organization.

Causes of crises

Crises are caused either by the actions of human beings or by natural disasters – fire, flood, earthquake, etc. If people are at the root of the crisis they may be deliberately inflicting harm on the organization from outside or, also externally, they may have taken actions which indirectly create a major problem. Internally, crises can be caused deliberately by people attempting to enforce their point of view or accidentally by some colossal misjudgement or a long history of compounded errors.

Crises may, however, be no more than sudden, unforeseen events which perhaps could have been anticipated. To dismiss strategy, as Macnamara did, is perhaps going too far, but Robert Burns did suggest that: 'The best laid schemes o' mice an' men gang aft a-gley', and this is as true today as when he wrote it in the eighteenth century.

In an ideal world, crises would not happen. You would know where you want to go and you would get there, with only minor deviations along the way. Problems would have been foreseen and contingency plans made to deal with them. This, of course, is not the way things are in real life. Murphy's law is always ready to strike again – if anything can go wrong it will.

Crises may appear to come suddenly, but this does not mean that they are unforeseeable. The Garcia Márquez novella, *Chronicle of a Death Foretold*, was written about a crisis, the murder of a young man, but, as the title implies, everyone knew it was going to happen only no one seemed able to stop it. Prior to a crisis there are often warning signs that disaster is about to strike. Even a volcanic explosion can be predicted.

There is a phenomenon which can be described as 'crisis slide'. Gradually, imperceptibly but inevitably, there is a build-up of events. Rain falls in ever-increasing volumes; the overflowing river is joined by equally overflowing streams, and the pressure increases. The force becomes progressively more irresistible until, under overwhelming pressure, the dam breaks. The crisis management process should, of course, have started as soon as observers had noticed the unusually heavy rainfall. Human error, however, creeps in and dams burst.

Steady slides down the slippery slope to an outright crisis can also happen, not because of human error, but because of human cussedness. If crisis management techniques are used coolly to assess potentially dangerous situations and bring the parties together in good time to discuss how to resolve the problems before they become critical, the dire effects of cussedness can be avoided. This can happen on the international scene as well as within organizations. Before Cuba, President Kennedy had been made aware of 60 nuclear near-disasters, including the launching of two missiles with nuclear warheads. He took steps not only to improve the US system of accident proofing but also to exchange information with the Russians. The Falklands crisis, however, was a sad story of a complete failure of the British both to understand how strongly the Argentines felt about the Malvinas and to appreciate that Galtieri was liable to go off the rails.

Management crises

In management all sorts of crises can happen: a takeover bid, a collapse in the foreign exchange rate, a drug which has disastrous side effects, a competitive product which suddenly appears on the market and wipes the floor with a market leader brand, an innovation which renders a product obsolete, a sudden damaging strike, a dishonest senior executive who gets the company into the headlines, a fire or a flood, the departure of key members of the management team to competitors, and so on. The list is endless.

Tolstoy said of marriages: 'All happy families resemble one another, but each unhappy family is unhappy in its own way.' The same can be said of crises. Each crisis is a unique event and has to be dealt with accordingly. However, there are certain types of behaviour which are appropriate in all critical situations and there are some general principles that can be followed in crises involving negotiation or conflict. There are also a number of crisis management techniques that are generally applicable, subject to modification to suit particular circumstances.

Crisis management behaviour

The most important thing to do in a crisis is to keep cool. As Kipling put it:

> If you can keep your head when all about you
> Are losing theirs and blaming it on you . . .
> Yours is the Earth and everything that's in it
> And – which is more – you'll be a Man, my son.

Perhaps the best exponent of this approach was Harold Macmillan who said at London Airport of a political crisis in his Cabinet: 'I thought the best thing to do was to settle up these little local difficulties, and then turn to the wider vision of the Commonwealth.' But another Prime Minister, James Callaghan, went too far when he said, also at London Airport (a great place for aphorisms), 'Crisis, what crisis?'

Statesmen, of course, have to give the impression of playing it cool. Henry Kissinger, who spent his whole diplomatic career in crisis management, said once: 'There cannot be a crisis next week. My schedule is already full.' But managers should play it cool too.

One of the arts of dealing with a crisis is to maintain the confidence of everyone around that you *are* managing it. Insouciance like Macmillan's, but not like Callaghan's, is one way of doing this. Another way is deliberately to give the impression that you are taking it easy – relaxing almost – when in actual fact you are working at top speed. Good crisis managers, in situations where all hell is let loose, and people and pieces of paper are being thrown about in all directions, and three telephones are ringing at once, will, from time to time, lean back in their chair, sip a cup of coffee, and idly gossip about last night's football game. They then resume work with redoubled energy. Robert Townsend (51) described this approach well in *Up the Organization* when he wrote: 'There is a time for engagement and a time for withdrawal. A time to contemplate it, and a time just to laugh at it.'

And in *The Right Stuff*, Tom Wolfe, in describing how Chuck Yeager (the man who broke the sound barrier for the first time with two broken ribs) influenced the crisis management style of airline pilots, wrote this about their approach:

> Anyone who travels very much on airlines in the United States soon gets to know the voice of the airline pilot . . . coming over the intercom . . . with a particular drawl, a particular folksiness, a particular down-home calmness that is so exaggerated it begins to parody itself (nevertheless! – it's reassuring) . . . the voice that tells you, as the airliner is caught in thunderheads and goes bolting up and down a thousand feet at a single gulp, to check your seat belt because 'it might get a little choppy'.

Negotiating situations

Crises concerning takeovers, industrial relations, legal disputes and other problems where the crunch has come because two sides have radically different views, will often involve negotiations. The normal negotiating tactics described in Chapter 33 will apply, although they may have to be speeded up.

In tense situations, special ploys may have to be used. For example, you can use the 'Trollope' ploy, which is the acceptance of an offer that has not been made in order to induce the adversary to accept the acceptance. Robert Kennedy coined this term, naming it after those Victorian heroines in the novels of Anthony Trollope who interpret a squeeze of the hand on the hero's part as a proposal of marriage and succeed in making this interpretation stick. It was used in the Cuban missile crisis where the ambiguity arose in communications from Mr Krushchev. He sent two letters, one implying a hard line about the American blockade, the other a mild and even yielding one. To deepen the confusion, it was not clear whether the 'hawklike' letter (which was received second) had been written before or after the 'dovelike' one. The American decision (the Trollope ploy) was to treat the dovelike letter as the true communication, ignoring the other hawklike one which was probably wirtten second as the Russian's final position. As reported by Robert Kennedy, it was this creative use of ambiguity which enabled the settlement to be reached.

In negotiations it can indeed be said that a shadow of ambiguity over a situation may be as effective as real strength. It gives you more room to manoeuvre and more scope to vary your tactics.

When to fight

In a crisis, the decision about when and how hard to fight is a matter of judgement. You can go in for aggressive brinkmanship or progressive appeasement, but either of these approaches will be inadequate if taken to an extreme.

At this stage it might be a good idea to remember Krushchev's message to Kennedy during the Cuban missile crisis: 'If people do not show wisdom, then in the final analysis they will come to a clash, like blind moles, and then reciprocal extermination will begin.'

The decision on tactics is never an easy one. It was said by Clausewitz that: 'War is nothing but the continuation of politics with the admixture of other means', and you should normally wait to launch an attack until you are certain that the normal process of peaceful negotiation is not going to get you anywhere.

The decision will also be affected by your ability to understand your opponent's strategy and tactics so that you can take pre-emptive action. Crisis management is very much about analysing other people's motives, intentions and ploys, and responding accordingly. Another adage from Clausewitz is worth bearing in mind: 'Despise the enemy strategically, respect him tactically.' In other words you may be quite certain that in the longer term your opponent will come to grief, but in the short term he may fight hard and you may have to fight back equally hard. Losing one battle may not lose the war but a succession of defeats must prejudice your chances, however just your cause and however superior your strategy.

Thomas Schelling, a leading commentator on crisis management, commented wisely on the fight or flight decision as follows:

> What is in dispute is usually not the momentary right of way, but everyone's expectations about how a participant will behave in the future. To yield is a signal that one can be expected to yield. To yield often or continuously may communicate an acknowledgement that that is one's role. To yield readily up to some limit, and then say 'enough', may guarantee that the first show of obduracy loses the game for both sides.

Crisis management may or may not take place within a well-defined strategy but, whatever happens, the tactics have got to be worked out on the basis of a complete understanding of the situation, especially those aspects of it which concern other people's intentions. If you yield, then, as Schelling says, take care to ensure that, because you have misunderstood or underestimated your opponent, he will not take advantage of it. Beware also of the possibility that both of you might lose in the end.

If you decide to fight, remember the following precepts of St Augustine and St Thomas Aquinas on what is a just war:

1. Just cause
2. Right intention
3. A reasonable chance of success
4. If successful, a better situation than would prevail in the absence of action
5. Force used (or threatened) should be proportional to the objective sought (or the evil repressed)
6. The intention should be to spare non-combatants or at least have a reasonable prospect of doing so.

Crisis management techniques

In *The Conventions of Crisis*, Coral Bell (7) wrote:

> Looking back over the history of the postwar crises as a whole, one is struck by a sense of how often the decision-makers seem to have been 'playing it off the cuff', acting on the promptings of intuition or temperament rather than plan or logic.

This highlights the biggest pitfall crisis managers can walk into in industry and commerce as well as in international affairs. All too easily they feel that instant and decisive action is required. Under acute pressure they do not look before they leap and they fall into the elephant trap.

Crisis management starts with avoiding action, keeping your finger on the pulse so that as soon as the pace hots up – at the first signs of the beginning of a crisis slide – you can take pre-emptive action. At this stage you have time to think, to consider contingency plans and to put them into effect.

If, however, in spite of all your efforts, you are faced with a crisis, the following is a checklist of the ten things you should do:

1. Sit back as coolly as you can and assess the situation. You may have to go through the analytical and thinking process five times as fast as usual, but do it. You need to establish:

   - What exactly is happening
   - Why it is happening
   - What is likely to happen unless something is done about it
   - How quickly you *have* to act to prevent further damage

- Who else is involved
- Who is likely to be involved
- What resources you have got – people, equipment, finance, back-up from other organizations, access to people with influence.

2. Draw up your preliminary plan of action – set it out step by step and prepare other contingency plans to deal with eventualities.

3. Line up a crisis management team to deal with the situation. Allocate roles and tasks and authorities to act (you may have to give emergency authority to some people).

4. Set up a crisis management centre (your office, the board room).

5. Set up a communications system so that you get instant intelligence on what is happening and can get your messages across to the members of your team and anyone else who you want to take action.

6. 'Load shed' when you can on the principle of the electrical system which sheds part of the load when the total load rises above a certain point. This means getting rid of any peripheral problems as quickly as possible.

7. But items on the 'back burner', ie relegate problems to a non-crisis area where they can be dealt with at leisure.

8. Prepare your detailed plans, which will include:

- time-scales – act now or later
- scope for a cooling-off period
- longer-term solutions to be prepared and implemented at the right time
- contingency plans to deal with new developments or emergencies.

9. Monitor continuously exactly what is happening. Ensure that you get the information you need fast so that you can react quickly but without panicking.

10. Evaluate actions and reactions continuously so that you can modify the plan and swiftly take corrective or pre-emptive steps.

Qualities of a crisis manager

Good crisis managers are decisive. They can react swiftly but their great skill is in being able to speed up the decision-making process. They will not miss out any steps in the standard problem-solving, decision-making sequence:

- Define the situation
- Specify objectives
- Develop hypotheses
- Get the facts
- Analyse the facts
- Consider possible courses of action
- Evaluate possible courses of action
- Decide and implement
- Monitor implementation.

Effective crisis managers will get through these stages more quickly, using their own experience and intelligence and that of their team.

Crisis managers buy time by putting things on the back burner but, like all good managers, they can make things happen fast when they want to. They are good leaders – providing inspiration to their team, encouraging their efforts and giving them confidence in the successful outcome of the crisis management process.

Finally, and most important, they keep cool. They do not panic, they do not over-react, they do not lose their heads. In fact, they deliberately slow down the pace, when they can, to give the impression that everything is under control and it is all going according to plan.

To sum up, crisis management is no more than good management under pressure. The adrenalin may flow faster but this concentrates the mind wonderfully. Good managers thrive under pressure and they are the good crisis managers.

Chapter 16
Delegation

You can't do everything yourself, so you have to delegate. At first sight delegation looks simple. Just tell someone what you want him to do and then let him do it. But there is more to it than that.

It may be that you would wish to delegate everything except what your subordinate cannot do. But you cannot then withdraw. You have arranged for someone else to do the job, but you have not passed on the responsibility for it. You are always accountable to your superior for what your subordinate does. Hence, as is often said, you can't delegate responsibility.

Delegation is difficult. It is perhaps the hardest thing that managers have to do. The problem is getting the balance right between delegating too much or too little and between over- or under-supervision. When you give someone something to do you have to make sure that it gets done. And you have to do that without breathing down his neck, wasting your time and his, and getting in the way. There has to be trust as well as guidance and supervision.

Advantages of delegation

- It relieves you of routine and less critical tasks
- It frees you for more important work – planning, organizing, motivating and controlling
- It extends your capacity to manage
- It reduces delay in decision-making – as long as authority is delegated close to the point of action
- It allows decisions to be taken at the level where the details are known
- It develops the capacity of staff to make decisions, get things done and take responsibility.

When to delegate

You should delegate when:

- You have more work than you can effectively carry out yourself
- You cannot allocate sufficient time to your priority tasks
- You want to develop your subordinate
- The job can be done adequately by your subordinate.

How to delegate

When you delegate you have to decide:

- What to delegate
- To whom you delegate – choosing who does the work
- How to inform or brief your subordinate – giving out the work
- How you will guide and develop your subordinate
- How you will monitor his performance.

What to delegate

You delegate tasks that you don't need to do yourself. You are not just ridding yourself of the difficult, tedious or unrewarding tasks. Neither are you trying to win for yourself an easier life. Delegation will, in fact, make your life more difficult, but also more rewarding.

Clearly, you delegate routine and repetitive tasks which you cannot reasonably be expected to do yourself – as long as you use the time you have won productively.

You also delegate specialist tasks to those who have the skills and know-how to do them. You cannot do it all yourself. Nor can you be expected to know it all yourself. You have to know how to select and use expertise. There will be no problem as long as you make it clear what you want from the experts and ask – if necessary force – them to present it to you in a usable way. As a manager you must know what specialists can do for you and you should be knowledgeable enough about the subject to understand whether or not what they produce is worth having.

Choosing who does the work

Ideally, the person you choose to do the work should have the knowledge, skills, motivation and time needed to get it done to your complete satisfaction. Frequently, however, you will have to use someone who has less than ideal experience, knowledge or skills. In these cases you should try to select an individual who has intelligence, natural aptitude and, above

117

all, willingness to learn how to do the job with help and guidance. This is how people develop, and the development of your staff should be your conscious aim whenever you delegate.

You are looking for someone you can trust. You don't want to over-supervise, so you have to believe that the person you select will get on with it and have the sense to come to you if he is stuck or before he makes a bad mistake.

How do you know whom you can trust? The best way is to try people out first on smaller and less important tasks, increasingly giving them more scope so that they learn how far they can go and you can observe how they do it. If they get on well, their sense of responsibility and powers of judgement will increase and improve and you will be able to trust them with more demanding and responsible tasks.

Giving out the work

When you delegate you should ensure that your subordinate understands:

- Why the work needs to be done
- What he is expected to do
- The date by which he is expected to do it
- The authority he has to make decisions
- The problems he must refer back
- The progress or completion reports he should submit
- How you propose to guide and monitor him
- The resources and help he will have to get the work done.

Your subordinate may need guidance on how the work should be done. The extent to which you spell it out will clearly depend on how much he already knows about how to do the work. You don't want to give directions in such laborious detail that you run the risk of stifling your subordinate's initiative. As long as you are sure he will get the job done without breaking the law, exceeding his budget, embarrassing you or seriously upsetting people, let him get on with it. Follow Robert Heller's golden rule: 'If you can't do something yourself, find someone who can – and then let him do it in his own sweet way.'

You can make a distinction between *hard* and *soft* delegation. Hard delegation takes place when you tell someone exactly what to do, how to do it and when you want the results. You spell it out, confirm it in writing and make a note in your diary of the date when you expect the job to be completed. And then you follow up regularly.

Soft delegation takes place when you agree generally what has to be achieved and leave your subordinate to get on with it. You should still agree limits of authority, define the decisions to be referred to you, say what exception reports you want (see Chapter 9), and indicate when and how you will review progress. Then you sit back until the results are due and observe from afar, only coming closer for periodical progress meetings, or when the exception reports suggest that something needs looking into, or when a problem or decision is referred to you.

You should always delegate by the results you expect. Even if you do not need to specify *exactly* how the results should be achieved, it is a good idea when delegating a problem to ask your subordinate to tell you how he proposes to solve it. You then have the opportunity to provide guidance at the outset; guidance at a later stage may be seen as interference.

Guidance and development

Delegation not only helps you to get your work done; it can be used to improve your subordinate's performance and therefore your trust in his ability to carry out more responsible work. Instruction, training and development are part of the process of delegation.

Monitoring performance

At first you may have to monitor a subordinate's performance carefully. But the sooner you can relax and watch progress informally the better.

You will have set target dates, and you should keep a reminder of these in your diary so that you can ensure they are achieved. Don't allow your subordinates to become careless about meeting deadlines.

Without being oppressive, you should ensure that progress reports are made when required and that you discuss deviations from the original plan in good time. You will have clearly indicated to your subordinate the extent of his authority to act without further reference to you. He must therefore expect to be reprimanded if on any occasion he exceeds his brief or fails to keep you informed. You don't want any surprises and your subordinate must understand that you will not tolerate being kept in the dark.

Try to restrain yourself from undue interference in the way the work is being done. It is, after all, the results that count. Of course, you must step in if there is any danger of things going off the rails. The Nelson touch is all right if your subordinate is a Nelson, but how many Nelsons have you got? Rash decisions, over-expenditure and ignoring defined and reasonable constraints and rules must be prevented.

There is a delicate balance to be achieved between hedging someone around with restrictions which may appear petty and allowing him licence to do what he likes. You must use your knowledge of the subordinate and the circumstances to decide where the balance should be struck. The best delegators are those who have a comprehensive understanding of the strengths and weaknesses of their staff and the situation in which they are working.

Above all, avoid 'river banking'. This happens when a boss gives his subordinate a task which is more or less impossible to do. As the subordinate is 'going down' for the third time his boss is observed in a remote and safe position on the river bank saying: 'It's easy really, all you need to do is to try a bit harder.'

The thoughts of some successful delegators

John H. Johnson, editor and publisher of Johnson Publishing Company, chief executive officer of Supreme Life Insurance Company and on the board of many large US corporations, said of his delegation techniques: 'I want to be big and I want to be bigger and I can't do it all by myself. So I try to do only those things that I can't get anyone else to do.'

Franklin D. Roosevelt used a particularly ruthless technique based on competition, when he requested his aides to find some information. One of his aides told the story as follows: 'He would call you in, and he'd ask you to get the story on some complicated business and you'd come back after a couple of days of hard labour and present the juicy morsel you'd uncovered under a stone somewhere and *then* you'd find out he knew all about it, along with something else you *didn't* know. Where he got this information from he wouldn't mention, usually, but after he had done this to you once or twice you got damn careful about your information.'

Robert Townsend's approach to delegation when he was chairman of Avis was to emphasize the need to delegate 'as many important matters as you can because that creates a climate in which people grow'.

Robert Magaven, when he started as the head of Safeway Food Stores, told his division managers: 'I don't know anything about the grocery business but you fellows do. From now on, you're running your division as if it were your own business. You don't take orders from anyone but me and I'm not going to give you orders. I'm going to hold you responsible.'

Franklin Moore related the following example of strong delegation: Ralf Cordiner, the head of General Electric in the US for ten years, had a vice president who wanted to see him urgently about a problem. The vice president explained his problem, and the choices he thought he had. 'Now, Mr Cordiner,' he said, 'What should I do?' 'Do?' Cordiner answered, 'You'd damn well better get on an airplane and get back to your office and decide. And if you can't decide we'd better get someone who can.'

Peter Drucker, writing about responsibility, referred to a newspaper interview with a young American infantry captain in the Vietnam jungle. The reporter asked: 'How in this confused situation can you retain command?' The captain replied: 'Around here, I am the only guy who is responsible. If these men don't know what to do when they run into an enemy in the jungle, I'm too far away to tell them. My job is to make sure they know. What they do depends on the situation which only they can judge. The responsibility is always mine, but the decision lies with whoever is on the spot.'

A case study

A group of researchers studying how managers delegate found that the following was happening in one of the companies they were studying:

In the situations in which the men we were interviewing found themselves, the boss was usually a hurried, and sometimes a harried, man. He gave out broad, briefly stated assignments, expecting his subordinates to make sense out of them. He also expected them to decide what information they needed, to get that information and then to go ahead and carry out their assignments. In the case of repetitive tasks, the typical boss assumed that after a few trials his subordinates would know for themselves when a job needed doing.

Frequently the boss wasn't sure himself about which things needed attention in his department. And although he knew what eventually had to be accomplished, often he had less idea than his subordinates about the approaches to take. It wasn't unusual, therefore, for the boss to be vague or even impatient when approached with questions about the job while it was going on. Usually he was much more assertive in describing what he wanted after a job was done than while it was in progress.

The production director came out of the board of directors' meeting where he had been roundly criticized for not getting the most out of his organization. He immediately called a meeting of his subordinates and told them: 'I don't intend to subject myself to such humiliation again. You men are paid to do your jobs; it's not up to me to do them for you. I don't know how you spend your time and I don't intend to try to find out. You know your responsibilities, and these figures bear out that you haven't discharged them properly. If the next report doesn't show a marked improvement, there will be some new faces around here.'

121

Chapter 17
Developing people

Investing in people

The chairman of an advertising firm once said that his 'inventory goes up and down in the lift'. His prime resource – his working capital – was people. The same applies in any other sort of organization. Money matters, but the human beings who work there matter even more.

If you want to take a pragmatic view of people, regard them as an investment. They cost money to acquire and maintain and they should provide a return on that outlay; their value increases as they become more effective in their jobs and capable of taking on greater responsibility. In accounting terms, people may be treated like any other asset on the balance sheet, taking into account acquisition costs and their increasing value as they gain experience.

The manager's contribution to effective training

The following are ten ways in which you can contribute to the effective training of your staff:

1. Determine the standards of performance required for each of the jobs you control.
2. Analyse the competences (knowledge and skills) relevant to the achievement of these standards. If necessary, seek help from specialized trainers to carry out this analysis.
3. Agree with the individuals concerned what these standards and competences are.
4. Review with these individuals their performance so that agreement can be reached on any gaps to be filled between what they can do and what they should be able to do.

5. Treat every time you give someone an instruction as a training opportunity. Get individuals to tell you how they would do the job. If they get it wrong, help them to work out the best way for themselves, progressively giving them less guidance so that they learn to stand on their own feet.

6. Allow for the learning curve. Don't expect too much, but do require trainees to improve at a pace which matches their natural aptitudes. Only bear down hard on people if they are clearly not trying – without any excuse.

7. Train and develop by example. Give people the opportunity to learn from the way you do things. Remember the truth of the saying that managers learn best how to manage by managing under a good manager. This principle applies equally well to other categories of job holders.

8. Remember that the prime responsibility for training and developing your staff rests with you. Your results depend on their competence. You neglect your training responsibilities at your peril. And you must not rely on the training department to do it for you. They can provide advice and help but cannot replace your capacity to train on the job.

9. Plan the training for your staff in accordance with a regular review of their training needs.

10. Remember to use a variety of training techniques such as job instruction, assignments, coaching, guided reading and computer-based training.

Management development

Management development is about improving the performance of existing managers, giving them opportunities for growth and development, and ensuring, as far as possible, that management succession is provided for.

Managers need to be given the opportunity to develop themselves. As Peter Drucker (16) wrote in *The Practice of Management*:

> Development is always self-development. Nothing could be more absurd than for the enterprise to assume responsibility for the development of a man. The responsibility rests with the individual, his abilities, his efforts . . . Every manager in a business has the opportunity to encourage self-development or to stifle it, to direct it or to misdirect it. He should be specifically assigned the responsibility for helping all men working with him to focus, direct and apply their self-development efforts productively. And every company can provide systematic development changes to its managers.

In Douglas McGregor's phrase, managers are grown – they are neither born nor made. And your role is to provide conditions favourable to faster growth. As McGregor (36) wrote in *The Human Side of Enterprise*:

> The job environment of the individual is the most important variable affecting his development. Unless that environment is conducive to his growth, none of the other things we do to him or for him will be effective. That is why the 'agricultural' approach to management development is preferable to the 'manufacturing' approach. The latter leads, among other things, to the unrealistic expectations that we can create and develop managers in the classroom.

There are two main activities in management development – performance management, discussed in Chapter 37, and planned experience, discussed below.

Planned experience

People learn mainly through experience. Surely, therefore, it is worth spending a little of your time planning the experience of anyone with potential for development.

Planning someone's experience means giving him extra tasks to do which provide a challenge or extend him into a new area. It could be a project which he has to complete himself or he could be included in a project team looking at a new development or problem which cuts across organizational boundaries. Projects which enlarge experience in unfamiliar areas, for example, a marketing executive in finance or vice versa, are particularly useful. Planned experience will work better if it is accompanied by coaching so that those undergoing it can receive the maximum benefit from expert advice.

Coaching

The best way to learn how to manage is to manage, under the guidance of a good manager. Coaching is an informal but deliberate way of providing this guidance. It should be linked to performance appraisal and the counselling that takes place as part of the appraisal procedure.

But coaching is a more continuous process. Every time you delegate a task to someone and discuss the outcome you are presented with a coaching opportunity. When you delegate you can provide guidance on how the job should be done. When you discuss progress with your subordinate or when he reports back to you, you can ask questions on how well he has thought through what he is doing, suggest alternative ways of looking at a problem (do not provide the solution), and provide constructive criticism if things are not going right.

You can help to develop people by discussing higher-level problems with them, involving them in your decisions and increasing their understanding of how to tackle a job senior to the areas for which they are responsible.

Chapter 18
Efficiency and effectiveness

In *Summer Lightning*, P G Wodehouse dubs Lord Emsworth's secretary 'the efficient Baxter'. He explains:

> We have called Rupert Baxter efficient and efficient he was. The word, as we interpret it, implies not only a capacity for performing the ordinary tasks of life with a smooth firmness of touch, but in addition a certain alertness of mind, a genius for opportunism, a genius for seeing clearly, thinking swiftly and Doing it Now.

Efficiency, as thus defined, is obviously an excellent characteristic. It includes the notion of effectiveness which is often emphasized less than it should be in the quest for efficiency.

Peter Drucker (15) in *The Effective Executive* pointed out forcibly that to concentrate on efficiency rather than effectiveness could be limiting and therefore dangerous. He wrote:

> Management, we are usually told, should concern itself with efficiency, that is with doing better what is already being done. It should therefore focus on costs. But the entrepreneurial approach focuses on effectiveness, that is, on the decision what to do. It focuses on opportunities to produce revenue, to create markets and to change the economic characteristics of existing products and markets. It asks not: how do we do this or that? It asks: which of the products really produce extraordinary economic results or are capable of producing them? Which of the markets and/or uses are capable of producing extraordinary results? It then asks: to what results should therefore the resources and efforts of the business be allocated so as to produce extraordinary results rather than the 'ordinary' ones which is all efficiency possibly can produce.

Developing this theme in *Managerial Effectiveness*, Bill Reddin (44) suggested that the manager who concentrates on efficiency instead of effectiveness tends to:

- Do things right rather than do right things
- Solve problems rather than produce creative alternatives
- Safeguard resources rather than optimize resource utilization
- Lower costs rather than increase profit.

The danger of laying too much emphasis on efficiency is that the object of the exercise becomes obscured by the bureaucratic machinery set up to achieve it. You should aim – in Drucker's phrase again – to manage for results. Clearly you adopt the most efficient way of getting there but never forget that it is the end that counts not the means.

Case studies

In an insurance company the 'efficiency' of inspectors (ie sales representatives) was measured by the number of policies they sold and the volume of premium income they generated. Naturally, they concentrated on selling the easiest forms of policy and generated lots of income. But volume, while a measure of efficiency, did not indicate effectiveness, which could only be assessed by the relative profitability of the different policies. Without guidance on which policies were most profitable the inspectors were efficient in volume terms but ineffective in terms of the only true measure of performance – profitability.

The accounts department prided itself on the efficiency with which it delivered voluminous printouts analysing costs incurred against budget for each cost centre within two weeks of the end of the month. But the information was not effective in that it did not help cost centre managers to control some of their crucial costs. This was because so many items were accrued (ie assumptions were made about expenditure because invoices had not yet been processed) that many of the figures in key expenditure areas were meaningless. As a result, cost centre managers maintained their own sets of duplicate accounts.

The chairman of an Industrial Training Board, which collected training levies from firms in the industry and redistributed them in the form of grants for approved training, was concerned because levy income was exceeding grant expenditure. Many of the firms in the industry complained bitterly that the Training Board was accumulating vast useless reserves at their expense. The chairman therefore launched a nationwide campaign under the slogan 'Get your whack back Jack', encouraging firms to do training and claim levy. With great efficiency the firms in the industry completed forms by the dozen, making grant claims for all sorts of training. But much of the training was irrelevant and for show.

A direct mail company decided to set up a 'party plan' type of operation to sell its products. It had no previous experience in this activity. Demonstrators had to be recruited, and it was decided that the current mailing list of people who had already shown some interest in the products would prove to be the best source of recruits. This seemed a less haphazard approach than advertising for demonstrators. The recruitment campaign was planned meticulously and executed with the utmost efficiency. Everything was thought of and everything happened as planned *except* that hardly anyone responded. The method proved to be totally ineffective because it was based on an incorrect assumption. The only ways to get good party plan demonstrators are by direct contact and classified advertising in the local press. An enquiry into why the mailing list members had not responded showed that the written approach through the mail failed to overcome their natural suspicions about party plan.

A government agency responsible for the recruitment of large numbers of staff had its procedures examined by an organization and methods team. It was noted that there were a number of directors of recruitment, each responsible for particular 'competitions' to get different categories of staff. Each director had a group of staff to administer the various stages of a competition. But there was duplication of work, such as the sifting and acknowledgement of applications, between the various directorates. The O & M team therefore hit on the 'efficient' solution, which was to have a number of units dealing with different activities; sifting, acknowledging, obtaining references, etc. Each of these units provided a service to all directors of recruitment but was controlled separately by a director of administration. This solution was certainly efficient in that it grouped associated activities together and saved staff. But it was also ineffective. Because there was no one person responsible for the control and coordination of individual competitions (the directors of recruitment sat on the sidelines as far as administration was concerned), delays took place at each stage. Competitions took much longer to complete and good recruits were being lost because they got tired of waiting.

An engineering firm ran into hard times and decided that a general cut of 20 per cent in all indirect staff was required. A senior manager was appointed to implement the cut. He conducted the assignment with great efficiency. Everyone was quite clear about what they had to do, the programme was implemented exactly as planned, and documentation was precise and complete. But the decision to make an all round 20 per cent cut had repercussions which had not been fully appreciated when the plans were made. A number of key research departments employing only indirect staff found that they had to dismiss key employees to achieve their targets. Their ability to provide for the longer-term development of the business was therefore seriously affected. The assignment was conducted efficiently but led to a significant decline in effectiveness where it really mattered – the future.

Chapter 19
Entrepreneurship

The French economist, J B Say, coined the word around 1800 when he wrote that: 'The entrepreneur shifts economic resources out of the area of lower and into an area of higher productivity and greater yield.' Closer to our own time, George Gilder (19) in *The Spirit of Enterprise*, said that: 'Entrepreneurs are innovators who evoke demand.' They are makers of markets, creators of capital, developers of opportunity and producers of new technology. They seek the unique product, the marketing breakthrough, the startling new feature or the novel design. They change technical frontiers and reshape public desires. They create wealth and employment. They take exception to the received view that companies should be market led. *They* lead the market.

Entrepreneurs are criticized as self-interested exploiters. Adam Smith, while recognizing that they do some good for society, partly reflected this view when he wrote in *The Wealth of Nations*:

> In spite of their natural selfishness and rapacity, though they mean only their convenience, though the sole end which they propose from the labours of all the thousands they employ be the gratification of their own vain and insatiable desires . . . they are led by a hidden hand, and without intending it, without knowing it, advance the interest of society.

What makes an entrepreneur?

An entrepreneur is someone who conceives business visions and turns them into business realities. Einstein used to say that he rode into the theory of relativity on a beam of light. Entrepreneurs base their achievements on the strength of their vision.

George Gilder (19) suggests that entrepreneurs prevail:

> not by understanding an existing situation in all its complexity, but by

creating a new situation which others must try to understand. Entrepreneurs inhabit a world where the last becomes first, where supply creates demand, where belief precedes knowledge.

The particular characteristics of successful entrepreneurs are that they:

- Are action orientated, in the words of Peters and Waterman (42) from *In Search of Excellence*, they 'do it, fix it, try it'
- Have the ability to visualize the steps from idea to actualization
- Are prepared to 'break the mould'
- Are both thinkers and doers, planners and workers
- Get involved – they adopt a 'hands-on' approach
- Can tolerate ambiguity – 'enterprise always consists of action in uncertainty' (Gilder)
- Accept risk but understand and manage it
- Overcome, rather than avoid, mistakes – they don't admit they are beaten
- See themselves as responsible for their own destiny – they are dedicated, setting self-determined goals
- Believe in creating markets for their ideas, not just in responding to existing market demands.

Intrapreneurship

Gifford Pinchot III (43) in *Intrapreneuring* has invented a new word to describe how the entrepreneurial drive for innovation can work within organizations. He defines an intrapreneur as,

> Any of the 'dreamers who do' – those who take hands-on responsibility for creating innovation of any kind in an organization. The intrapreneur may be the creator or inventor but is always the dreamer who figures how to turn an idea into a profitable reality.

His recipe for success as an intrapreneur is:

1. Choose a good idea.
2. Produce a business plan which:

   - evaluates your idea – why is it a good one?
   - states where you want to go and how you are going to get there;
   - defines the resources (investment) required;
   - sets out the costs and benefits, the latter in terms of return on investment.
3. Get other people involved.

4. Find a sponsor who will see that your idea gets the backing it deserves.
5. Build a team to develop the idea – enthuse them with your vision and lead them positively to success.

Entrepreneurship – how it is done

Success as an entrepreneur depends very much on the intelligence, imagination and strength of purpose of the individual. A little bit of luck may be thought necessary, but it can be argued that there is no luck in achieving success – you *make* your own luck. Turning visions into realities is more about hard work than good luck.

Japan is a place where entrepreneurs have achieved huge success by hard work as well as imagination and ability, and two of the most notable have been Sony and Honda.

The Sony story

Akio Monto, the head of Sony, used to say: 'Sony does what others don't, we lead, they follow.' Oddly enough, Sony's success did not depend on technological breakthroughs in the field of semi-conductors; American firms such as Texas Instruments were more innovative. The genius of Sony was in linking its understanding of the technology to a clear vision of what the market wanted or could be persuaded to want. This led Sony away from the more exciting realms of semi-conductor development to focus on the transistor radio as its main product, and on satisfying customers as its primary aim. Monto tells a story to illustrate this. 'Two shoe salesmen find themselves in a backward part of Africa. The first salesman wires his head office: "There is no prospect of sales. Natives do not wear shoes." The other wires: "No one wears shoes here. We can dominate the market. Send all possible stock."'

The key difference between Sony and other electronics firms is that, as their American sales director put it: 'Others see a market and come up with a product to fit it. Sony's philosophy is to develop a product when there is *no* market, and then create one.'

Sony used its mastery of transistors and miniaturization to develop a long series of consumer products starting with the first transistor television set in 1960, and then going on to the unique Trinitron, one-gun, one-lens colour television in 1968, the Betamax video cassette recorder in 1975, and, of course, the Walkman in 1980. In each case, the inspiration behind the development was not simply to produce a less expensive product, but to increase customer satisfaction. The question put at Sony was: 'How well does this product fulfil the customer's "objective function"?' In other words, could Sony achieve more hours of satisfying performance per yen, dollar or pound than its competitors?

Sony's entrepreneurial achievement can be summed up, in the words of George Gilder, as: 'Doing what others don't, making markets out of human needs, finding opportunity in the expert's despair.'

The Honda story

Honda is one of those great entrepreneurial companies that seem to feed on resistance and grow stronger. Honda himself was the world's single most brilliant and successful entrepreneur in the field of mechanical engineering since Henry Ford. He started, in effect, on the shop floor, developing his own version of piston rings for Toyota. He then moved away from the automobile industry into designing textile machinery but ran out of funds. This sort of setback is characteristic of the careers of many entrepreneurs, which often consist of a continuing series of setbacks and failures which by sheer guts and determination they are able to overcome. Soichira Honda's comment on this was: 'Many people dream of success. To me, success can be achieved only through repeated failure and introspection. In fact, success represents 1 per cent of your work which results from the 99 per cent that is called failure.'

After his setback in textiles. Honda got back into the motorcycle business almost by accident. He started during a fuel crisis by attaching a motor to his bicycle. It worked. So he contrived a makeshift motorbike using surplus motors, and sold them from his repair shop until the motors ran out. With the income generated from this venture he set out to design a real motorcycle. There was no demand for such things in Japan at the time, but, as Honda said: 'We do not make something because of the demand, the market is there. With our technology, we can create demand, we can create the market.' In fact, in the words of George Gilder: 'Supply creates its own demand.'

Honda's success in transforming the moribund motorcycle industry into one of the most glamorous growth products of the late twentieth century is well known. But an even more remarkable achievement was the way he broke into the motorcar market. He started in motor racing and his strategy was to make a series of technological breakthroughs with the help of the best engineering talent he could find in Japan. The venture was a success. As a journalist on the *Sunday Times* wrote at the time: 'The precision of Honda's engineering, almost like a jewelled watch, has astonished every engineer I spoke to.'

Honda then made the classic entrepreneurial move of 'going where they ain't.' He developed a non-polluting car. He quickly demonstrated that he

133

had acquired a unique technology and boldly constructed a huge new factory to meet his anticipated sales. He had reserves, but having taken the risk of plunging into an unfamiliar market with a brand new product, he took a further risk by undercutting his rivals – he held his prices while they increased theirs. And in spite of a more or less complete lack of market power, he succeeded. Within a year, Nissan and Toyota saw their sales drop by 40 per cent. Honda's sales rose by 76 per cent over the same period.

The Honda success story continues, although it was his protégé, Kiyoshi Kawashima, who took Honda to a position where, in terms of brand image and quality, they are regarded worldwide as among the market leaders in the motor industry.

Chapter 20
Excellence and how to achieve it

Robert Townsend (51) said almost all that needs to be said about excellence in *Up the Organization* when he wrote: 'If you can't do it excellently, don't do it at all. Because if it is not excellent it won't be profitable or fun, and if you're not in business for fun or profit, what the hell are you doing here?'

Excellence is doing things well and thereby getting the results you have to achieve.

A number of recipes for achieving excellence have been developed recently and the following is a summary of the messages derived from three key studies.

In Search of Excellence

In its sub-title, this book by Tom Peters and Robert Waterman (42) is described as 'lessons from America's best-run companies'. The analytical framework they used was based on the seven elements, described as the 'seven S's', which Richard Pascale and Anthony Athos (38) used in *The Art of Japanese Management*. These are:

1. *Strategy*   – the plan to reach identified goals.
2. *Structure*   – the characteristics of the organization structure – functional, decentralized, etc.
3. *Systems*   – the routine for processing and communicating information.
4. *Staff*   – the categories of people employed.
5. *Style*   – how managers behave in achieving the organization's goals.
6. *Skills*   – the capabilities of key people.
7. *Superordinate goals* – the significant meanings or guiding concepts that an organization imbues its members with (ie values).

A distinction was made between the 'hard' elements – strategy, structure and systems – on which UK and American companies concentrate, and the remaining 'soft' elements which Pascale and Athos claimed the Japanese manage particularly well.

Using these factors in their research into 75 highly regarded companies, Peters and Waterman identified the following eight attributes which characterized the excellent innovation companies:

1. *A bias for action.* The excellent companies get on with it. They are analytical in their decision-making but this does not paralyse them, as it does some companies.
2. *Close to the customer.* They get to know their customers and provide them with quality, reliability and service.
3. *Autonomy and entrepreneurship.* Leaders and innovators are fostered and given scope.
4. *Productivity through people.* They really believe that the basis for quality and productivity gain is the rank and file. They do not just pay lip service to the slogan 'people are our most important asset'. They do something about it by encouraging commitment and getting everyone involved.
5. *Hands-on, value-driven.* The people who run the organization get close to those who work for them and ensure that the organization's values are understood and acted upon.
6. *Stick to the knitting.* The successful organizations stay reasonably close to the businesses they know.
7. *Simple form, lean staff.* The organization structure is simple and corporate staff are kept to a minimum.
8. *Simultaneous loose-tight properties.* They are both decentralized and centralized. They push decisions and autonomy as far down the organization as they can get into individual units and profit centres. But, as Peters and Waterman say, 'they are fanatic centralists around the few core values they hold dear'.

The Winning Streak

Walter Goldsmith and David Clutterbuck (20) based their book on an analysis of a number of successful British companies. From this they listed eight winning characteristics.

1. *Leadership.* This was regarded as central to business growth. As Goldsmith and Clutterbuck wrote:

> The business leader need not be charismatic (indeed, if he fails to combine charisma with wisdom, disaster is almost inevitable). But he must be able to motivate those around him, to provide a sense of

mission for the organization as a whole, and to ensure that all the middle and junior management leaders down the line have clear objectives they can work to, to motivate and direct their own subordinates' efforts.

2. *Autonomy.* This is giving people the freedom they need to do their job most effectively. The right blend has to be achieved between autonomy and control, and this varies a lot, even within one company.

3. *Control.* Effective controls allow autonomy to take place. Neither too much nor too little is the aim. A balance must be struck, but rather a limited number of good controls than too many loose ones. As Tom Peters (41) wrote: 'A few (controls) that are believed in are much more effective than numerous controls that are honoured mainly in the breach.'

4. *Involvement.* The successful companies extract a great deal of commitment and loyalty from staff at all levels. They do this by getting them closely involved with the organization and its aims.

5. *Market orientation.* As Goldsmith and Clutterbuck wrote: 'The unsuccessful companies lived in their markets; the successful ones lived them.'

6. *Getting back to basics and staying there.* Winners know what business they are in and why they are in it. And they know how to position it and target its market sector.

7. *Innovation.* Successful companies create a climate which encourages innovation. And they act on promising ideas.

8. *Integrity.* The best companies build up and maintain a reputation for fair-dealing and trustworthiness with staff, customers, suppliers and the public at large.

The Business of Success

In *The Business of Success* Robert Heller (24) commented on the results of a study of 250 firms in the printing industry. The stars in this group as measured by return on capital employed, ratio of profit to sales and value added, had five common features which make up the acronym OMMIT.

1. *Objectives* – business objectives were defined and the business operated to meet them.

2. *Market* – market opportunities were identified and commercial efforts coordinated to achieve planned business results.

3. *Money* – its role and use as a resource was clearly understood.

4. *Information* – there were good information systems in support of good decision-making procedures.

137

5. *Team* – management were organized to operate as a team, executives being developed to meet the changing needs of the business.

Heller says that any company omits any one of these factors at its peril. Note, however, that he does not specifically refer to people. But the effective management of human resources is implied in each one of them. Even money only gets results if *people* use it properly.

Chapter 21
Getting on

Getting on is first about knowing what you can do – your strengths and weaknesses. Then you can decide what you want to do and set out to do it.

You can start in the right direction, therefore, by trying to analyse yourself and the situation which you are in.

Beyond that there are certain actions you can take which will help you to get on. Some are obvious, others less so. How you apply them must depend on your assessment of where you are and what you can do. With due acknowledgement to the two men who have written the most sense on this subject – Peter Drucker and Robert Townsend – the list of things to do is set out below under four main headings:

- Knowing yourself
- Knowing what you want
- Developing and deploying the skills required to get what you want
- Displaying the personal qualities and behaving in the ways that will contribute to your success.

Knowing yourself

Carlyle once described the saying 'know thyself' as an impossible precept. He felt that to 'know what thou canst work at' would be better advice. Therefore, the starting point in career management is what you can do – your strengths and your weaknesses. This means developing self-awareness by analysing your achievements, skills and knowledge and by assessing your own performance.

Achievement, skills and knowledge

The questions to ask yourself are:

1. *What have I achieved so far?* Answer this question by looking back on your life and list the key events, happenings, incidents and turning points that have taken place. Whenever you have succeeded in doing something new or better than ever before, analyse the factors which contributed to that success. Was it initiative, hard work, determination, the correct application of skills and knowledge based on a searching analysis of the situation, the ability to work in a team, the exercise of leadership, the capacity to seize an opportunity (another and better word for luck) and exploit it, the ability to articulate a need and get into action to satisfy it, the ability to make things happen – or any other factor you can think of?

2. *When have I failed to achieve what I wanted?* You do not want to dwell too much on failure but it can be treated positively, as long as you analyse dispassionately where you went wrong and assess what you might have been able to do to put it right.

3. *What am I good or bad at doing?* What are your distinctive competences? Consider these in terms of professional, technical or managerial know-how as well as the exercise of such skills as communicating, decision-making, problem-solving, teamworking, exercising leadership, delegating, coordinating, meeting deadlines, managing time, planning, organizing and controlling work, dealing with crises.

4. *How well do I know my chosen area of expertise?* Have you got the right qualifications? Have you acquired the right know-how through study, training and relevant experience?

5. *What sort of person am I?* (This is the most difficult question of all to answer truthfully.) The following is a checklist of the points you should consider, based on Cattell's classification of primary personality factors. In each case, assess the extent to which either of the paired descriptions applies to you:

- *Outgoing* – warm-hearted, easy-going, participating, extroverted; or
- *Reserved* – detached, critical, cool, introverted.

- *Intellectual* – good at abstract thinking; or
- *Non-intellectual* – better at concrete thinking.

- *Emotionally stable* – calm, able to face reality; or
- *Affected by feelings* – emotionally unstable, easily upset.

- *Assertive* – independent, aggressive, stubborn; or
- *Submissive* – mild, obedient, conforming.

- *Enthusiastic* – lively, happy-go-lucky, heedless, talkative; or

- *Sober* – prudent, serious, taciturn.

- *Conscientious* – persevering, staid, rule-bound; or
- *Expedient* – 'a law unto yourself', by-passes obligations.

- *Venturesome* – bold, uninhibited, spontaneous; or
- *Shy* – restrained, diffident, timid.

- *Tender-minded* – dependent, over-protected, sensitive; or
- *Tough-minded* – self-reliant, realistic, a no-nonsense approach.

- *Suspicious* – self-opinionated, distrustful, hard to fool; or
- *Trusting* – free of suspicion or jealously, adaptable, easy to get on with.

- *Imaginative* – speculative, careless of practical matters, wrapped up in inner urgencies; or
- *Practical* – inclined to action rather than speculation, regulated by external realities, careful, conventional.

- *Shrewd* – calculating, penetrating, worldly; or
- *Artless* – guileless, ingenuous, natural.

- *Apprehensive* – a worrier, depressive, troubled; or
- *Confident* – self-assured, serene, placid.

- *Experimenting* – critical, liberal, analytical, free-thinking; or
- *Conservative* – respecter of established ideas, tolerant of traditional practices.

- *Self-sufficient* – resilient, resourceful, prefers own decisions; or
- *Group-dependent* – a 'joiner', happiest in a group, reliant on the support of others.

- *Controlled* – socially precise, self-disciplined, compulsive; or
- *Casual* – careless of protocol, untidy, follows own inclinations.

- *Tense* – driven, overwrought, fretful; or
- *Relaxed* – tranquil, unfrustrated, calm.

Assess your managerial competences

While self-awareness is the basis for a more specific assessment of your strengths and weaknesses as a manager, you need also to consider your basic managerial qualities and the competences required to operate effectively.

In analysing your effectiveness as a manager it is useful to look at the criteria used by major organizations in measuring the competence of their managers at their assessment or development centres (two- to three-day

141

affairs where managers are subjected to a number of tests and undertake various exercises to demonstrate their skills). The headings used by two organizations in their assessment centres are set out below:

1. The National Westminster Bank

Effective managers:

- *Are achievement orientated* – they are strongly motivated by achievement, recognition and reward, and possess internal drive that continually urges them forward to higher levels
- *Have a positive outlook* – they are energetic, enthusiastic and want to make a unique personal contribution to every job they do
- *Are reliable* – they are noted for always doing a job properly with attention to relevant detail
- *Are adaptable* – they are flexible, self-organized and self-monitoring
- *Are good organizers* – they are able to organize themselves and those around them to meet targets effectively and on time
- *Have a natural affinity with people* – they possess well-developed leadership skills and a high degree of maturity in dealing with others
- *Are good team builders* – they understand that their progress can be enhanced by building up the performance of their teams. They are therefore keen to advance the interests of others as well as themselves
- *Are good communicators* – both face to face and on paper.

2. W H Smith

The performance areas used in W H Smith's general management assessment centre are:

- *Self-management* – the ability to organize, plan and manage time.
- *Interactive management and leadership* – the ability to work constructively with peers and seniors.
- *Financial management* – financial knowledge and the ability to make sound financial judgements.
- *Marketing management* – the ability to consider and approve strategic marketing issues, recognizing and responding to strengths and opportunities.
- *Strategic planning* – the ability to think and act at a strategic level and to define clear longer-range business-related objectives.
- *Situation assessment* – the ability to make an analysis of a business situation, to identify its key variables and to generate appropriate objectives and courses of action.
- *Staff management* – the ability to work successfully with subordinates and/or experts to obtain information and understanding of unfamiliar subjects.

- *Manpower planning* – the ability to determine future requirements against available resources, identifying training and development needs.
- *Oral communications* – the ability to speak clearly and present or argue a situation in a logical and positive manner which gains commitment and support.
- *Written communications* – the ability to create business-like correspondence and, where appropriate, present well-argued proposals supported by relevant data.

You can assess your competence as a manager against these criteria giving yourself marks between 1 and 10 for each item relating to a classification along these lines:

A = outstanding   (9–10 points)
B = very effective   (7–8 points)
C = satisfactory   (5–6 points)
D = barely satisfactory (3–4 points)
E = unsatisfactory   (0–2 points)

On completing this assessment, note the particularly high and low scores in each list and draw up a schedule of your strengths and weaknesses as a manager. You can complete this 'SWOT' analysis (Strengths and Weaknesses, Opportunities and Threats) by considering your opportunities for advancement in your present organization (or elsewhere) and assessing any threats that might prevent you from realizing your ambitions.

Knowing what you want

1. Find out what you are good at doing and then do it.
2. Analyse not only your strengths but also your weaknesses: 'There is nothing that helps a man in his conduct through life more than a knowledge of his own characteristic weaknesses' (William Hazlitt).
3. Decide what you want to do and then go for it. Believe that if you really want something you can get it, and act accordingly.
4. Set demanding targets and deadlines for yourself. 'People grow according to the demands they make on themselves' (Drucker). But don't over-commit yourself. Be realistic about what you can achieve.
5. Pursue excellence. 'If you can't do it excellently don't do it at all' (Townsend).

6. Focus on what *you* can contribute. 'To ask "what can I contribute?" is to look for the unused potential in a job' (Drucker).
7. Get your priorities right. Adapt Drucker's rules for identifying them:

   - pick the future as against the past
   - focus on opportunities rather than on problems
   - choose your own direction - rather than climb on the bandwagon
   - aim high, aim for something that will make a difference rather than something that is 'safe' and easy to do.

8. Be specific about what you want to do yourself and what you want others to do for you.
9. Keep it simple. Concentrate. Consider all your tasks and eliminate the irrelevant ones. Slough off old activities before you start new ones. 'Concentration is the key to economic results . . . no other principle of effectiveness is violated as constantly today as the basic principle of concentration . . . Our motto seems to be: "let's do a little bit of everything"' (Drucker).
10. Take the broad view but don't ignore the significant detail: 'Ill can he rule the great, that cannot reach the small' (Spenser). It is sometimes necessary to penetrate beneath the surface to find out what is really happening - on the shop floor or in the field. But do this selectively.
11. Adapt to changing demands. 'The executive who keeps on doing what he has done successfully before is almost bound to fail' (Drucker).

Develop skills

Every chapter in this book refers to an area of management skill that you need to develop if you want to get on. The key areas are:

- Communicating - express yourself clearly, concisely and persuasively.
- Problem-solving - adopt a logical approach to problem-solving but don't forget that lateral thinking can be very productive of new ideas.
- Decision-making - develop the analytical skills and confidence in yourself to enable you to make incisive judgements.
- Listening - listen to ideas and act on the good ones. Hear what is said, let the other person know that you have heard, show an interest, let him feel important.

- Motivating – understand what your people can do and what makes them tick, make clear what you expect them to do, setting standards which are grounded on the requirement of the task and not personal, reward them or otherwise according to their contribution.
- Staffing – select people for their strengths, accept that everyone has some weakness or other, don't go for mediocrity.
- Managing yourself – achieve control over your work day. Separate the essentials from the inessentials that litter your desk. Know how to simplify your workload – where appropriate cut corners.

Personal qualities and behaviour

- Be enthusiastic and show it.
- Innovate and create – come up with new ideas and react positively to other people's ideas. Don't sulk if your ideas are not accepted. Try again another way.
- Show willing – there is nothing worse than the person who always moans when he is given something to do. Don't say: 'How can I possibly do that?' Instead, respond immediately with something like this: 'Right, this is what I propose to do – is that what you want?'
- Be positive – in the words of the old Bing Crosby song: 'accentuate the positive and eliminate the negative.'
- Work hard – people who get on are hard workers. But they don't work for work's sake. Effectiveness is never a function of how late you stay in the office. It's what you do while you are there that counts.
- Present yourself well – life is not all about making a good impression but you might as well make sure that your achievements are known and appreciated. And if people are impressed by executives who are decisive, punctual and answer promptly, why not impress them that way? More good than harm will come of it.
- Be ambitious – 'A man's reach should exceed his grasp, or what's a heaven for?' (Robert Browning). But don't overdo it. Don't appear to be more concerned about your future status than with present effectiveness.
- Be courageous – take calculated risks, believe in what you are doing and stick to your guns.
- Be assertive but not aggressive.
- Get your points across firmly and succinctly.
- Don't talk too much. Never over-commit yourself. Save up what you want to say until the right moment. Keep your powder dry.

145

Don't shoot your mouth off. 'Whereoff one cannot speak, thereon one must remain silent' (Wittgenstein).

- Learn to cope with stress. You won't avoid it and you have to live with it. If things are coming at you thick and fast try to slow down. Relax. Take a little time off. Give yourself a chance to put things in perspective. (See also Chapter 47.)
- If things go wrong, bounce back. Accept reverses calmly. Think about what you need to do and then get into action – fast. There is nothing like purposeful activity in these circumstances.
- Get people to trust you – you will do this if you never lie or even shade the truth, if you avoid playing politics and if you always deliver what you promise.
- Accept constructive criticism.
- 'Admit your own mistakes openly, even joyfully' (Townsend). Never make an excuse. Accept the responsibility *and* the blame if you make a mistake.

Chapter 22
How things go wrong and how to put them right

Theodore Roosevelt once said: 'Do what you can, with what you have, where you are.' The trouble is, people don't always take this advice. Things go wrong because people do less than they are capable of, misuse their resources or choose an inappropriate time or place in which to do it. Situations are misjudged and the wrong action is taken.

There have been two interesting analyses of incompetence which, if studied, will give you some clues about how to avoid or at least minimize mistakes. The first of these is *The Peter Principle* by Dr Lawrence J Peter (40); the second is *On the Psychology of Military Incompetence* by Norman F Dixon (12).

The Peter Principle

In *The Peter Principle*, Dr Lawrence Peter suggested that in a hierarchy, individuals tend to rise to the level of their own incompetence. This somewhat pessimistic view was based on his experience that the system encourages this to happen because people are told that if they are doing their job efficiently and with ease, the job lacks challenge and they should move up. However, as Peter says: 'The problem is that when you find something you can't do very well, that is where you stay, bungling your job, frustrating your co-workers, and eroding the effectiveness of the organization.'

The Peter Principle has only been accepted as common parlance because it reflects a fundamental problem when assessing potential. We know, or we think we know, that someone is good at his present job. But does this predicate success in the next one up? Perhaps yes, perhaps no; however, we

147

cannot be sure because the skills needed by, for example, a first-rate research scientist are quite different from those required by the leader of a research team. Technical competence does not necessarily indicate managerial competence.

Beating the Peter Principle – for yourself

Can the Peter Principle be beaten? The answer is yes, but with difficulty. People don't usually refuse promotion. If they do, they become suspect. It is thought that they should be made of sterner stuff. It is, however, perfectly reasonable to check on what is involved if you are promoted. You should get precise answers to questions on what you will be expected to achieve, the resources you will be given to achieve it and the problems you will meet. If you think these demands are unreasonable, discuss the job to see if they can be modified.

Don't take a job unless you are satisfied that you can do it, or at least that you can learn how to do it within an acceptable period of time. You can quite properly ask what training and help you will be given in the early stages. If your predecessor failed, you can ask what went wrong so that you can avoid making the same mistakes.

Beating the Peter Principle – for others

If you are in a position of offering promotion or a new job, you have to be aware of the Peter Principle and how to circumvent it. You need to match the capacities of the candidate to the demands of the job, and your starting point for this process should be an analysis in depth of the skills required. These should be classified under the headings of MATCH:

1. *Managerial* – making things happen, leading, inspiring and motivating people, team building and maintaining morale, coordinating and directing effort, using resources productively, and controlling events to achieve the required results.
2. *Analytical* – dissecting problems and coming up with the right conclusions about what is happening and what should happen.
3. *Technical/professional* – an understanding not only of all the tricks of the trade but also of how to use other people's knowledge effectively.
4. *Communications* – getting the message across.
5. *Human resource management/personal* – the ability to persuade, enthuse and motivate, trustworthiness, integrity, dedication.

When you have drawn up the specifications, measure the candidate against each of these criteria. Obtain whatever evidence you can about his performance in the present job which gives any indication of potential competence in these areas. Ask for information on successes and failures and why they occurred.

This matching process should identify any potential weaknesses. You can then discuss these and decide on any help the individual needs in the shape of coaching, training or further experience.

Monitor the progress of the individual carefully in the initial months. Your aim should be to spot dangerous tendencies in good time so that swift remedial action can be taken.

Military incompetence

Norman Dixon suggests that there are two basic types of military incompetence. The first group includes Generals Elphinstone (first Afghan war), Raglan (the Crimean War), Butler (Boer War) and Percival (Singapore). These were all mild, courteous and peaceful men, paralysed by the burden of decision-making under fire. The second group includes people like Haig, Joffre, and a number of the other First World War generals. They are characterized by overweening ambition coupled with a terrifying insensitivity to the suffering of others. Far from being paralysed by decisions, they were active, but active in vain, devious, scheming and dishonest ways. Alastair Mant in *Leaders We Deserve* quotes the example of the catastrophic results achieved in the Crimean War when an incompetent in the first group (Raglan) has authority over someone in the second group (the Earl of Cardigan, reputed by one contemporary to possess the 'brains of a horse').

The elements of military incompetence are listed by Norman Dixon as:

- Serious wastage of human resources
- Fundamental conservatism and clinging to outworn tradition or to past successes
- Tendency to reject or ignore information which is unpalatable or which conflicts with preconceptions (eg, company yes men)
- Tendency to underestimate the enemy
- Indecisiveness and a tendency to abdicate from the role of decision-maker
- Obstinate persistence in a given task despite strong contrary evidence
- Failure to exploit a situation gained and a tendency to 'pull punches'
- Failure to make adequate reconnaissance
- A predilection for frontal assaults, often against the enemy's strongest point (reference the gross overcrowding of once profitable markets)
- Belief in brute force rather than the clever ruse

- Failure to make use of surprise or deception
- Undue readiness to find scapegoats
- Suppression or distortion of news from the Front, usually deemed necessary for morale or security
- Belief in mystical forces – fate, bad luck, etc.

Examples of all these can be found in the actions or inactions of business leaders and managers.

1. *Wasting resources.* Most factories and offices are overmanned, to the tune of 10 per cent or more.
2. *Conservatism.* 'That's the way it always worked.' We have been market leaders for the last 20 years, why change?
3. *Rejecting unpalatable information.* 'What did you say about our losing market share? I don't believe it; these desk surveys are always inaccurate.'
4. *Underestimating the enemy.* 'What's this? Bloggs & Co have introduced a new product in our range. And you think it will compete? Forget it. They're useless. They couldn't run a winkle stall.'
5. *Indecisiveness.* 'We need to think a bit more about this.' 'I need more information.' 'I sometimes think that if you put problems like this in the "too difficult" section of your pending tray, they will go away.' 'It seems to me that we have several alternative routes (*sic*) ahead of us. Let's call a meeting next week or sometime to look at the pros and cons.' 'This is something for the Board.'
6. *Obstinate persistence.* 'Don't confuse me with the facts.' 'That's the way it's going to be.'
7. *Failure to exploit a situation.* 'Okay, you think we're going to exceed budget on our launch and you want to accelerate the programme. But let's not get too excited, we mustn't overstretch ourselves.'
8. *Failure to reconnoitre.* 'I don't believe in market research.'
9. *A predilection for frontal assaults.* 'Bloggs are doing particularly well in widgets. Yes, I appreciate we know nothing about widgets, but we can soon find out. Let's get in their fast and topple them from their perch.'
10. *A belief in brute force.* 'Tell the union they can either take 5 per cent or do the other thing . . . What's this about a productivity package? I don't believe in messing about. It's a straight offer or nothing . . . They'll come out? I don't believe it, not with unemployment levels round here topping 15 per cent.'
11. *A failure to make use of surprise.* 'I don't like playing about. Let's get this show on the road . . . You think we'll get off to a better

start if we keep the competition guessing? Forget it, we're miles better than they are!'

12. *Scapegoating.* 'It's not us, it's the rate of exchange.' 'This xxxx government has screwed us up!' 'Why am I surrounded by incompetent fools?'

13. *Suppression of news.* 'Don't tell them about how well we're doing. They'll only ask for more money.'

14. *A belief in mystical forces.* 'I just *feel* in my bones we must do this thing.'

Why things go wrong – a summary

The main reasons for things going wrong are:

- Inability to learn from mistakes
- Sheer incompetence through over-promotion
- Poor selection, inadequate training
- Over-confidence
- Under-confidence
- Laziness
- Lack of foresight.

What can you do about it?

Inability to learn from mistakes

Remember Murphy's Law, which states that if anything can go wrong it will. Mistakes will happen. The unforgivable thing is to make the same mistake twice. You learn from your mistakes by analysing what went wrong – no excuses, no alibis – and making notes of what to do and what not to do next time.

Incompetence

This is something you should minimize in your subordinates by a constant drive to improve selection and performance standards and by training and coaching aimed at correcting specified weaknesses.

If you have doubts about your own ability, analyse your own strengths and weaknesses and grab every opportunity you can to get extra training and advice from people you believe in. If that still does not work, get out in good time.

151

Over-confidence

This is the most difficult problem to eradicate. It is always said in the Royal Air Force that the most accident-prone pilots are the over-confident ones. You need confidence in yourself and your staff. How can it be controlled from going over the edge?

It takes time to understand or demonstrate that misjudgements occur because you are so certain that you know all the answers that no attempt is made to foresee or take care of the unexpected. Over-confident people tend to have tunnel vision – they can see quite clearly to the end but they take no notice of what is happening on either side or beyond. And if they see the light at the end of the tunnel they may not appreciate that it is the light of the oncoming train.

Under-confidence

This can be overcome as long as the individual is fundamentally competent. An under-confident person often needs help from someone who can underline achievements and provide encouragement to do more of the same. Mentors can help, as can a deliberate policy of extending people steadily so that they are not suddenly faced with a daunting leap in the level of work they have to do. Start by giving the under-confident tasks that are well within his capabilities and progressively increase demands, but only in achievable steps.

Carelessness

This is a universal problem. It can happen through over-confidence, but we all make mistakes under pressure or because we think the task is easier than it is. Sadly, reputations can be damaged, even destroyed by relatively minor mistakes. If you submit a report to your board with a glaring arithmetical error in it, the credibility of your whole report may be damaged, even if the mistake, although obvious, was not significant. Never submit a report or write a key letter without checking every figure and every fact at least once. If possible, get someone else to do it as well.

Laziness

No one would ever admit to being lazy. But lazy people do exist, either because they are naturally indolent or they have not been given sufficient leadership and a well-defined role in the organization. If one of your staff is lazy, put the boot in. It cannot be tolerated.

Lack of foresight

This is a common reason for errors. As a manager, one of your prime responsibilities is to think ahead. You must try to anticipate all the eventualities and make contingency plans accordingly. You won't get it right every time and you may find yourself occasionally in a crisis-management situation. But you will at least be better prepared if thought has been given to some of the eventualities, even if you could not anticipate them all.

Chapter 23
Innovating

Innovation is the life-blood of an organization. There is nothing so stultifying to a company – or the people in it – as a belief that the old ways must be the best ways. An organization which tries to stand still will not survive.

Innovation requires a blend of creativity, clear thinking and the ability to get things done. It requires thinkers and doers to work closely together. Top management must create a climate in which managers have the scope to develop new ideas and the resources to implement them.

The success of innovative projects, therefore, can be seen to depend on two things: the characteristics of the individual manager and the climate of the organization.

Individual characteristics

To be an effective innovator you need:

- To have a clear initial view of the results you want to achieve – you should not worry too much to begin with about the ways of achieving them.
- To define clearly the aims and benefits of the project.
- To argue the case for the project persuasively.
- To get support not only from your boss but also from your colleagues and subordinates – you need to build a coalition in which everyone shares equally in the belief that the project is worthwhile.
- Courage – to take calculated risks and to weather the storm when the inevitable setbacks occur.
- To be good at getting people into action – to mobilize people to contribute fully to the project means using a participative management style.

- Power to mobilize support and resources and to get things done.
- The ability to handle interference or opposition to the project – resistance can be open, but it often takes a passive or covert form: criticism of the plan's details, foot-dragging, late responses to requests, or arguments over allocation of time and resources among projects. Covert resistance can be the most dangerous.
- The force of character to maintain momentum, especially after the initial enthusiasm for the project has waned and the team is involved in more tedious work.

Organizational characteristics

The organizational characteristics which encourage innovation are:

- A free flow of information which allows executives to find ideas in unexpected places and pushes them to combine fragments of information
- Close and frequent contact between departments, and an emphasis on lateral as well as vertical relationships providing resources, information and support
- A tradition of working in teams and sharing credit
- Senior executives who believe in innovation and will make the necessary resources available
- Managers with the ability and desire to seize opportunities and to make time available for innovation.

Case studies

Float glass

The development at Pilkington's is sometimes described as a one-man campaign by Alistair Pilkington. This is not entirely correct. Alistair Pilkington did indeed have and deploy the qualities of a successful innovator. He knew what he wanted, he knew it was worthwhile and he was quite ruthless in getting his own way against opposition. But he had the advantage of working in a company where the climate was conducive to innovation. One of the most impressive research establishments in the world was there to provide the skills and facilities required for the enormous development programme. And of equal importance was the tradition at Pilkingtons of management by committee. Often considered to act as a brake on innovation and achievement, the committee system did in fact work well for research and development. Because all relevant departments were represented – research, development, production and sales – the float glass project was a fully integrated affair from the very beginning. The problems of cooperation and the misunderstandings that are inevitable in any major new project did not get a chance to flare up. The traditional rivalries between research, development and production did not, of course, vanish overnight, but the will and the machinery were there to minimize tension. The project was a triumph.

Innovation in management development

John Raimes was personnel manager in the Filton division of the British Aircraft Corporation. He successfully introduced project and do-it-yourself training a dozen years before various management development pundits announced this approach as a major new discovery.

Raimes was dissatisfied with the traditional type of management training course. He believed that managers would get much more out of being involved in a project which dealt with a real issue of immediate concern to the company. If the right group of managers were brought together they could benefit the company with their ideas as well as learning from and about each other, extending their understanding of how a firm is managed and testing their ability to analyse problems and think through new ideas. A do-it-yourself element could be introduced by giving the managers taking part in a project the scope to attend courses, call for outside advice (within limits) and extend their reading on the subject.

Raimes had to sell his idea to top management. He had to exercise all his considerable powers of persuasion to convince them that his concept would be much more beneficial to the company and its managers than conventional training. He had no proof that this would be the case. He could only carry his point by demonstrating his total conviction that he was right. Which he did.

Raimes' own belief in what he was doing was the main reason why he succeeded. But he was helped by the climate in the firm which, as part of the aerospace industry, lived by innovation and creativity. There were people on the board who recognized that the needs of management in this type of industry were different and had to be catered for in an original way.

Chapter 24
Integrating

An organization will only function effectively as a system of coordinated activities if the groups of people within it are able to cooperate effectively. They will not necessarily do this unless you consciously work at improving the integration of their activities.

Vertical and horizontal integration

Integration needs to take place both vertically and horizontally. Douglas McGregor (35) said of vertical integration in the *Harvard Business Review*:

> The outstanding fact about relationships in the modern industrial organization is that they involve a high degree of interdependence. Not only are subordinates dependent upon those above them in the organization for satisfying their needs and achieving their goals, but managers at every level are dependent upon all those below them for achieving both their own and organizational goals.

The achievement of satisfactory vertical integration is largely a matter of the way in which people are managed. It is not so much a structural affair, although integration will be more difficult if there are too many layers of management or if spans of control are too wide.

Problems arise because vertical integration is largely dependent on management style. The quality of managers as leaders and motivators varies considerably. It is the bad and indifferent ones who inhibit vertical integration (see Chapter 26).

Horizontal integration needs to take place between different functions or organizational units. It is not just a matter of coordinating activities; it is much more concerned with getting people to work well together. Problems arise because people tend to be more aware of the need to be independent rather than recognizing the importance of interdependence.

This applies particularly to relationships between line departments, such as production and staff, or functional departments, such as finance.

Improved horizontal integration has to be worked for, and there is a choice of methods you can use to achieve it. The main ones are listed below:

- *Coordination.* This is the traditional method. Managers coordinate different units or people carrying out related activities. It should work but often does not, either because the span of control is inappropriate or because people will not necessarily work well together simply because they are told to.
- *Structural integration.* Group activities by product or customer, so that people can easily relate their tasks to a common objective, rather than by process, where work is more likely to be seen as an end in itself.
- *Voluntary integration.* Encourage people to communicate with each other and to integrate their activities without reference to higher authority, except where a decision is needed to resolve differences of opinion.
- *Meetings.* Set up meetings or committees to deal with planning and operational matters requiring integration. To avoid the dangers inherent in 'management by committee' you should ensure that meetings concentrate on resolving policy issues where joint decisions are required rather than attempting to usurp the normal role of management.
- *Project teams.* Set up teams or working parties to deal with specific issues or problems outside the normal routine; for example, product development, quality control and systems development. Getting people from different departments to work together is a good way of increasing understanding and developing a sense of common purpose.
- *Communications.* Improve the quality of communications throughout the organization. This is partly a matter of attitude (there has to be the will to communicate and to listen to communications), partly a matter of structure (too many levels of management or too many separate units or departments will inhibit communications), and partly a matter of the systems and techniques used (the more effective use of the spoken or written word). All this is easier said than done. You cannot force people to communicate; you can only encourage them and try to remove barriers of misunderstanding.
- *Training.* Training can help to make people more aware of the need to integrate and can improve techniques (communications and getting the most out of meetings). Courses attended by members of

different departments can increase understanding. Team-building training, which concentrates on helping people to work better together in groups, can help.

- *Understanding of roles.* Help interrelated functions, units and individuals to be aware of their respective roles. This can be achieved by various informal means, as mentioned above. You can also produce more formal definitions and circulate them to all concerned, but this seldom works: it is just possible that the missives will be read by the recipients, but it is most unlikely that they will take any notice of impersonal exhortations. Management by exhortation is the last refuge of the incompetent manager.
- *Planning.* Set up planning procedures which involve people in different units and at different levels in jointly formulating policies and preparing plans.
- *Management information.* Install management information systems which help to identify areas where joint action is required.

A case study

Two professional institutions had merged, one of which had two sections and the other three, catering for different branches of the profession. The new institution therefore had five sections, each anxious to promote its own interests.

The governing body of the institution, the council, was well aware of the fact that while the members of each section recognized that there were financial advantages in being formed into one body, they did not want to lose any of their independence or separate identity.

But there were a number of areas, such as relationships with the government, professional ethics, public image and educational standards, where the institution had to present a cohesive front even if the various sections differed in their views about the subject. An integrated approach was therefore required to reconcile the conflicting aims of unity and independence. Unrest and dissent were already in evidence and had to be stopped.

The obvious solution was to integrate activities through the elaborate committee structure of the institution. Overall, there was a general council dealing with policy matters while each sector had its own council which concerned itself with policy issues specific to that sector.

To integrate the many forms of educational activities of which the institution was rightly proud, a general education committee was set up under the general council. Each sector had its own education committee which sent representatives to the general committee. Similar patterns were evolved for other key areas.

But this solution did not work. The sector committees continued to go their own way, ignoring the need to integrate their activities with those of the other sectors. The central specialist committees were emasculated because the sector representatives were not interested in agreeing or even discussing policies which in any way impinged on sectional interests. The general council was not aware of what the sectors were up to in a number of areas and felt it was in danger of losing control.

Other methods of integration had to be attempted. First, extensive discussions led by senior council members took place at all levels to get sector members to recognize the value to them of having a strong united institute to represent their interests. Next, a working party was formed to conduct a detailed analysis of each of the main policy areas to determine which decisions could be made at sectional or council level. Finally, the working party devised a system of strategic planning which started at sector level and, for those issues which were of general interest, proceeded to council level. The planning procedure was devised on an iterative basis, ie initial ideas were floated at sector level and, if they affected the institution as a whole, were then discussed at the appropriate central committee. If there was any dissent the issue was referred back to the sector committee for further discussion before being reconsidered at the centre. To coordinate this whole process for the general council a planning committee was set up to review and integrate plans for each area for submission to the council for its final decision.

The advantage of the approach was not so much the planning procedure itself which did prove to be somewhat elaborate. The great benefit was that issues of general interest were discussed at all levels. No decisions were made about the future of the institution without attention being given to the views of each sector. The council was in a position to pronounce authoritatively on matters of overall concern, in the knowledge that the sector had been given every opportunity to participate in the formulation of the policies of the institution. A sense of common purpose was therefore developed which provided a firm basis for the integration of the institutional activities.

Chapter 25
Interviewing

Everyone believes that he is a good interviewer. Like everyone believes he is a good driver. But bad drivers abound, as road accident statistics prove. And the record of job failures in most organizations can often be attributed to poor selection in the first place. Many research studies have shown that predictions made at interviews often fail because of bias, failure to get the information required, or inability to interpret the information. To minimize these problems you need to adopt a systematic approach, based on a job description and a specification of the sort of person you need to fill the job. You then need to consider the method of interviewing you use, how to conduct the interview and how to evaluate the results.

Approach to the interview

An interview has been described as a conversation with a purpose. It is a conversation in which the candidate should be drawn out to talk freely about himself and his career. Apart from the time when he is talking about the job and the company, the interviewer should restrict himself to asking questions and making encouraging grunts. Open-ended questions will produce the most informative answers; 'yes or no' questions should be avoided as far as possible. If you simply say 'tell me about your present job' you will get most of what you want to know. Gaps can be filled in by asking follow-up questions. Avoid leading questions which indicate the answer you are expecting.

The interview's principal purpose is to provide evidence upon which a prediction can be made of a candidate's suitability for the job. It does, however, have two other aims: to provide the candidate with information about the job and the company, and to give him a favourable impression of the company. This should encourage the good candidate to join and should leave the rejected candidate without any ill-feelings.

Conducting the interview

The interview must be planned to elicit information from the candidate which will enable his experience, qualifications and personal qualities to be measured against the requirements set out in the job specification. There is no one best way of sequencing an interview. A fairly typical approach would be:

1. Put the candidate at his ease – he will be nervous and you want him to relax so that he will express himself freely.
2. Explain how you are going to handle the interview.
3. Start with a brief description of the job and the company. Do not spend too long over this, especially if the candidate is a marginal one. You can elaborate at the end of the interview.
4. Use a biographical approach, inviting the candidate to describe in his own words his education and career to date. Do not delve too deeply into the distant past – spend most time on the current job. Probe if necessary to ensure that the candidate is giving you the full picture. He will naturally try to gloss over any less successful episodes in his career. Get him to tell you not only what he did but why he did it. This is particularly relevant when discussing choice of career and reasons for leaving jobs. It will give you a chance to assess how well he is motivated.
5. Give him the opportunity to talk about his achievements and to explain any setbacks.
6. Allow time at the end of the interview for him to ask questions.

The information-gathering part of the interview should last between 20 and 40 minutes, depending on the level of the job.

For key jobs, a second interview by a more senior person is desirable.

Evaluating the interview

The only questions you need to answer at the end of the interview are:

- Does this candidate measure up to the job?
- How does this candidate compare with other candidates?

Qualifications are relatively easy to assess unless they have been obtained from some obscure institution. Experience should not be too difficult to evaluate once you have taken steps to assure yourself that the candidate has really done what he claims. Job titles are misleading; you must have information on the actual level of responsibility and compare this with what he will be expected to do in each of the key areas of the job for which he is being considered. Information on specific tasks and achievements is helpful.

His progress to date will give you some indication of how he will perform in the future. A steady progression in line with his ambitions is obviously what you are looking for. Anyone can fail once for reasons which are not particularly blameworthy. A pattern of failure, character-ized by short stays in jobs, is highly suspect. If any gaps in the candidate's career emerge, find out where he was and what he was doing.

A candidate's personal qualities are difficult to assess at an interview. You may be able to decide quickly whether you like his manner or not, but it is much harder to assess qualities such as drive, ability to work with others and leadership.

Interviewers are always warned about the 'halo effect' which means allowing a favourable impression of, for instance, a candidate's appear-ance or manner to override judgement on other aspects of his character and ability. Equally dangerous is the 'horns effect' by which too much attention is paid to one unattractive feature. A balanced view must be achieved, which means looking at all aspects of the candidate's career as well as the initial impression he makes, even though this may be a very important part of the job itself.

Information on personality strengths and weaknesses can be obtained by analysing the applicant's career and interests. Someone with high aspirations who has consistently achieved what he set out to do is clearly well motivated. Someone from a poor background who has triumphed over early setbacks has obviously more drive than someone who has not made the most of the opportunities given to him. The candidate's interests may indicate the extent to which he likes mixing with people and taking up leadership positions. An indication of a person's drive and determina-tion can be seen by how energetically he pursues his spare-time activities. Stamp collecting may sound pretty pedestrian but, if the candidate reveals that by sheer application he has become the leading authority in Britain on colonial stamps in the mid-nineteenth century, this will tell you about his ability to achieve something.

Candidates can make revealing statements about themselves if you allow them to talk – they may indeed talk themselves out of a job. If, for example, someone says that he left his last three jobs because his boss didn't appreciate him, this suggests an inability to get on with superiors or a tendency towards paranoia or both. He has drawn attention to a pattern which could well be repeated.

The final assessment

The evidence required to make an assessment of the candidate comes from various aspects of the interview and from the letter of application or application form. It needs to be looked at against the specification and summarized on an assessment form, especially if there are a number of candidates.

Dos and don'ts of interviewing

DO	DON'T
Plan the interview	Start the interview unprepared
Establish an easy and informal relationship	Plunge too quickly into demanding questions
Encourage the candidate to talk	Ask leading questions
Cover the ground as planned	Jump to conclusions on inadequate evidence
Probe as necessary	
Analyse career and interests to reveal strengths, weaknesses and patterns of behaviour	Pay too much attention to isolated strengths or weaknesses
Maintain control over the direction and time taken by the interview	Allow the candidate to gloss over important facts
	Talk too much

Chapter 26
Leadership

What is leadership?

Leadership is getting things done through people. It happens when there is an objective to be achieved, or a task to be carried out, and when more than one person is needed to do it. All managers are by definition leaders in that they can only do what they have to do with the support of their team, who must be inspired or persuaded to follow them. Leadership is therefore about encouraging and inspiring individuals and teams to give their best to achieve a desired result.

Leadership is required because someone has to point the way and that same person has to ensure that everyone concerned gets there. Organizational effectiveness depends on the quality of leadership.

Objectives of a leader

The overall aim of a leader is to achieve the task with the help of his group. To meet this overall aim, the leader has three main objectives:

1. To gain the commitment and cooperation of his team.
2. To get the group into action to achieve agreed objectives.
3. To make the best use of the skills, energies and talents of the team.

A leader's aim is to get people to do what he wants by obtaining willing cooperation, not grudging submission. He must also build up the morale of his group, which will be high when the group is productive and the people in it work well together. They don't need to feel comfortable; in fact, they will often be under pressure to do more than they would if left to their own devices. But they will feel that they are achieving something worthwhile together and gain satisfaction from that.

How are these objectives achieved?

The most familiar saying about leadership is that 'leaders are born not made'. Like all clichés there is some truth in it although it cannot be taken literally. There are many successful leaders around who demonstrated their abilities at an early age and have never looked back since. They have natural talents and, although they may not have actually been born with them, these talents have been fostered by their early upbringing and experiences at school, university or in the armed forces. Their charisma, inspirational qualities and ways of handling people combine to produce a person about whom everyone says 'he's a natural leader'.

It can seem effortless, but of course it isn't. As Lao Tzu wrote in the sixth century BC: 'The great rulers – the people do not notice their existence.'

Effective leaders start with some natural talents, and then they build on them. They are good at observing how to do it and how not to do it. They learn from their experience and they keep on learning. It cannot be said of one of them that 'here is a man whose 20 years' experience is one year's experience repeated 20 times'. Good leaders take pains to analyse their successes and failures and learn from them.

Given certain natural leadership abilities, how do you improve them? By practice, of course, but also by observation and analysis of one's self as well as of others. The rest of this chapter aims to help you by providing an analytical framework for this purpose. This is done by answering three key questions about leadership:

1. What is a leader?
2. What does a leader do?
3. How do leaders do it?

It will then be possible to summarize the ways in which leadership effectiveness can be maximized.

What is a leader?

There are many answers to this question. According to the American management writers Warren Bennis and Burt Vanus, about 250 definitions have been produced by writers on leadership. Not one of them achieved the necessary combination of clarity and completeness.

Most attempts to define a leader concentrate on the qualities required, the factors influencing success, the personality traits of successful leaders, or the types of leader that exist. Each of these approaches to defining a leader will be considered in this section. All of them look at the leader from his or the organization's point of view but, by definition, leaders have followers and further insight into what leaders are can be gained by considering them from the standpoint of their subordinates.

Leadership qualities

The British expert on leadership, John Adair (2), quotes the following ranking of the 12 attributes rated most valuable at the top level of management by successful chief executives.

1. Decisiveness
2. Leadership
3. Integrity
4. Enthusiasm
5. Imagination
6. Willingness to work hard
7. Analytical ability
8. Understanding of others
9. Ability to spot opportunities
10. Ability to meet unpleasant situations
11. Ability to adapt quickly to change
12. Willingness to take risks.

One of the problems with this sort of list is that the qualities are often difficult to define. John Adair points out that another survey of 75 top executives revealed that the definition of dependability included 147 different concepts.

Another difficulty is that the qualities may have to be used in different ways in different circumstances and they need to be deployed judiciously. For example, consistency is a good thing if it means that people know where they stand, don't get unpleasant surprises from your decisions and think that you act fairly. But paying excessive homage to the principle of consistency can lead to inflexibility and being over-predictable. And there is not one type of leader who is equally successful in all circumstances. Winston Churchill was the right war-time leader because he had the natural qualities required by the situation such as audacity, pugnacity and tenacity. But they did not serve him particularly well in peace time.

His successor, Clement Attlee, had none of the charisma of Churchill and would not have made an effective war-time leader, but it is generally recognized that he was one of the best peace-time cabinet leaders in living memory.

Leaders emerge in certain situations because they have the qualities or the know-how needed – authority flows to the one who knows. In Barrie's *The Admirable Crichton*, the butler became the leader when the family

167

was shipwrecked on a desert island, because he was the man of the moment, the only one who could cope with the situation.

Factors influencing success

Successful leadership, therefore, seems to depend on having the right qualities at the right time. But what are the factors that influence and develop these qualities? A study of chief executives in the UK by Charles Margerison produced the following ranked list of influences on success:

		Rating out of 100
1.	Ability to work with people	78
2.	Early responsibility for important tasks	75
3.	A need to achieve results	75
4.	Leadership experiences early in career	74
5.	Wide experience in many functions before age of 35	68
6.	Ability to do deals and negotiate	66
7.	Willingness to take risks	63
8.	Ability to have more ideas than colleagues	62
9.	Having talents 'stretched' by immediate bosses	60
10.	Ability to change managerial style to suit occasion	58

This list is a mix of abilities or skills (1, 3, 6, 7, 8 and 10) and the types of experience that have developed those abilities (2, 4, 5 and 9). It highlights the fact that natural abilities are only part of the picture. They are nurtured by experience and the situations in which potential and existing leaders have found themselves.

Lance Secretan in his book *Managerial Moxie* (46) emphasizes the last point when he says that leadership is largely an acquired skill. To start with, he wrote, a leader needs intelligence, a positive attitude, and a combination of the qualities of courage, shrewdness and common sense (moxie is a slang word for these qualities). Successful leaders as they gain experience build on these natural talents and develop the wide range of skills they need.

Personality traits of successful leaders

To develop Secretan's point, while it may not be possible to be definite about the abilities or skills that unequivocally characterize effective leaders in all situations, there is good evidence that there are certain basic personality traits which tend to characterize leaders in a wide variety of situations. In general, leaders are more intelligent than their followers, although not too much so as they might appear to be remote and could have difficulties in communicating and getting their views accepted. Leaders also tend to be better adjusted, more dominant, more extroverted, less conservative, and to have a better understanding of people than the rank and file. It is interesting to note that these characteristics are sometimes latent, only emerging when people are put into leadership positions: 'some are born great, some achieve greatness and some have greatness thrust upon them.'

Types of leader

Leaders can be defined in terms of characteristics, success factors and personality traits. To answer the question, 'Who is a leader?' it is also helpful to explore how these combine to produce different types of leader.

Leadership types can be classified in a number of ways and the following are some of the most typical categorizations:

1. *Charismatic/non-charismatic.* The charismatic leader relies on his aura, his personality and his inspirational qualities. These are natural characteristics, although experience may have taught him how best to project himself. The non-charismatic leader relies mainly on his know-how, his ability to give an impression of quiet confidence, and his cool, analytical approach to dealing with problems.

2. *Autocratic/democratic.* The autocratic leader imposes his decisions and surrounds himself with yes-men. He uses his position to force people to do what they are told. The democratic leader encourages people to participate and involve themselves in decision-making. He will exert his authority to get things done but he will rely more on know-how and persuasive ability than the use of position power.

3. *The visionary/enabler or the controller/manipulator.* Dr John Nicholls identifies the visionary/enabler as the true leader, inspiring people with his vision of the future and using 'tender loving care' to encourage them to participate and to generate commitment. In contrast, the controller/manipulator is the administrator who is concerned essentially with operating the internal system and treating his subordinates with 'thinly disguised contempt'.

Of course, not one of the three contrasting types can be used as a description of a typical leader. Most leaders combine something of all these approaches in the way in which they carry out their task. The mix will depend on the make-up of the leader but also on the conditions under which he operates.

The worm's-eye view – what followers expect from leaders

Basically, followers want to feel that they are being led in the right direction. They want to be told where they are going and why. They need

169

to know where they stand, what is going to happen and what is in it for them. They want to feel that it is all worthwhile. That is why the visionary leader, who can somehow get across his inspiration to his team, usually gets the best results.

Research into the follower's perception of the leader has indicated four requirements if the leader is to be successful.

1. *The leader must be perceived as 'one of us'.* He shares certain characteristics with the members of his group and is not perceived as an outsider.
2. *The leader must be perceived as the 'most of us'.* He must incorporate to a special degree the norms and values which are central to the group. He can influence values by his visionary powers but he may fail as a leader if he moves too far away from them.
3. *The leader must be perceived as the 'best of us'.* He has to demonstrate that he is an expert in the task facing the group, indeed that he is superior to his team in those abilities which are relevant to the group task, ie getting the group working purposefully together. He need not necessarily have more expertise than each of his team members in particular aspects of the task, but he must prove that he can direct and harness this expertise in obtaining results.
4. *The leader must fit the followers' expectations.* He is more likely to gain the respect and cooperation of his followers if he behaves in a way which they expect of good leaders. These expectations will vary according to the group but will often include being straight, fair and firm as well as being considerate, friendly and approachable.

It is not enough, however, to define a leader in terms of who he is or what his followers think of him. He must also be considered from the point of view of what he does – his roles, the demands made upon him and the type of authority he exercises. These aspects of leadership are considered in the next section of this chapter.

What do leaders do?

Leadership is a complex process because it is dealing with complex situations and complex human beings. And the leader has many different roles to play.

Leadership roles

Leadership roles can be classified into two groups:

1. *Primary functions* which are essential to the process of leadership, namely:

- *The leader as visionary.* He has a vision of the future and conveys his belief to his team.
- *The leader as executive.* He determines the objectives of the group and directs and coordinates the group's activities in achieving them.
- *The leader as planner.* He decides how the group should achieve its ends.
- *The leader as policy-maker.* He participates in formulating policies in the shape of continuing guidelines on what the group does.
- *The leader as expert.* He has the expertise and information required by the group.
- *The leader as controller of relationships in the group.* He decides how the group should be organized and influences how people in the group work together.
- *The leader as purveyor of rewards and punishments.* He has the power to apply rewards and punishments and thus exercise control over group members.

2. *Accessory functions* which are those a leader may assume or be assigned because of his leadership position, namely:

- *The leader as exemplar.* He serves as a model of behaviour for the group members.
- *The leader as symbol of the group.* He provides a focus for group unity.
- *The leader as father figure.* He can become an object for identification or even submissiveness.
- *The leader as scapegoat.* He may become the target for the aggressions of a frustrated, disappointed, disillusioned group.

Demands made on the leader

The way in which a leader carries out these roles will be dependent on the two essential demands made on him. He has to:

1. *Achieve the task* – that is why he and his group exist. The leader's role is to ensure that the group's purpose is fulfilled. If it is not, the result is frustration, disharmony, criticism and, eventually, perhaps, disintegration of the group.
2. *Maintain effective relationships* – between himself and the group and the people in it, and within the group. These relationships are

171

effective if they are conducive to achieving the task. They can be divided into those concerned with the team and its morale and sense of common purpose, and those concerned with the individual and how he is motivated.

In *Action Centred Leadership* John Adair (1) has suggested that these demands are best expressed as three areas of need which the leader is there to satisfy. These are:

1. *Task needs* – to get the job done.
2. *Group needs* – to build up and maintain team spirit.
3. *Individual needs* – to harmonize the needs of the individual with the needs of the task and the group.

These three needs are interdependent and are best expressed as three overlapping circles.

The three-circles model of leadership needs (John Adair)

The leader's action in one area affects the others. Successful achievement of the task is essential if his team is to be held together or the individual is to be motivated to give his best efforts to the job. Efforts directed at meeting group or individual needs stem directly from the needs of the leader to achieve the task. If any need is neglected, one of the others will suffer and the leader will be less successful.

The authority of a leader

In taking action in each of these areas, but especially when satisfying task needs, the leader exercises authority, of which there are three types:

172

1. The authority of *position* – job title or rank.
2. The authority of *personality* – the ability to inspire, to persuade, to get people to 'follow my leader'.
3. The authority of *knowledge* – managerial, technical or professional.

Position authority may provide the starting point but it can only be sustained and used effectively by deploying the second and third kinds of authority. And this means using natural abilities and know-how in the light of an understanding of how leaders carry out their functions, with particular reference to their methods of dealing with task and people needs in accordance with the demands of the situation, as discussed in the next section of this chapter.

How leaders do it

In *Functions of the Executive* Chester Barnard (4), chief executive of General Electric, said that:

> A good leader may sometimes give the impression that he is a rather stupid fellow, an arbitrary functionary, a mere channel of communication, and a filcher of ideas. In a measure this is correct. He has to be stupid enough to listen a good deal, he certainly must arbitrate to maintain order and he has to be at times a mere centre of communication. If he used only his own ideas he would be somewhat like a one-man orchestra, rather than a good conductor, who is, or should be, the very essence of a leader.

The analysis of what leaders do underlines the important point that the leader and his group are interdependent. He leads, they follow. But he depends just as much on them as they do on him. Ed Carlson, the man who successfully turned United Airlines around, believes that the leader, while influencing his subordinates, has to treat them as respected and trusted. And he shares Chester Barnard's view that employees in a sense delegate upwards to management the authority for organizational decisions and in so doing legitimize the right of those above to command those below.

The analysis does not, however, tell us exactly how it is done. Leadership still seems a somewhat abstract notion, and one of the dangers in trying to analyse leadership in these terms is that you end up by being mystified by it as Robert Graves' commanding officer found in the First World War, when he said that 'soldiers will follow this young officer if only to find out where he is going'.

A number of theories about leadership behaviour have been developed by academics. And when you read the word theory, before reaching for your gun like Goering confronted with culture, remember that there is nothing so practical as a *good* theory, ie one based on proper observation, research and analysis where actual results and the behaviours contributing to these results are studied by qualified people. Two of these research projects are described below. They expand on the distinction between task and people needs referred to above and consider relationships between leadership behaviour and productivity. These researches contribute to a better understanding of how leaders function in different situations and point the way to an analysis of the 'law of the situation' and the need for what has been described as situational leadership.

Leadership in the air

Two American researchers, Halpin and Winer, were asked to study leadership in aircrews in order to help in the selection of captains. The study was conducted by obtaining data on how existing commanders carried out their leadership functions, and what both their superiors and subordinates thought about them.

The research revealed two main dimensions of leadership which were described as:

1. *Initiating structure* (task-orientated) – organizing and defining the task and the relationships between the captain and the crew.
2. *Consideration* (people orientation) – behaviour indicative of friendship, trust, respect and warmth in relationships between captain and crew. This is called the 'maintenance' function, ie the emphasis is on maintaining good relationships. ·

Typical actions under the heading of initiating structure included:

- He makes his attitude clear to his crew
- He rules with an iron hand
- He makes sure his role is understood by the crew
- He maintains definite standards of performance.

Typical actions under the heading of consideration included:

- He finds time to listen to crew members
- He looks out for the welfare of individual crew members
- He treats crew members as his equals
- He is friendly and cooperative.

One of the most interesting things about this study was that, while superiors thought that the most effective captains were strongest in initiating structure, crew members thought that the best captains were equally strong on structure and consideration.

This distinction between being task- and people-orientated is not a black and white one; most managers fall between these extremes. Blake

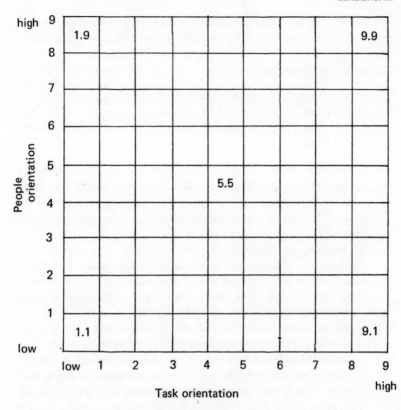

The managerial grid

and Mouton produced a grid against which managers are able to determine where they stand.

According to their position on the grid, Blake and Mouton characterized management styles as:

9:1 style.   Concentrates on the task, ignores the people. 'I get my job done in spite of my subordinates.'

1:9 style.   Runs a cosy country club, looks after people and values friendly relations more than productivity. 'We have a cheerful crew but we haven't repaired many engines.'

1:1 style.   Has little concern for people or production. 'My main aim is to keep my job and stay out of trouble.'

9:9 style.   Obtains high productivity through gaining commitment. 'How can I harness group energy to achieve high productivity?'

5:5 style.   Is the compromise man who produces as much as possible

175

without upsetting people. 'Let's not be too demanding as long as we get a reasonable day's work.'

Leadership and productivity

A number of studies in leadership and productivity have been carried out by Katz and Kahn (29) among railway, engineering and insurance workers. They found that three dimensions of leadership behaviour were consistently related to productivity.

1. *Assumption of leadership role.* Managers who actively assumed the functions of leadership were found to get better results than those who performed more or less the same functions as members of the group. The leader has to distance himself somewhat from the team. He cannot be one of the boys.
2. *Closeness of supervision.* High-producing supervisors were found to supervise less closely than low-producing supervisors. The latter tended, in various ways, to limit the freedom of the workers to do their jobs in their own way. Those who were allowed some autonomy on the job were more productive.
3. *Employee orientation.* High-producing supervisors were consistently found to be more employee-orientated and less production-orientated than low-production supervisors. But employee orientation could be overdone. The best supervisors were interested in their staff in so far as they were effective producers. They did not coddle them nor did they set out to be liked. They maintained what Fiedler (17) in *A Theory of Leadership Effectiveness* terms 'psychological distance' between themselves and members of the group. They made it clear who was boss and discriminated sharply between competent and incompetent workers, encouraging and looking after the former and giving them considerable freedom to act, applying sanctions to the latter and restraining their autonomy.

The law of the situation

The type of leadership you exercise and your success as a leader depends to a large extent on the situation and your ability to understand it and act accordingly. The situation comprises the nature of the task, the impact of the organization – its policies, culture and environment – the degree to which the situation is structured or ambiguous, the sort of people you have in your working group, and the type of authority the leader has, given or assumed.

The performance of a group, as Fiedler pointed out, is related to both the leadership style and the degree to which the situation provides the leader with the opportunity to exert influence. His research indicated that a task-orientated/initiating structure approach worked best for leaders in situations which are highly favourable. In the very favourable conditions when the leader has power, formal backing and a relatively well-structured task, the group is ready to be directed and told what to do.

In unfavourable conditions, such as an emergency, the task-orientated leader will be more effective than the considerate leader who is concerned with interpersonal relationships. The latter will do better in a somewhat unstructured or ambiguous situation, or where his power as a leader is restricted.

Fiedler (17) called this his contingency theory of leadership and emphasized the situational aspects of being a leader:

> Leadership performance then depends as much on the organization as on the leader's own attributes. Except perhaps for the unusual case, it is simply not meaningful to speak of an effective leader or an ineffective leader, we can only speak of a leader who tends to be effective in one situation and ineffective in another.

The point was made earlier that not only does the situation affect the type of leadership required but that it will also create conditions under which new and different types of leaders will emerge who are appropriately qualified to meet changing demands. Business leaders like Lee Iacocca of Chrysler, John Harvey-Jones of ICI and Michael Edwardes at British Leyland were put in positions where somehow they had to transform ailing organizations. Transformational leaders have a fresh vision of the future and then take steps to communicate and institutionalize it. They do not wait for the danger to strike. Instead they create a sense of urgency in the organization before an emergency occurs. If there is a threat, they sense it first and then transmit it to the rest of the organization so that all the people who matter can pre-empt it.

Leadership skills

If you want to be an effective leader you have to do six things:

1. Know yourself
2. Know your situation
3. Select management styles which are appropriate to the situation (these are discussed in the final section of this chapter)
4. Satisfy task needs
5. Satisfy team needs
6. Satisfy individual needs.

Know yourself

As a leader, you will start with certain natural abilities and by experience you will have developed certain skills. To improve your leadership qualities your first step is an analytical one – know yourself. Check each of the ten qualities and skills listed below and see how you measure up to them:

1. Ability to work with people
2. Ability to gain the respect and support of people
3. Decisiveness
4. Enthusiasm
5. Imagination (vision)
6. Ability to inspire others with your enthusiasm and vision
7. Willingness to work hard
8. Analytical ability
9. Integrity
10. Ability to change leadership style to suit occasion.

Assess your strengths and weaknesses under each heading. Analyse the occasions when you have succeeded *or failed* and why. Try to assess how you exercised these abilities or skills and answer these questions:

- Was it directive?
- Was it supportive?
- Was it appropriate to the situation?
- Did it work? And if so, why? And if not, why not?

If, following this analysis, you know your strengths, you can develop them, and if you know what works in particular circumstances you have a good idea of the approach you should adopt in similar situations (as long as they *are* similar). If you are aware of your weaknesses, you can do your best to manage them, remembering, however, that there is no point in trying to invent an entirely new persona. As Robert Browning said: 'Best be yourself, imperial, plain and true.'

Know your situation

Having got to know something about yourself as a leader – your strengths and weaknesses – you have to carry on using your analytical powers to understand the situation so that you can exploit your strengths, minimize your weaknesses and adopt the most appropriate management style. Your situational analysis should answer the following questions:

1. *The task*

    - What needs to be done and why?

- What results have to be achieved?
- What problems have to be overcome?
- Is the solution to these problems straightforward or is there a measure of ambiguity?
- Is this a crisis situation?
- What is the time-scale for completing the task?
- What pressures are going to be exerted on me?

2. *The team*

- What is the composition of the team?
- How well is the team organized?
- Do the members of the team work well together?
- What will they want to get out of this?
- How am I to get this particular team's commitment?
- How am I to get results by satisfying their needs?
- How are they likely to respond to the various leadership styles or approaches I might adopt?

3. *The individuals in the team*

- What are the strengths and weaknesses of each member of the team?
- What sort of things are likely to motivate them?
- How are they likely to respond individually to the various leadership techniques or styles I might adopt?

Select an appropriate management style

Adopt a situational approach to leadership by using your analyses of yourself, the task, the team and its individual members to decide on the most appropriate style or styles to adopt.

Case studies

The following are descriptions of the leadership style deployed by three highly effective managers. In each case the style was influenced by three factors: the environment, the people involved, and the personality of the manager.

Edward Smith

Ted Smith was the planning manager in a large engineering works. He had some 200 people working in the departments under his control who dealt

179

with process planning, shop loading and production control. It was a highly responsible job and his staff included highly qualified engineers as well as large numbers of clerks doing routine work.

Ted's job was to make sure that his departments ran like clockwork. Everyone had to know exactly what to do and when they had to do it. Close cooperation between the three areas under his control was essential. Charismatic-type leadership was out. He had to be cool, calm, measured and a little bit distant. Everyone in the department had to believe he knew what he was doing and what he wanted.

He therefore held regular meetings with all his subordinates at which he quickly and efficiently reviewed progress, gave instructions and, as and when necessary, discussed problems. At these meetings he was prepared to switch quickly from being someone who knew exactly what he wanted and expected people to do exactly as they were told (because it was sensible and right for them to do so) to someone who was prepared to listen to different views, weigh them up and decide. Sometimes he would deliberately throw his managers a problem and tell them to go away and solve it, and let him know the outcome of their actions.

Ted also ensured that his managers transmitted the content of these meetings down to first line supervisor level. And the latter were encouraged to meet their sections regularly. He emphasized throughout the need for teamwork and demonstrated his commitment by ensuring that at inter-departmental meetings problems of lack of cooperation or poor communications were given priority. The only time he was ever seen to express anger was when work suffered because of feuds between departments.

Elwyn Jones

Elwyn Jones was the personnel director of a large conglomerate in the food industry with over 80,000 employees. The firm had grown fast by acquisition and was highly decentralized. Staff were deliberately kept to a minimum at headquarters and Jones had only four executives responsible directly to him. He was, however, also responsible for the implementation of group personnel policies in each of the divisions and on these matters the divisional personnel directors were responsible to him.

Jones was not in a position to dictate to divisions what he wanted them to do. He could only influence them, and he felt that he had to get genuine acceptance for new policies before they could be introduced. He therefore had to consult on any changes or innovations he wished to introduce and, in most cases, he had to solicit cooperation on the testing of new ideas.

With his headquarters staff, Jones adopted a highly informal, almost permissive approach. He gave them broad guidelines on how they should develop their ideas in the divisions but encouraged them to think and act for themselves. He never called a formal meeting. He was more likely to withdraw to the local pub where, under the watchful eyes of 'big fat Nellie' behind the bar, he consumed pink gins with his colleagues and discussed strategies on entirely equal terms. He adopted precisely the same approach with the divisional personnel directors, although once or twice a year they all got together in a country hotel (one recommended by the *Good Food Guide*, of course) and spent a pleasant couple of days talking generally about their mutual interests.

James Robinson

Jim Robinson was the managing director of a medium-sized business (1000 employees) in the fast-moving consumer goods sector of industry. He had come up the hard way and his experience had always been in similar firms. Business was highly competitive and the pressures on maintaining, never mind increasing, market share were considerable. Tough decisions about products, markets and people had to be made often and quickly. There was a non-executive chairman and three outside non-executive directors on the board, but they let Robinson get on with it as long as he delivered the results they wanted – which he did.

Robinson was a despot, although a benevolent one. He knew much more about the business as a whole than any of the other four executive directors, and the chairman and the key institutions (who were represented by the non-executive directors on the board) relied implicitly on his judgement.

Robinson's management style was rumbustious. He did not suffer fools gladly and he cracked down on any repeated inefficiencies or mistakes. He made the key decisions himself. At meetings of the executive directors he would sometimes say that he wanted the views of those present but stated quite clearly that he had already made up his mind and would need a lot of convincing to change it.

But his deep understanding of the business and his ability to think faster on his feet than anyone else meant that, while his autocratic behaviour was sometimes resented at the time, those subjected to it would say on almost every occasion 'you've got to give it to the old so-and-so – he knows his stuff and he's right'. He led, they followed. This was simply because they knew he could accomplish whatever was required in the volatile environment in which they worked.

Chapter 27
Listening skills

There are many good writers and speakers but few good listeners. Most of us filter the spoken words addressed to us so that we absorb only some of them – frequently those we want to hear. Listening is an art which not many people cultivate. But it is a very necessary one, because a good listener will gather more information and achieve better rapport with the other person. And both these effects of good listening are essential to good communications.

Why people don't listen effectively

People don't listen effectively because they are:

- Unable to concentrate, for whatever reason
- Too preoccupied with themselves
- Over-concerned with what they are going to say next
- Uncertain about what they are listening to or why they are listening to it
- Unable to follow the points or arguments made by the speaker
- Simply not interested in what is being said.

Effective listeners:

- Concentrate on the speaker, following not only words but also body language which, through the use of eyes or gestures, often underlines meaning and gives life to the message
- Respond quickly to points made by the speaker, if only in the shape of encouraging grunts
- Ask questions frequently to elucidate meaning and to give the speaker an opportunity to rephrase or underline a point
- Comment on the points made by the speaker, without interrupting

the flow, in order to test understanding and demonstrate that the speaker and listener are still on the same wavelength. These comments may reflect back or summarize something the speaker has said, thus giving an opportunity for him to reconsider or elucidate the point made

- Make notes on the key points – even if the notes are not referred to later they will help to concentrate the mind
- Are continuously evaluating the messages being delivered to check that they are understood and relevant to the purpose of the meeting
- Are alert at all times to the nuances of what the speaker is saying
- Do not slump in their chairs – they lean forward, show interest and maintain contact through their oral responses and by means of body language
- Are prepared to let the speaker go on with the minimum of interruption.

Chapter 28
Managerial planning

As a manager you will normally plan ahead over a relatively short period of time – up to one or, at most, two years. And your objectives, targets and budgets will probably have been fixed by the corporate plan or company budget.

You plan to get things done on time without using more resources than you were allowed. Your aim should be to avoid crises and the high costs that they cause; to have fewer 'drop everything and rush this' problems. Planning warns you about possible crises and gives you a chance to avoid them. Contingency or fall-back plans should be prepared if you have any reason to believe that your initial plan may fail for reasons beyond your control.

When you plan, you choose certain courses of action and rule out others; that is to say, you lose flexibility. This will be a disadvantage if the future turns out differently from what you expected – which is only too likely. Try to make plans that you can change at reasonable cost if you have to. It is a bad plan that admits no change.

Planning activities

As a manager, there are eight planning activities you need to carry out:

- *Forecasting*
  - What sort of work has to be done, how much and by when
  - How the workload might change
  - The likelihood of the department being called on to undertake specialized or rush jobs
  - Possible changes within or outside the department which might affect priorities, the activities carried out, or the workload

- *Programming* – deciding the sequence and time-scale of operations and events required to produce results on time

- *Staffing* – deciding how many and what type of staff are needed and considering the feasibility of absorbing peak loads by means of overtime or temporary staff

- *Setting standards and targets* – for output, sales, times, quality, costs or for any other aspect of the work where performance should be planned, measured and controlled

- *Procedure planning* – deciding how the work should be done and planning the actual operations by defining the systems and procedures required

- *Materials planning* – deciding what materials, bought-in parts or subcontracted work are required and ensuring that it is made available in the right quantity at the right time

- *Facilities planning* – deciding on the plant, equipment, tools and space required

- *Budgeting.*

Planning techniques

Most of the planning you do as a manager is simply a matter of thinking systematically and using your common sense. Every plan contains three key ingredients:

- Objective – the innovation or improvement to be achieved
- Action programme – the specific steps required to achieve the right objective
- Financial impact – the effect of the action on sales, turnover, costs and, ultimately, profit.

Overleaf is an example of how a manufacturing plan could be set out.

Bar charts should be used to express plans more graphically wherever there is more than one activity and care has to be taken to sequence them correctly. The manufacturing plan illustrated overleaf could be expressed as a Gantt chart (page 187).

A more refined method of planning activities in a complex programme, where many interdependent events have to take place, is network planning. This requires the recording of the component parts and their representation in a diagram as a network of interrelated activities. Events are represented

185

Manufacturing Plan

Objective

To reduce the frequency and cost of faulty castings received from the XYZ Company.

Action Programme

Steps	Responsibility	Completion by
1. Ensure recognition by supplier of problem with 'hard spots' in castings.	Purchasing Manager Production Manager	15 January
2. Negotiate price concession on all castings received during weeks when we return more than ten bad castings.	Purchasing Manager	31 January
3. Set up storage area to accumulate ruined castings.	Facilities Manager	15 February
4. Establish procedures to record machine downtime and cutter breakage with individual castings.	Production Controller	1 March
5. Ensure XYZ Company agrees new arrangements.	Purchasing Manager	15 March

Profit Impact

		£ 19.. Profit Increase (Decrease)
Price concessions		7,000
Effect of improved quality	Scrap	8,500
	Overtime	3,500
	Expense tools	9,000
	Lost production	20,000
	Other	12,000
Modifications in storage area		(2,000)
Recording procedures		(1,000)
Other costs		(3,000)
	Total profit impact	£54,000

Step (detailed in action programme)	Responsibility	January	February	March
1. Get XYZ Company to recognize problem.	Purchasing Manager	▭		
2. Negotiate price concession.	Purchasing Manager		▭	
3. Set up storage area.	Facilities Manager		▭	
4. Establish downtime recording procedures.	Production Controller		▭	
5. Get XYZ Company to agree new arrangements.	Purchasing Manager			▭

by circles, activities by arrows, and the time taken by activities by the length of the arrows. There can also be dotted arrows for dummy activities between events that have a time rather than activity relationship. A critical path can be derived which highlights those operations or activities which are essential for the completion of the project within the allocated time-scale. An illustration of part of a basic network is given below.

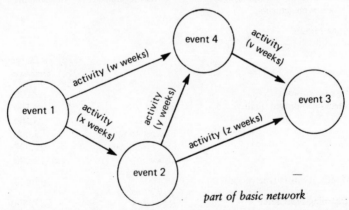

part of basic network

There may be occasions when even more sophisticated planning tech-niques, using computer models, can be made available to help the manager, especially when large quantities of information have to be processed against a number of fixed assumptions or parameters, or where alternative assumptions have to be assessed. In Book Club Associates, for example, the loading required in the warehouse in terms of machine time

187

HOW TO BE AN EVEN BETTER MANAGER

and man hours can be projected two years ahead by feeding parameters for projected activity levels into the programme. Plans can then be made to ensure that manpower and machine capacity are available to deal with forecast work levels.

Chapter 29
Managing your boss

If you want to achieve results, innovate and get on, you have to learn how to manage your boss. The word 'manage' is defined in the *Oxford English Dictionary* as:

● To conduct affairs
● To control; cause to submit to one's rule
● To bring (a person) to consent to one's wishes by artifice, flattery, or judicious suggestion of motives
● To operate upon, manipulate for a purpose
● To bring to pass by contrivance; to succeed in accomplishing
● To deal with or treat carefully.

Although such concepts as artifice, flattery and manipulation would not normally play any part, all these definitions provide clues as to the various aspects of managing one's boss.

If you really believe that something needs to be done and you cannot do it without the consent of your boss, you have to work out how you are going to manage him. And it is worth careful and continuous thought. It is too easy to neglect this essential part of the art of management.

To manage your boss you need to know how to:

● Get agreement from him on what you want to do
● Deal with him over problems
● Impress him, so that he is more likely to accept your proposals and to place his trust in you.

Getting agreement

Getting agreement from your boss is in many ways like getting agreement from anyone else. You need to be good at case presentation and at persuasion. More specifically you need to do the following things:

1. Find out what he expects.
2. Learn about his likes and dislikes, his quirks and his prejudices.
3. Establish how he likes things presented to him. Does he like long, carefully worked out, written reports? Or does he prefer a succinct proposal on one side of one sheet of paper? Perhaps he is more likely to be persuaded if he is introduced gradually to a proposal – a softening-up process, as it were. It is often advisable to test the water before plunging straight in. Some people prefer to start by talking all the way round a problem before getting down to its essential elements. They don't like surprises.
4. Get to know how he likes things done – by observation and by asking other people. If something goes wrong, choose the right moment and ask his advice on how to do it better next time (most people love being asked for their advice).
5. Find out the right time to approach him. Some people are at their best first thing. Others take time to warm up. It is obviously inadvisable to spring surprises if he is at the end of a long hard day. Check on his mood in advance. His secretary can help. And it is always worthwhile having her on your side. Secretaries can be good friends but bad enemies.
6. Work out the best circumstances in which to tackle him. Alone in his office, or over lunch, or driving him at speed along a motorway (there is a lot to be said for making him a captive audience). Getting away from the office may be an advantage: there will be no interruptions and your boss is less likely to call in his henchman, and you will not then have to persuade two people at once. (Picking them off one at a time is much more likely to be successful.) Beware of the 'abominable no-man'. Most organizations have at least one – often the head of finance. He no doubt performs a useful role but keep him out of your way if you can.
7. Decide whether you want support. You may be able to make a better case on a one-for-one basis. There is a lot to be said for standing firmly on your own two feet.
8. Don't go in for open confrontation if you cannot get your own way at first. Get your boss to agree with what he is prepared to agree and then turn to the problem areas. Impress upon him that you want the two of you to cover every possible angle. Emphasize joint responsibility.
9. Leave him an escape route – a way open to consent without his

having to climb down. Don't beat him into the ground – you might win this one but what about the next time?

10. Don't overwhelm him with your ideas. Don't expect to achieve everything at once. Tackle one important thing at a time. Keep it simple. If you come up against a strong objection don't fight it for too long. Survive to fight another day. This does not mean that you should not argue your case strongly, but that you should avoid giving the impression of being pig-headed.

11. Keep in reserve alternative proposals or modifications to your original idea to use if you are getting nowhere.

12. If your boss comes up with a better idea than yours, recognize and accept it. Everybody likes recognition. There is no need to flatter him. You are only reacting to him the way you would like him to react to you.

13. If you can't convince him first time remember that he's the boss. He makes the ultimate decisions. If he says 'that's the way it's going to be' you *may* have to accept it. In the end he could say to you 'we're in a two-horse race and only one can win and that's going to be me'. But you don't have to give up completely. Watch for any signs that he might be prepared to change his mind – given time and a revision to your argument or proposal. Don't nag. If you press too hard he will become stubborn and begin to think that you are challenging his authority and his position. Retire in good order and re-open your campaign at the right moment.

Dealing with problems

Things are going wrong. You've made a mistake. You need your boss's help in sorting out a problem. How do you tackle him? You should adopt the following approach.

1. Keep him informed. Never let him be taken by surprise. Prepare him in advance for the bad news. If 'troubles come not in single spies but in battalions', don't let him have it all at once. Let him down as gently as possible. Don't use the 'first the good news then the bad news' line too crudely, but don't be too gloomy. Give him hope.

2. If something has gone wrong, explain what has happened, why it has happened (no excuses) and what you would like to do about it. Don't dump the problem in his lap in a 'take it or leave it' spirit.

3. Emphasize that you are seeking his views on what you propose, as well as his agreement.

191

4. If you think he is to blame, never say 'I told you so'. If you do, you will make an enemy for life.
5. If you admit responsibility, try to stop your boss keeping on at you. Steer him away from recriminations into a positive attitude on what you can *jointly* do to solve the problem.

Impressing your boss

Your purpose as a manager is not solely to impress your boss. Nor is it to make him like you. But you will get more done and get on better if you impress him. And why make an enemy of your boss when you can have him as a friend?

Your boss needs to trust you, to rely upon you and to believe in your capacity to come up with good ideas and to make things happen. He doesn't want to wet-nurse you or to spend his time correcting your mistakes or covering up.

To succeed in impressing your boss without really trying – it's fatal to push too much – you should:

1. Always be frank and open. Admit mistakes. Never lie or even shade the truth. If there is the faintest suspicion that you are not perfectly straightforward, your boss will never trust you again.
2. Aim to help your boss to be right. This does not mean being subservient or time-serving. Recognize, however, that you exist to give him support – in the right direction.
3. Respond fast to his requests on a can do/will do basis.
4. Don't trouble him unnecessarily with your problems.
5. Provide him with protection where required. Loyalty is an old-fashioned virtue, but you owe it to your boss. If you cannot be loyal to him then you should get out from under as quick as you can.
6. Provide your boss with what the army calls 'completed staff work'. This means that if you are asked to do something you should do it thoroughly. Come up with solutions, not problems. Test your ideas in draft form if you like but, having done so, present a complete proposal with whatever supporting arguments or evidence you need. Avoid half-baked suggestions. Your boss wants answers not questions. When you have finished your report and studied your conclusions and recommendations, ask yourself the question: 'If I were my boss would I stake my reputation on this piece of work and put my name to it?' If the answer is 'No', tear up your report and do it again. It's not completed staff work.

Chapter 30
Meetings

Down with meetings

Meetings bloody meetings, the title of a well-known training film, strikes a familiar chord with us all. When you think how many committees exist and how many meetings are held in any organization, it is remarkable how hard it is to find anyone who has a good word to say for them.

It has been said that committees are made up of the unfit appointed by the incompetent to do the unnecessary, and, again, that a camel is a horse designed by a committee. Experience of badly organized and pointless meetings is so widespread that, for many people, these cynical comments come very close to the truth.

What's wrong with meetings?

Meetings are criticized because they:

- Waste time – too many people talk too much
- Fail to produce decisions and can be slow, exasperating and frustrating – they legitimize procrastination and indecisiveness
- Tend to be dominated by a few people with strong personalities
- Make lowest common denominator recommendations
- Encourage political decisions where vested interests can prevail by means of lobbying and pressure
- Dilute responsibility
- Are costly in time and money
- Concentrate on trivialities they can grasp rather than big issues beyond their scope. Northcote Parkinson cited as an example of this a committee which approved a £1 million capital development

project (which it couldn't properly understand) in ten minutes flat yet spent two hours arguing about a new cycle shed costing £800.

What's right with meetings?

Meetings tend to incite such criticism because they are not properly organized. Many of the criticisms levelled at meetings are really criticisms of their misuse, not their proper use. A well-organized meeting held at the right time for the right reasons can bring a number of benefits. It can:

- Ensure that important matters get proper consideration from all involved
- Clarify thinking in that members have to justify their positions before the others present
- Ensure that different viewpoints are aired
- Act as a medium for the exchange of information
- Save time by getting a number of people together
- Promote coordination
- Create something as a group which the individuals could not have achieved working separately – this is the process of synergy, where the whole is greater than the parts.

To make meetings work there are three things that must happen:

- They should be set up properly
- There should be a good chairman
- The members should be able to participate effectively.

Dos and don'ts of meetings

DO	DON'T
Use a meeting if the information or the judgement is too great for one person	Use a meeting if one person can do the job better
Set up committees only when it is essential to assemble people with different viewpoints in one place at one time	Set up a committee if you want sharp, clear responsibility
	Use a committee to administrate anything
Appoint a chairman who is going to be able to control the meeting and get the best out of it	Use a meeting or committee if you need speedy action
	Appoint a bigger committee than you need – over ten people can become unwieldy

DO	DON'T
Put people with different backgrounds who can contribute ideas on the committee	Hold unnecessary meetings – it may be a good thing to meet regularly on the first Friday of every month but it may be an even better thing to meet only when you have something to discuss.
Tell committees what they are to do and what their authority is	
Be explicit about when you want the meeting to report back	
Use meetings where they work best – reviewing or developing policies, coordinating decisions, ensuring that all concerned with a programme are consulted and kept informed	
Wind up committees as soon as they have served their purpose.	

Chairmanship

The success or failure of a meeting largely depends on the chairman. If you are chairing a meeting this is what you must do:

Prior to the meeting

Before the meeting starts ensure that it has proper terms of reference and that the members are briefed on what to expect and what they should be prepared to contribute. Plan the agenda to provide for a structured meeting, covering all the issues in a logical order. Prepare and issue briefing papers which will structure the meeting and spell out the background, thus saving time going into detail or reviewing purely factual information during the meeting.

During the meeting

1. Start by clearly defining the objective of the meeting, setting a time-scale which you intend to keep.
2. Go through each item of the agenda in turn ensuring that a firm conclusion is reached and recorded.
3. Initiate the discussion on each item by setting the scene very briefly and asking for contributions – ask for answers to specific questions (which you should have prepared in advance) or you may refer the matter first to a member of the meeting who can make the best

initial contribution (ideally, you should have briefed that individual in advance).

4. Invite contributions from other members of the meeting, taking care not to allow anyone to dominate the discussions.
5. Bring people back to order if they drift from the point.
6. If there is too much talk, remind members that they are there to make progress.
7. Encourage the expression of different points of view and avoid crushing anyone too obviously if he has not made a sensible comment.
8. Allow disagreement between members of the meeting but step in smartly if the atmosphere becomes too contentious.
9. Chip in with questions or brief comments from time to time, but do not dominate the discussion.
10. At appropriate moments during the meeting summarize the discussion, express views on where the committee has got to and outline your perception of the interim or final decision that has been made. Then check that the meeting agrees, amending the conclusion as necessary, and ensure that the decision is recorded exactly as made.
11. Summarize what has been achieved at the end of the meeting, indicating who has to do what by when.
12. If a further meeting is needed, agree the purpose of the meeting and what has to be done by those present before it takes place.

Members

If you are a member of a meeting you should:

1. Prepare thoroughly – have all the facts at your fingertips, with any supporting data you need.
2. Make your points clearly, succinctly and positively – try to resist the temptation of talking too much.
3. Remain silent if you have nothing to say.
4. Keep your powder dry if you are not leading the discussion or if it is a subject you are not knowledgeable about. Listen, observe and save your arguments until you can make a really telling point. Don't plunge in too quickly or comprehensively – there may be other compelling arguments.
5. If you are not too sure of your ground, avoid making statements such as 'I think we must do this'. Instead, pose a question to the chairman

or other member of the meeting such as, 'Do you think there is a case for doing this?'

6. Be prepared to argue your case firmly, but don't persist in fighting for a lost cause. Don't retire in a sulk because you cannot get your own way; accept defeat gracefully.

7. Remember that if you are defeated in committee, there may still be a chance for you to fight another day in a different setting.

Chapter 31
Mission and value statements

Mission and value statements are valuable as a means of developing a sense of purpose in an organization and of defining acceptable types of behaviour. Managers need to understand their function and to know the part they can play in formulating and implementing them.

Mission statements

A mission statement defines the business the organization is in and where it is going.

Mission statements can:

- Focus attention on purpose – what the organization exists to do
- Convey top management's vision about the future of the organization
- Provide a foundation upon which strategic plans can be built
- Lead to the development of explicit statements defining the core values of the organization and the guiding principles that are adopted to implement them
- Be used as levers for change by acting as the starting point for programmes designed to develop new structures and systems, achieve innovations and improve performance.

Preparation

A mission statement is best developed at a management workshop in which plenty of time can be spent in examining the issues and their implications thoroughly.

The statement should be prepared as follows:

- It should have 'personality'. In other words, it should reflect the realities in the organization and should not simply consist of bland pieces of prose reached down from the shelf.

- There should be top management consensus about the statement and commitment to its message.
- The formulation of a mission statement should go hand-in-hand with the definition of strategies, core values and critical success factors – what the business intends to do, the way it intends to go about doing it and the criteria for accomplishment.
- The mission statement should take account of the external environment and the corporate culture.
- Management behaviour must be consistent with its declared mission, otherwise the statement is devalued and loses credibility.
- Specific action in the shape of briefings, discussions and workshops should be taken to ensure that the mission statement and its supporting strategies, core values and critical success factors are disseminated and discussed throughout the organization.

The IBM approach

Defining the mission as part of the strategic planning process is essential to the IBM approach at corporate level. This involves the following steps:

1. Define the mission statement.
2. Evolve a corporate strategy which will enable the company to achieve its mission.
3. Define the corporate critical success factors which will determine what issues need to be addressed to achieve strategic aims. (This activity is described in more detail in Chapter 46.)
4. Define within each function the critical success factors which will ensure that it provides the right level of support to cooperative effort.

Example of a mission statement – Ford Motor Company

Ford Motor Company is a worldwide leader in automotive and automotive-related products and services as well as in newer industries such as aerospace, communications and financial services. Our mission is to improve continually our products and services to meet our customers' needs, allowing us to prosper as a business and to provide a reasonable return for our stockholders, the owners of our business.

Functional approach

Managers can and should develop mission statements for their own functions, as in the following example for the personnel department of the International Stock Exchange:

> The mission of the personnel department is to develop and promote the highest quality personnel and human resource practices and initiatives in an ethical, cost-effective and timely manner to support the current and future business objectives of the International Stock Exchange, and to enable the managers to maximize the calibre, effectiveness and development of their human resources.

Value systems and statements

A value system expresses basic beliefs in the behaviour which is believed to be good for an organization and in what the organization considers to be important. It is expressed in a value statement.

Uses of value statements

The purpose of a value statement is to help to develop a value-driven and committed organization which conducts its business successfully by reference to shared beliefs and an understanding of what is best for the enterprise. Value statements are therefore an integral part of strategic planning as a means of guiding the direction of effort in the longer term.

Value statements are closely associated with mission statements and like them can be used as levers for change, getting people to act differently in ways which will support the attainment of the organization's objectives.

Content

A value statement defines core values in such areas as:

- Care and consideration for people
- Care for customers
- Competitiveness
- Enterprise
- Excellence
- Flexibility
- Growth as a major objective
- Innovation
- Market/customer orientation
- Performance orientation
- Productivity
- Quality
- Teamwork.

Examples of value statements

Book Club Associates – Core Values

The core values of BCA are:

- *Excellence*. Anything we do well now we can do better.
- *Profitable growth*. We aim to ensure the profitable expansion of the business to generate the return our owners want on their investment and to ensure the continued prosperity and security of our employees.
- *Enterprise*. We thrive by innovation, by creativity and by seizing opportunities whenever they arise.
- *Customer service*. We depend on our customers and maintaining and improving levels of service to them is a continuing priority.
- *Reward*. Achievement brings reward to everyone in the firm.
- *Teamwork*. BCA is an organization which relies on teamwork to get results.
- *Professionalism*. The effective and dedicated use and development of skills is a prime requirement in the firm.
- *Productivity through people*. Higher productivity and therefore profitability is achieved by effective leadership and the development of a committed and well-trained workforce.
- *Partnership*. All employees are treated as partners in the enterprise, to be involved in matters that affect them and to be informed of how the firm is doing and of its plans for the future.
- *People*. Employees are treated fairly and as responsible human beings. They are given the opportunity to develop their skills and careers in the firm, the management of which is constantly aware of the need to improve the quality of working life.

Ford Motor Company – Values

How we accomplish our mission is as important as the mission itself. Fundamental to success for the Company are these basic values:

- *People*. Our people are the source of our strength. They provide our corporate intelligence and determine our reputation and

HOW TO BE AN EVEN BETTER MANAGER

> vitality. Involvement and teamwork are our core human values.
>
> - *Products*. Our products are the end result of our efforts, and they should be the best in serving customers worldwide. As our products are viewed, so are we viewed.
> - *Profits*. Profits are the ultimate measure of how efficiently we provide customers with the best products for their needs. Profits are required to survive and grow.

Guiding principles

Value statements are often supplemented by a list of guiding principles as in the following example from Ford Motor Company:

- Quality comes first – to achieve customer satisfaction, the quality of our products and services must be our number one priority.
- Customers are the focus of everything we do – our work must be done with our customers in mind, providing better products and services than our competition.
- Continuous improvement is essential to our success – we must strive for excellence in everything we do: in our products, in their safety and value, and in our services, our human relations, our competitiveness, and our profitability.
- Employee involvement is our way of life – we are a team; we must treat each other with trust and respect.
- Dealers and suppliers are our partners – the Company must maintain mutually beneficial relationships with dealers, suppliers and our other business associates.
- Integrity is never compromised – the conduct of our Company worldwide must be pursued in a manner that is socially responsible and commands respect for its integrity and for its positive contributions to society. Our doors are open to men and women alike without discrimination and without regard to ethnic origin or personal beliefs.

Espoused values

It is important to distinguish between the values a company espouses and the actual behaviour of management and the members of the organization. It is easy enough to produce high-sounding value statements but they are meaningless if management does not practise what it preaches or takes no steps, through the development and implementation of supporting policies, to ensure that they are enforced. Management must also do its best to ensure that the values are understood, accepted and followed throughout the organization by example, by education and by insisting that certain standards of behaviour are adhered to.

Chapter 32
Motivating

If your staff are going to achieve the results you are aiming at, they must be well motivated. That is, they must be made to want what you want them to want.

Ensuring that your staff are well motivated is essentially a matter of using the leadership skills and appropriate management style discussed in earlier chapters. An understanding of the process of motivation will greatly enhance your chances of success.

What is motivation?

Motivation is what makes people act or behave in the way they do. When we observe people behaving in a certain way, we ask: 'What are their motives?' If we want them to do something, we ask: 'How can we motivate them?'

Motivation and needs

Motivation begins with the needs that exist within us all. If these are unsatisfied we establish a goal, consciously or unconsciously, and take action to achieve that goal. The basic motivation model therefore looks like the diagram opposite.

Most people make the mistake of trying to motivate others on the basis of faulty assumptions about their future behaviour. People's needs and the ways in which they are satisfied are much more complex than we tend to think. We observe behaviour and draw conclusions from it, but very often we do not really know what the motivating factor is.

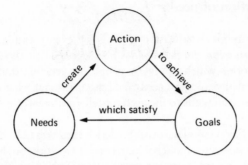

The following is an example of how a superficial analysis of needs can lead a company astray:

The management of an aircraft assembly plant in the UK fell into this trap a few years ago when they were in the happy position of having a full order book and a shortage of skilled craftsmen. To achieve production deadlines, they recruited fitters from all parts of the country, promising help with settling-in costs and removal expenses. Unfortunately, a very high proportion of the fitters (nearly 50 per cent) left within three months when they were just beginning to become effective. Heavy recruitment costs had to be written off and production suffered.

The immediate reaction of the factory manager was that the newly engaged fitters needed more money. He could not alter basic rates but he encouraged his rate fixers to relax times and so increase bonus earnings. But labour turnover carried on at the same high rate, although earnings were increased all round.

The factory manager therefore asked · the personnel manager to investigate the problem more thoroughly. The latter interviewed every fitter who was leaving and also a large sample of existing workers. He got the same story from everybody. Because this was the first production run there were many modifications and design changes. This led to shortages of tools and parts. The fitters felt they were being messed about and were utterly frustrated by the constant interruptions and delays. Moreover, their earnings fluctuated considerably. They never knew what was going into their pay packets from one week to the next and this caused great difficulties with their wives, who were trying to adjust to new surroundings and expenditures.

Hardly any of the fitters complained about the level of earnings; it was their unpredictability that concerned them. Their basic needs were for a settled working environment and an end to wildly fluctuating pay packets, not extra cash.

To avoid this sort of problem you need to know more about the needs affecting motivation – how they are classified and how they operate.

Classification of needs

The most famous classification of needs is the one formulated by Maslow (33) in *Motivation and Personality*. He suggested that there are five major need categories which apply to people in general, starting from the fundamental physiological needs and leading through a hierarchy of safety, social and esteem needs to the need for self-fulfilment, the highest need of all.

Another behavioural scientist, Frederick Herzberg (25), developed what he called a two-factor model of human needs at work, on the basis of what some people regard as rather spurious research. One group of factors revolves around the need for people to develop in their job as a source of personal growth – it includes the needs for achievement, responsibility and recognition. The second group is associated with the needs for fair treatment in pay, supervision, working conditions and administrative practices.

How needs operate

According to Maslow, man is a wanting animal. It is unsatisfied needs that drive him forward. As one need is satisfied, the next one in the hierarchy emerges.

Herzberg looked at needs another way. He suggested that his first group of needs – those associated with the work itself: responsibility, achievement, etc – are the real satisfiers because they seem to be effective in motivating the individual to superior performance and effort. The second group of needs – those associated with the environment in which work is carried out: pay, conditions, etc – serve primarily to prevent job dissatisfaction, while having little effect on positive job attitudes. Herzberg christened this second group the 'hygiene' factors.

Herzberg and many others who have followed him thus distinguished between the *intrinsic* factors arising from the work itself and the *extrinsic* factors provided by the employer, such as pay. The claim has been made that while extrinsic rewards can be important in increasing effort and minimizing dissatisfaction, intrinsic rewards relating to responsibility and achievement may have a longer and deeper effect in creating and increasing job satisfaction. The whole creed of 'job enrichment' (giving people more responsibility and scope in their jobs) has been founded on this belief.

While classifications of needs may be helpful, their use in understanding the complex nature of motivation is limited. For instance, even Herzberg had to admit that money 'takes on some of the properties of a motivator with dynamics similar to recognition for achievement', and neither he nor anyone else has been able to prove a significant relationship between satisfaction of needs and performance. We therefore need to look at other aspects of motivation.

The relationship between satisfaction and performance

It is clearly simplistic to believe that a happy worker is a productive worker. There are some people who are quite happy to do nothing. But it could be equally simplistic to think that a satisfied worker is *necessarily* a productive worker. There is such a thing as being self-satisfied. Moreover, the numerous research projects on motivation carried out within factories and offices over the last 50 years have failed to produce convincing evidence that satisfaction leads to good performance. It has been shown that satisfaction explains less than 20 per cent of variances in performance. Indeed, it is possible to say that it is not satisfaction that produces good performance, but good performance that produces satisfaction.

We must therefore reject the theory that passive and historical feelings of job satisfaction are the key motivators – an essentially static theory – and look at the more dynamic aspects of motivation in the shape of what people are seeking in the future – their expectations.

The role of expectations

Motivation is a forward-looking process. The degree to which we are motivated depends very much on our perception of the likelihood that certain behaviour will achieve the results we want. Motivation is much more about expectations than about satisfactions. This concept of expectancy was formulated by Vroom, among others. He wrote in *Work and Motivation* (52):

> Whenever an individual chooses between alternatives which involve certain outcomes, it seems clear that his behaviour is affected not only by his preference among these outcomes but also by the degree to which he believes these outcomes to be probable . . . An expectancy is defined as a momentary belief that a particular act will be followed by a particular outcome.

Thus, in the case of the aircraft company mentioned earlier, the fitters were de-motivated because their expectations about a steady flow of earnings were disappointed, not because they were not enough.

It follows from this commonsense proposition – people will only be motivated if they think they are going to get what they want (or avoid what they don't want) – that expectations about rewards have an

207

important impact on motivation. We must therefore consider the role of the reward system.

The reward system

It was suggested above that good performance causes satisfaction – a sense of achievement. And in *The Human Side of Enterprise* (36) Douglas McGregor said that: 'Commitment to objectives is a function of the rewards associated with their achievement.'

If we want effort from the people who work for us there are two factors we must consider:

- The value of the rewards to the individual in so far as they are likely to satisfy his needs for security, social esteem and self-fulfilment
- The probability that rewards depend on effort, as perceived by the individual; in other words, his expectations about the relationship between his effort and his reward.

Thus, the greater the value of a set of rewards and the higher the probability that receiving each of these rewards depends upon effort, the greater the effort that will be made in a given situation.

The painstaking research of countless behavioural scientists seems therefore to have resulted in the 'discovery' that effort depends on the rewards people can expect to get – a fact which any sensible line manager knows without resort to research. But effort is not enough. It has to be effective effort if it is to produce what we want. And there are a number of additional factors which affect motivation.

Other factors affecting motivation

- *Ability* – the individual's intelligence, skills and know-how.
- *Perceptions about the job* – what the individual wants to do or thinks he is required to do. From the organization's point of view, it is desirable that the individual's perceptions should coincide with what it believes he ought to be doing.
- *Influence of other people* – the pressures exerted on a person by fellow employees, family and other social groups to which he belongs. Group pressures are important because they affect social needs and the need for esteem.
- *The work itself* – the extent to which the work itself gives people an opportunity for achievement, responsibility and satisfaction. The

following story is an example of how the quality of working life, resulting from the way jobs are designed, can affect performance.

In the new policies department of an insurance company, output, as measured by policies issued per clerk, was falling badly. A preliminary investigation suggested that high labour turnover was a major causal factor. A further investigation indicated that the nature of the work itself was the problem. The qualification level for new entrants was fairly high – four or more GCSEs. But the clerks were put on absolutely routine work. Each one dealt with a single stage in the process of dealing with new insurance policies. Their work was then checked by another section. Some people therefore spent their whole day checking or rechecking other people's work – a soul-destroying occupation. If any interesting work needed to be done it was hived off to a department of specialists. Only routine work went down what was aptly called 'the pipeline'. The answer to the problem was to give each clerk whole segments of work, including the interesting bits. There was a significant reduction in staff turnover and improvement in performance.

These variables affecting performance can be expressed in the model shown below, which is based on the important work of Lawler and Porter (31) in this field:

Motivation in practice

The analysis of the process of motivation in this chapter suggests certain things that you can do as a manager to improve your ability to motivate. These are:

1. Try to understand what the needs of your subordinates are in terms of Maslow's categories of need: security, social, esteem and self-fulfilment.

2. Find out not only what they need but also what they want. You may not be able to give it to them but you might at least be able to modify your approach to motivation in the light of this knowledge.

3. Use financial rewards as a prime motivator. Money is important because it satisfies so many needs – it provides what people want to increase their standard of living, but it also serves as the most effective way of recognizing achievement (self-fulfilment) and enabling people to demonstrate their achievement to others (esteem).

4. Bear in mind, however, that money is not the only reward that people need and want. They can also be motivated by recognition, praise, promotion and the work itself – the opportunity to achieve something extra or to take on greater responsibility. And this sort of reward can sometimes be more effective than money. It depends on their individual needs, and the reason you should try to identify these needs is that you can be more discriminating in the use of rewards.

5. Remember the importance of expectations as an influence on motivation. A reward will be much more effective when people know what they can get if they work hard and well enough. You should therefore:

- Ensure that the relationship between effort and reward is clearly defined in any financial reward system – payment by results, commission or bonus schemes
- Set your subordinates targets and standards which are achievable but not too easily
- Make them aware that their achievements will be recognized by praise, a special reward or the opportunity to do better – but don't cheapen the reward, give praise only when praise is due
- Make it known, as far as possible, what people have to do to gain promotion or take on greater responsibility
- Spell out not only what they can get if they do well but also what they won't get if they do badly. This is not a crude carrot and stick tactic but a clarification of the fact that what they achieve or don't achieve is up to them.

6. Always keep in mind that your aim, as defined by Douglas McGregor, is 'the creation of conditions such that the members of the organization can achieve their own goals *best* by directing their efforts towards the success of the enterprise'. Hence the value of:

- Identifying people's needs, so that you can try to adjust rewards to meet those needs

- Getting people to think for themselves about what they can and should do and agreeing targets and standards with them.

7. Recognize the fact that people can be motivated by the work itself if it satisfies their needs for responsibility and achievement. Do this by using the following job enrichment techniques:

   - Increasing the responsibility of individuals (as in the insurance company case mentioned earlier)
   - Giving people more scope to vary the methods, sequence and pace of their work
   - Giving a person or group a complete natural unit of work, thus reducing specialization
   - Removing some controls from above while ensuring that individuals or groups are clearly accountable for achieving defined targets or standards
   - Giving people the control information needed to monitor their own performance
   - Encouraging the participation of employees in planning work and innovating new techniques
   - Assigning projects to individuals or groups which give them more responsibility and help them to increase their expertise.

8. Remember that group pressures can affect motivation, for good or ill. Take steps to get groups on your side by involving them in key decisions which affect their work.

Chapter 33
Negotiating

Negotiation is the process of coming to terms and, in so doing, getting the best deal possible for your firm, your union or yourself.

Negotiations involve a conflict of interest. Sellers prefer a high price to a low one and buyers prefer a low price to a high one. Unions want the highest settlement they can get, management wants the lowest. What one side gains the other loses. No one likes to lose, so there is conflict, which has to be managed if an amicable agreement is to be achieved. And negotiators do, or should, try to end up on friendly terms, whatever differences of opinion have occurred on the way. After all, they may well meet again.

Another important feature of negotiations is that they take place in an atmosphere of uncertainty. Neither side necessarily knows what the other wants or will give.

There are two main types of negotiation – commercial and trade union.

Commercial negotiations

Commercial negotiations are mainly about the price and the terms for supplying goods or services.

In their simplest form they are no more than a haggle between buyer and seller, much the same as what happens when you trade in your car for a new one. At their more complex they concern a package in which a number of extras are on offer along with the basic product. Sellers can usually offer a range of prices to suit the needs of the buyer: an 'ex-works' price, a delivered price, an installed price and a price which includes service. Various methods of staging payments or providing credit may also be offered.

Negotiations of this type usually start with the buyer producing his specification. The seller then produces a proposal and negotiation starts.

The seller will have included a negotiating margin in his proposal and will be prepared to vary his price according to the package required.

Commercial negotiations are usually conducted in a friendly manner, and that's your major problem. You can too easily be seduced into accepting a less than satisfactory deal by the blandishments of the negotiator.

Trade union negotiations

Trade union negotiations can be much tougher. They may involve a simple pay settlement, but usually they involve a package. Extra benefits will be at issue, which can be traded for concessions if need be.

In this type of negotiation, both parties are probably quite clear as to the maximum they will give or the minimum they will accept. They will have predetermined their opening demands and offers and their shopping list of extras will have been analysed to determine which points can be conceded in return for some benefit.

There are a number of bargaining conventions used in union negotiations, of which the following are the most generally accepted:

- Whatever happens during the bargaining, both parties hope to come to a settlement.
- Attacks, hard words, threats and (controlled) losses of temper are treated by both sides as legitimate tactics and should not be allowed to shake either party's belief in the other's integrity, or their desire to settle without taking drastic action.
- Off-the-record discussions (beneficial as a means of probing attitudes and intentions) should not be referred to specifically in formal bargaining sessions, unless both sides agree in advance.
- Each side should be prepared to move from its original position.
- It is normal, although not inevitable, for the negotiation to proceed by a series of offers and counter-offers which lead steadily towards a settlement.
- Concessions, once made, cannot be withdrawn.
- Firm offers must not be withdrawn, although it is legitimate to make and withdraw conditional offers.
- A third party should not be brought in until both parties are agreed that no further progress would be made without one.
- The final agreement should mean exactly what it says. There should be no trickery and the terms agreed should be implemented without amendment.

- If possible, the final settlement should be framed so that both sides can save face and credibility.

The process of negotiation

In both cases the process is much the same. Here each stage is illustrated by a summary of what took place in an actual trade union negotiation.

Stage 1: Preparation – Setting objectives (or drawing up specifications), assembling data, and deciding on negotiating strategy
The union's aim was to achieve a settlement at, or above, the current rate of inflation (8 per cent). Its strategy was to force management on to the defensive by asking them to make an offer without divulging what the union wanted. In addition, the union asked for a reduction of one hour in the working week, an extra three days' holiday and a Christmas bonus of one week's pay.

The management's objective was to settle at no more than the rate of inflation, and to concede nothing that would raise the total cost of the package above 8 per cent. There was some debate within the management team about strategy. One hawk wanted to pre-empt the union claim by starting with the final offer, allowing no room for bargaining. He was overruled on the grounds that this would cause a confrontation and hence long-term damage to relations with the union. The next question was how much room for manoeuvre should be allowed between the opening and closing offer. Some wanted to start as low as possible, say 3 per cent, so as to close well below the 15 per cent claim expected from the union. The prevailing view, however, was that too low an offer would prolong the negotiations unnecessarily. It was thought better to start at 5 per cent, so that, if it had to, the firm could take two steps of 1½ per cent before reaching its maximum of 8 per cent.

Stage 2: Opening – Negotiators reveal their initial bargaining positions to their opposite numbers
The union started by stating its case. It wanted a substantial increase to protect its members from inflation and to restore the differentials lost over the previous three years. The extras (reduced working week, etc) were thrown in almost as make-weights, giving management the clue that there might be scope for some trading later on.

Management stated that no 'substantial offer' could be expected. It emphasized the poor trading results of the firm and the fact that, overall, the pay of the union's members compared favourably with other workers. The point was also made (it was to be repeated many times in ensuing meetings) that the firm could not guarantee that pay increases would match inflation. Having set out their opening positions and their main arguments the two parties agreed to adjourn the meeting.

Stage 3: Bargaining – At this stage both parties have the same aims. As a negotiator you will be trying: (a) to probe the weaknesses in the other side's case, and (b) to convince the other side that they must abandon their position and move closer to your own. You will also be checking to see if your own position holds good in the light of information received from your opponents and their reactions to your case. Your original judgement may be confirmed or you may have to adjust it now. You may also decide to apply pressure or give concessions now in order to move towards a satisfactory conclusion.

In the bargaining stage three meetings were held. At each of them the arguments of both management and union teams were the same as in the opening phase.

Each party aimed to discover how strongly the other believed in his arguments and to what extent he was prepared to shift his position. Every phrase was analysed to discover just what was behind it, both sides seeking hints as to how much support the other was getting – from the shop floor and top management respectively.

Management opened with a 5 per cent offer and got the usual reaction: it was 'derisory', 'insulting', and so on. The union refused to state exactly what it wanted, hoping to mystify and wrong-foot the management.

Between the second and third meetings the management team were agreed in the belief that the union was hoping to get 10 per cent but, if pushed, might settle for eight. It was decided that an offer to reduce the working week by 30 minutes might be made, but only as a last-minute trade-off if a reasonable settlement seemed unlikely.

At the third meeting, management increased its offer to 7 per cent, saying that this was as far as it could go. When pressed to state whether this was, or was not, their final offer, the management team refused to elucidate. The union rightly interpreted this to mean that there was more in the kitty and that top management would release it if pressed hard enough. The union demanded 10 per cent *and* the other concessions.

Stage 4: Closing – Each party judges whether the other side is determined to stick to its position or will settle for a compromise. The final moves are made. It is during this stage that final 'trade-offs' may lead to a settlement.

The final meeting lasted all day and into the night. Management stuck to its 7 per cent offer and made no other concessions. The union tried several tactics. Pleading, controlled loss of temper and threats of industrial action were all used. The management team finally judged that the only way to get a settlement was to attempt a trade-off. They offered 7 per cent plus one hour off the working week, in return for an agreement to abolish the customary five minutes' 'wash-up' time (a practice that had been consistently abused).

Management reiterated that this was the final offer and was as much as the firm could afford and managed to convince the union by sheer force of argument that it meant what it said. The union accepted the offer after ballotting its members.

Negotiating tactics

(a) Preparation

1. Define your bargaining objectives as follows:

   - *Ideal* – the best you can hope to achieve
   - *Minimum* – the least you would be prepared to settle for
   - *Target* – what you are going to try for and believe, realistically, you have a good chance of achieving.

2. Consider how you might build up a package which would allow concessions to be exchanged. For example, could you accept a higher price for a concession on payment terms, or increase a pay offer if the union agrees to remove a restrictive practice?

3. Assess what the other party wants or is prepared to offer. For example, if you are a manufacturer negotiating terms with a store it pays to know, say, that the buyer is constrained by his company policy which insists on a three times mark-up. Knowing the retail price that the store will want to charge you will have a good idea of the maximum the buyer will pay. You can then judge whether you should press for a larger order to justify a lower selling price than you would normally accept.

   In a typical wage negotiation the union or representative body making the claim will come to the table with a predetermined target, minimum and opening claims. Similarly, you, as the employer, will have your own target, maximum and opening offer.

   The difference between their claim and your offer is the negotiating range. If your maximum exceeds their minimum this will indicate the settlement zone. This is demonstrated in the top diagram opposite. In this example the chance of settlement without too much trouble is fairly high. It is when your maximum is less than their minimum, as in the lower diagram opposite, that the trouble starts.

4. Decide on your strategy and tactics – your opening offer, the steps

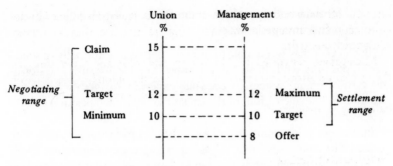

Negotiating range with a settlement zone

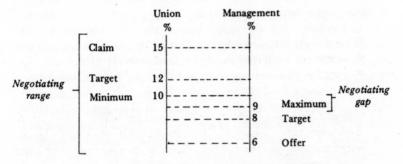

Negotiating range without a settlement zone

you are going to take, the concessions you are prepared to offer and the arguments you are going to use.

5. Collect the facts needed to support your case.
6. Assemble any documents you need, such as standard contract terms.
7. In a trade union negotiation:

- Select the negotiating team. This should never have fewer than two members, and for major negotiations should have three or more: one to take the lead, one to take notes and feed the negotiator with any supporting information he needs, and the others to observe their opposite numbers and play a specific part in negotiations in accordance with their brief.
- Brief the members of the negotiating team on their roles and the negotiating strategy and tactics that are to be adopted. If appropriate, prepared statements or arguments should be issued at this stage to be used as required by the strategic plan.
- Rehearse the members of the team in their roles. They can be asked to repeat their points to other members and deal with responses from them; or someone can act as devil's advocate and

217

force the leader or other members of the team to handle awkward points or negotiating ploys.

At this stage it may be possible to meet the opponent informally to sound out his position, while he sounds out yours. You can use such a session as an 'early warning' system to get your opponent to modify his initial demands by convincing him of the strength of your own position or your determination to resist.

In a recent trade union negotiation these 'corridor tactics' met with success. The union concerned had asked management to introduce a new technology agreement with the usual clauses about consultation, job protection and health precautions.

During the first two meetings management stuck firmly to its view that all these requirements were catered for by existing agreements and published policies. But the union insisted that this was not so. The negotiation seemed to have reached an impasse. Whatever the union leader felt, he could not weaken too obviously during the actual meetings. Neither could the general manager who was heading the management team.

To break the impasse the general manager asked his industrial relations manager to hold an off-the-record meeting with the trade union leader. At this meeting it was made clear that the company would not agree to a separate new technology agreement in any circumstances. But the industrial relations manager suggested that the company would be prepared to add a stronger prior consultation clause to the existing agreement.

From previous experience, the union leader knew this man meant what he said. He saw no point in having a major confrontation on this issue and knew he would get little support from his members, who did not see new technology as a real issue. But he felt that if he had to give a concession he should get something back. In other words, he wanted a trade-off.

He therefore agreed to go along with the idea, so long as the company let the union monitor the introduction of any major new technology schemes over the next six months. This was accepted by the industrial relations manager. Both parties understood the convention that there was no commitment and that no reference would be made to their discussion in future formal meetings. They then cleared the informal understanding with their respective committees and, at the subsequent formal meeting, the terms were agreed without any difficulty. What looked like being a major problem had been solved by corridor negotiations.

(b) Opening

Your tactics when opening the negotiation should be to:

- Open realistically and move moderately
- Challenge your opponent's position as it stands; but on no account to limit his ability to move
- Explore attitudes, ask questions, observe behaviour and, above all, listen; assess your opponent's strengths and weaknesses, his tactics and the extent to which he may be bluffing
- Make no concessions of any kind at this stage
- Be non-committal about proposals and explanations (do not talk too much).

(c) Bargaining

Your aim is to narrow the gap between the two initial positions and to persuade your opponent that your case is so strong that he must accept less than he had planned. You should:

- Always make conditional proposals: 'If you will do this I will consider doing that'
- Never make one-sided concessions: always trade-off against a concession from the other party: 'If I concede x then I expect you to concede y'
- Negotiate on the whole package: never allow your opponent to pick you off item by item; keep all the issues open so as to extract the maximum benefit from potential trade-offs.

Reading the signals

During the bargaining stage you must be sensitive to any signals made by the other party. Every time he makes a conditional statement it shows that he is prepared to move. Explore the possibilities with questions. Try to get behind what people *say* and understand what they really *mean*. For example:

What they say	What they mean
That's as far as I can go.	I might be able to persuade my boss to go further.
We don't usually give more than 5 per cent discount.	We're prepared to give more if you give us something in return.
Let's think about that point.	I'm prepared to negotiate.
I need notice of that question.	It's difficult, but not impossible. Try again.
It will be very difficult for us to meet that requirement.	It's not impossible but we'll want a trade-off.

219

What they say	What they mean
I shall certainly consider your offer.	I am going to accept it but I don't want to appear to be too easy a touch.
This is our standard contract.	We're prepared to negotiate on the terms.
We're prepared to offer you £x per 1000 units.	The price is negotiable.
That's my final offer.	My boss *might* go further if pushed (or if it is made worth his while).
We couldn't meet your delivery requirements at that price.	I will negotiate on delivery or price.

Arguing

During the bargaining stage much of your time will be spent in arguing. Clear thinking (see Chapter 6) will help you to present your case and expose the fallacies in your opponent's arguments.

You should also consider the *manner* in which you argue. You are not there to beat your opponent into the ground. In fact, in the interests of future good relationships (which will benefit *you* as well as him) it is wise to provide him with an escape route. As Victor Feather said: 'Always leave the other fellow the price of his bus ticket home.'

Avoid brow-beating your opponent. Disagree with him firmly, but don't shoot him down. Don't try to make him look small. Score points over him, if you must, to discredit his arguments or expose fallacious reasoning but never in order to discredit him as a person. If you indulge in personal attacks or abuse, your opponents will close ranks.

To argue effectively you must be prepared to listen both to the stated, and to the implied, points made by your opponent. Don't talk too much yourself; it will prevent you reading signals, and you may give too much away. Wherever you can, challenge your opponent to justify his case on an item-by-item basis. Put the onus on him by questioning for clarification. Answer a question with another question if you want time to consider.

Argue calmly and without emotion, but emphasize the points you really want to ram home either by raising your voice slightly and slowing down to highlight your argument, or by repetition.

Control your anger. Express yourself strongly, by all means, but you will lose everything if you lose your temper.

Always remember that you are *not* trying to win at all costs. If he wants something which you cannot give, don't just say no. Offer an alternative package. If he is asking for a higher specification than you normally provide for the price and wants a delivery date which you cannot meet without incurring extra overtime costs, tell him that you can meet the specifications and the delivery deadline as long as he is prepared to cover the costs.

Gambits

There are a number of standard bargaining gambits. Here are a few of the more common ones:

- *Uttering threats* – 'Agree to what I want or I'll call out the lads'; or '. . . I'll take my custom elsewhere'. Never react to such threats and never utter empty ones.
- *No negotiation under duress* – 'We refuse to discuss your claim unless and until you cancel your overtime ban.' An excellent approach, if you can get away with it.
- *It will reflect badly on you* – 'Do you really want to get the reputation of being a heartless employer?' This is an emotional appeal and, as such, should be discounted.
- *The bluff direct* – 'I have two or three quotations lower than yours.' The answer to this gambit is to call his bluff – 'What are they offering for the price?' 'OK, why not accept them, why bother talking to me?'
- *The leading question* – 'Do you think it is a good idea to reward people according to merit?' 'Yes.' 'Then why do you insist on retaining this fixed incremental scheme which benefits everybody irrespective of how well they've done?' Never fall for a leading question.
- *The piecemeal or 'salami' technique* – In this your opponent will try to pick off the items one by one. 'That's the price agreed, now we can deliver in three months, OK?' 'Right, we've agreed the delivery terms, now this is how we charge for maintenance.' Always negotiate the whole package. Don't allow yourself to be railroaded into a piecemeal approach.
- *The yes, but . . . approach* – 'Yes, we agree to accept an increase of 8 per cent but before we can agree to everything there is this other problem of compensation for redundancy we must tackle.' To avoid being caught in a yes/but trap, always make offers on one part of a package conditional on accepting another part: 'We are prepared to consider an 8 per cent offer but only if you agree to drop your claim for enhanced redundancy pay.'

(d) Closing

When and how you close depends on your assessment of the strength of your opponent's case and his determination to see it through. You may close by:

1. Making a concession, preferably a minor one, and trading it off against an agreement to settle. The concession can be offered more positively than at the bargaining stage: 'If you will agree to settle at x, I will concede y.'
2. Doing a deal: You might split the difference, or bring in something new – such as extending the settlement time-scale, agreeing to back payments, phasing increases, making a joint declaration of intent to do something in the future (for example to introduce a productivity plan), or offering an incentive discount.
3. Summarizing what has happened to date, emphasizing the concessions that have been made and the extent to which you have moved, and stating that you have reached your final position.
4. Applying pressure through a threat of the consequences which will follow if your offer is not accepted.
5. Giving your opponent a choice between two courses of action.

Do not make a final offer unless you mean it. If it is not really your final offer and your opponent calls your bluff, you will have to make further concessions and your credibility will be undermined. He will, of course, attempt to force you into revealing how close you are to your final position. Do not allow him to hurry you. If you want to avoid committing yourself and thus devaluing the word 'final', state as positively as you can that this is as far as *you* are prepared to go.

Chapter 34
Objectives

> Objectives are needed in every area where performance and results directly and vitally affect the survival and prosperity of a business (Peter Drucker, *The Practice of Management* (16))

In theory at least, the better you know where you are going, the more likely you are to get there. However, no organization has one simple objective such as to maximize profits. High profits in the short run would mean running down stocks and cutting back on investments which would endanger the company's future existence. A book club, for example, can only survive in the long run by 'investing' in new members. If it lived off the fat of existing members it could make more money in the short term but as these members left it would run out of income and go out of business. Survival and growth are thus prime objectives, along with that of maximizing profit.

The problem facing most organizations – profit or non-profit making – and their managers is one of balancing the various objectives and deciding on priorities.

A company may express its objectives under a number of headings, for instance:

- To increase market share to x per cent
- To maintain return on capital employed at its present level
- To increase turnover in real terms by x per cent
- To maintain profit as a percentage of sales at its present level
- To launch product A by a given date, achieving a return on investment of £x in the first year.

Stating objectives in this way is only a starting point. Policies and plans on how to achieve objectives and reconcile conflicts between them will have to be evolved. And this will mean evaluating alternatives and, sometimes, keeping options open when the information is not available on which an immediate decision can be made.

Why have objectives?

As Peter Drucker points out, objectives in a business enterprise enable management to explain, predict and control activities in a way which single ideas like profit maximization do not. More specifically, objectives:

- Enable the organization to explain the whole range of business phenomena in a small number of general statements
- Allow the testing of those statements in actual performance
- Enable decisions to be examined while they are still being made rather than after they have been effected
- Help to improve future performance by the analysis of past experience.

Corporate objectives

Peter Drucker has suggested that there are eight areas in which performance objectives should be set: market standing, innovation, productivity, physical and financial resources, profitability, manager performance and development, worker performance and attitude, and public responsibility. One other key area is overall activity levels as measured by sales. Any board would be well advised to sit down at least once a year and use these headings as an agenda for considering the future. Then they should review achievements against objectives at regular intervals during the year.

Some objectives such as market share, profits as a percentage of turnover, sales turnover, and sales turnover per employee are quantifiable as targets. Others, such as launching a new product, can be set as aims to be achieved by a certain date. In areas such as manager and worker performance where a target cannot be quantified or defined, it is still useful to have a broad statement of aims.

Individual objectives

There is no doubt that as a manager you will be in a better position to plan your work and monitor progress if you have clear objectives which have been agreed with your boss. It is equally certain that your subordinates will be more effective if they also understand and accept their objectives.

The table shows some of the headings under which objectives can be formulated in different jobs.

General Manager	Works Manager	Sales Manager
Profitability	Achievement of factory output targets	Achievement of sales targets
Volume and growth of business	Control of costs	Contribution to profits and fixed overheads
Provision and utilization of fixed assets	Utilization of plant and machinery	Development of new accounts
Provision and utilization of current assets	Control of stocks	Extension of existing business
Product innovation	Product quality	Customer satisfaction
Customer satisfaction	Labour productivity	Identification of new products
Operating costs	Industrial relations	Introduction of new products
Management effectiveness	Management effectiveness	Effectiveness of sales force
Employee productivity and attitude	Safety	Control of costs

When setting your own or other people's objectives you should avoid quantification for quantification's sake. Artificial figures attached to objectives are unhelpful. To ask a personnel manager to reduce the rate of absenteeism from 4.3 per cent to 4.0 per cent is to give him a meaningless objective. He cannot predict with precision how any action he takes will affect absentee levels. It would be far better to set a broad objective such as 'to work with line management and the company's medical officer to develop procedures which will reduce the level of absenteeism'. His success can then be measured by the extent to which absenteeism has been reduced, not by his ability to achieve an arbitrary figure.

The other thing to avoid in setting individual objectives is to create too much paperwork. Discuss and agree objectives with your subordinates; review results against those objectives; agree what has to be done to improve performance and what changes need to be made to current

225

objectives. But don't use elaborate forms for the purpose. All you need to record can be put down on one side of one sheet of paper – in handwriting.

Above all, remember that what you are trying to do is to provide a guideline for future action. Objectives are only worth setting for yourself or other people if they are used as the basis for plans and for monitoring performance.

Chapter 35
Organizational effectiveness

Features of an effective organization

The effectiveness of an organization depends on:

1. Strong visionary leadership from the top.
2. A powerful management team.
3. A well-motivated, committed, skilled and flexible workforce.
4. Good teamwork throughout the organization.
5. A continuous pressure to innovate coupled with the ability to manage and thrive on change
6. Clearly defined goals and strategies to accomplish them.
7. A positive corporate culture.
8. A value system which emphasizes performance, quality and the responsibilities of the organization to its stakeholders – shareholders, managers, suppliers, customers and the community.
9. An ability to get into action fast.
10. A sound financial base.

Improving organizational effectiveness

Improved organizational effectiveness is achieved by:

1. Analysing the existing situation with regard to each of the ten headings listed above.
2. Conducting a management audit as described below.
3. Taking whatever steps are necessary in the light of these analyses.

Management audit

The main areas covered in a management audit are as follows:

- *Top management's vision.* The quality of the vision of top management about the future of the company.
- *Top management's concept of function.* The extent to which top management have a clear view of their role and carry it out effectively.
- *Strategy.* The extent to which a clear sense of direction has been established by means of a strategic management approach.
- *Objectives.* Whether or not objectives are appropriate, clearly defined and understood.
- *Plans.* The extent to which they are considered, realistic, adventurous and acted upon.
- *Corporate culture.* The degree to which the corporate culture is functional or dysfunctional in assisting the organization to achieve its objectives.
- *Values.* The existence of an appropriate value system which is understood and acted upon.
- *Organization climate.* The degree to which there is evidence of cooperation and trust between managers and those who work for them.
- *Management style.* The appropriateness of the management style adopted by the chief executive and senior managers, with specific reference to the provisions of clear leadership and a strongly developed sense of direction, with a willingness to communicate to all levels and listen to what people have to say.
- *Innovation.* The amount of innovation that takes place and its effectiveness in preventing stagnation and furthering the objectives of the company.
- *Organization.* The degree to which it contributes to the achievement of objectives and the extent to which the structure is logical and facilitates the processes of communication, coordination and control.
- *Human resource management.* The ability of the company to attract, retain, develop and motivate the quality and quantity of people it needs and the quality of the relationships maintained with employees.
- *Management.* The strengths and weaknesses of the management team, the extent to which managers understand their objectives, have a sense of purpose and are committed to achieving their targets and standards, and the quality of the provisions made for management succession and development.
- *Employees.* The quality, commitment and morale of employees.
- *Finance.* The strength of the financial base of the company, the degree to which financial targets are achieved, the inferences that can

be obtained from an examination of financial ratio trends (especially those dealing with return on capital, liquidity, inventory and overheads), the control of cash and working capital, and the effectiveness of budgetary control procedures.

- *Marketing.* The importance attached to the concept that the purpose of the business is to create and keep a customer, and to do that, the business must produce and deliver goods and services which people want and value at prices that represent good value to them compared with those they can get elsewhere.

- *Operations.* The efficiency with which manufacturing and distribution operations are planned and controlled and inventory is managed, the levels of quality and customer service achieved; the extent to which higher levels of productivity are being achieved by automation, mechanization and more effective management; the extent to which wasteful practices and inefficiencies exist.

- *Management science.* The use to which operations research and other quantitative methods are being put to increase the effectiveness with which the company's operations are planned and controlled.

- *Information technology.* The efficiency and effectiveness of computers and other information technology systems in processing information and providing data which is needed by management.

- *Control.* The effectiveness of control procedures in measuring results against budgets and targets, identifying variances, and indicating where corrective action is required.

Chapter 36
Organizing

The task

Your job as a manager is to develop an organization which gets the work done as you want it to get done. Organizing is basically about who does what. It means defining responsibilities, building structures and developing relationships. The essential element is people: what they do and how they work together.

Organizations are not static things. Changes are continually taking place in the business itself, in the environment in which the business operates, and in the people who work in the business. This makes it difficult, if not impossible, to achieve an ideal organization. It is a good thing to have an ideal structure in mind, but you will have to modify it. How you modify it depends on the circumstances, and, especially, on people. For example, you will probably be forced to accept the fact that at senior levels you are going to have to build your organization around the capacities, strengths and even weaknesses of the people you've got – in the short term at least.

Basic approaches to organization design

When you are setting up a new organization structure or considering the effectiveness of an existing one, it is advisable to:

1. Define what the organization is there to do
2. Analyse the circumstances in which the activities are carried out – the technology, the rate of growth or change, the sort of management and its management style, and the outside environment

3. Identify the activities required to achieve the aims of the organization
4. Group related activities logically together into organizational units and, within these units, into individual positions
5. Establish the relationships that should exist in the organization – vertically within functions and horizontally between functions – paying particular attention to the need to integrate the work of related activities
6. Ensure that everyone in the organization understands what they have to do (responsibilities), how far they can go in doing it (authority), the structure in which they operate, and the relationships they are expected to maintain.

The process of structuring a new organization or restructuring an existing one is akin to building something with a box of bricks. The bricks are the key activities or groups of closely related activities. So the first thing to do is to define what these bricks are. In other words, you carry out an activity analysis. You then need to fit them together to build your structure. And there will be several ways in which the bricks – ie the discrete activities – can be grouped together. You may have to experiment with alternative arrangements to decide which pattern looks the best. It may well be a matter of choosing between two or three structures which look equally good, and the decisive factor is likely to be the quality of the people you have got or can obtain.

Organization guidelines

The following guidelines are intended to help you to deal with organizational problems.

Formal and informal organizations

A formal organization can be described as a system of coordinated activities in which groups of people work cooperatively under authority and leadership towards a common goal. Formal structures aim to achieve orderly relationships between functions, but they also have the added value of providing people with a sense of security. The boundaries between functions should never be allowed to become barriers to communication.

An informal organization always exists alongside the formal one. People behave and interact in ways which cannot be defined in manuals, charts and job descriptions. They cross lines and cut corners. They set up informal groups which extend over organizational boundaries. This fluidity within the organization is a valuable characteristic. It nearly always helps the organization to achieve its aims. If, on occasion, it creates confusion and conflict, something has to be done to resolve these problems without jeopardizing people's freedom to organize themselves informally.

Structure and function

The appropriate type of organizational structure is determined by the nature of the work carried out, and the conditions in which the company operates. The structure should be designed to facilitate the identification and accomplishment of work and to enhance the ability of employees to work together.

Formal, well-defined and highly structured or bureaucratic organizations may well be appropriate where conditions are stable and predictable. Changeable situations may demand organizations which are more fluid, less rigidly defined and organic in the sense that their form develops in line with changes in their functions.

Different structures can exist in the same organization: a bureaucratic (formal) structure may be appropriate for some tasks and a non-bureaucratic (informal) structure for others.

Allocation of work

The work that needs to be done has to be defined and allocated to the appropriate job holders or departments. Related activities should be grouped together to avoid unnecessary overlap and duplication of work.

Matters requiring a decision should be dealt with as near to the point of action as possible.

Managers should not try to do too much themselves. Neither should they exercise too close supervision.

Levels in the structure

Too many levels of management and supervision inhibit communication and create unnecessary work (and jobs). Your aim should be to reduce the number of levels to a minimum, bearing in mind always that organizations are like india rubber – if you squeeze them they will expand sideways, ie at some levels the number of subordinates directly reporting to one manager will increase.

Span of control

There are limits to the number of people anyone can manage or supervise well. These vary considerably between different jobs. Most people can work with a far greater span of control than they think they can, as long as they are prepared to delegate more effectively and avoid getting into too much detail.

One man–one boss

Generally speaking, individuals should report to only one boss. This avoids conflicting orders being given to one person. If a manager bypasses his immediate subordinate when issuing instructions, it can cause confusion, and it undermines authority. If it happens too often, you will need to question the abilities of the manager and his subordinate, and the existence of the intermediate layer of management. Of course, there may be occasions when bypassing has to take place to deal with an emergency, but these should be exceptional.

The exception to the 'one man–one boss' principle is the case of 'functional authority'. For instance, the finance director may lay down methods of preparing budgets and pass instructions on budgeting direct to managers in other departments. But functional authority should only be exercised as a means of getting company-wide policies, which have been agreed at top level, implemented consistently.

As long as the nature of the authority is understood by all concerned, there should be no confusion. If, however, anyone feels that he has received an unreasonable request from a functional manager, he is at liberty to appeal to his own line manager.

Organization charts

Charts are sometimes useful in planning and reviewing large organizations. They indicate how work is allocated and how activities are grouped together, they show who is responsible to whom and they illustrate lines of authority. Drawing up a chart can be a good way of clarifying what is currently happening: the mere process of putting the organization down on paper will highlight any problems. And when you come to considering changes, charts are the best way of illustrating alternatives.

The danger with organization charts is that they can be mistaken for the organization itself. They are a snapshot of what is supposed to be happening at a given moment. They are out of date as soon as they are drawn and they leave out the informal organization. If you use little boxes to represent people, they may behave as if they were indeed little boxes, sticking too closely to the book of rules.

Charts can make people very conscious of their superiority or inferiority to others. They can make it harder to change things, they can freeze relationships, and they can show relationships as they are supposed to be, not as they are. Townsend (51) said of organization charts in *Up the Organization*: 'Never formalize, print and circulate them. Good organizations are living bodies that grow new muscles to meet challenges.'

Use organization charts carefully if at all. They can do more harm than good.

Job descriptions

Like organization charts, job descriptions can be too rigid and stifle initiative. If kept brief (one side of one sheet of paper) they have their uses: to define the sort of job for which you are recruiting – and the sort of person you want to find; to provide a basis for training programmes and performance appraisal and to help slot jobs into a pay structure.

But the elaborate, three-, four- and five-page efforts that are produced in some companies are a waste of time, especially at senior levels. Townsend again: 'Judgement jobs are constantly changing in nature and the good people should be allowed to use their jobs to see how good they are.' If, say, a production manager needs a four-page job description to tell him how to make widgets, he should not be a production manager.

The danger of written job descriptions is that people feel restricted by them. They might feel that they ought not to do unspecified work because they have no responsibility or authority beyond their written list of duties. Of course, any able executive who tries to can bend a job description to suit his own purposes. And the problem can be avoided altogether by inserting a catch-all phrase into the job description to the effect that the job holder will 'carry out such other duties as are required to achieve the overall purpose of the job'.

Job descriptions are frequently consigned to the files and forgotten about as soon as they are written. If and when they are resurrected, they are out of date. This is the most powerful argument against lengthy job descriptions – they are a waste of time and money.

Job descriptions should be brief, handwritten, used for a specific purpose such as those mentioned above, and then scrapped.

Case studies

The type of organization structure you need will depend on the type of operation you are in. The following two cases were mentioned by Honor Croome in *The Human Problems of Innovation* (9). They were based on research carried out in Scotland by Tom Burns and G M Stalker (8).

The first case illustrates organization problems as perceived by a manager in a firm which was mainly engaged in high technology development and batch production work. The second is a description of how organization in a process plant operated smoothly.

The case of the harassed high technology manager

Here, in interview, is an executive concerned with the design, production and sale of an advanced product; his department produces, designs, controls progress through the works, buys in stock and parts, and runs a separate assembly plant, using components produced elsewhere in the works. He has been having trouble in sales and production and he ascribes these troubles to the lack of a clear-cut, up-and-down, structure of responsibility.

'Well, to my mind, the most important thing is delegation of authority and responsibility to the different levels from whoever is resident at the top. In our case it would be the managing director. Now the authority must be in line with the responsibility that you expect the individual to take . . . One man holding all the strings and under him a sound team of people who are specialists in the various fields and in the various management functions which they are to exercise . . .

'What happens in our case, the way I see it, is that this top management layer is missing and you're jumping virtually from managing director to a number of senior technicians in charge of sections . . . who haven't got anyone coordinating their efforts except the managing director by his occasional appearances and periodic meetings . . . Now to take one instance, we do have meetings. They are fashionable now. Something goes wrong and then it's decided that a weekly meeting should take place.'

'What kind of things go wrong?'

'Well, supposing that a delivery goes wrong, or a design is put into production and is functionally not quite what it ought to be, then there is the usual post-mortem and it usually boils down to everybody realizing that there hasn't been enough control. People have gone too far and got rather wrapped up in their own particular small aspect of the overall project. It's then realized that there hasn't been any one body keeping an overall eye on things, and the usual scheme is to inaugurate a weekly meeting at which various points can be raised and discussed. Now, in theory, that's a very desirable thing so long as it discusses matters relative to its function. Also that the plan of attack for the following week's work is clearly laid down and it is stated who will do what and they report back. It shouldn't just amount to a weekly gathering of bodies who, half-way through the meeting, drink a cup of tea and then break up and that's that . . .'

'What kind of things go wrong that are not put right at such meetings?'

'Well, when you start a new design there are certain steps you must go through to get a new production batch on the go. Those steps involve the drawing office, purchasing, and planning and progress. That in turn will require examination of the capacity within the plant, machine loading and the rest . . . To get the whole thing going needs one instruction to one man who, in turn, will see that the wheels are set in motion. Well, that doesn't normally happen here. There is no one man. What it amounts to is that it's announced "Wouldn't it be a good idea if we produced another ten of such and such a type?" and everybody says, "Yes, Sir, it's a jolly good idea. Let's do that." The meeting breaks up, and a few days later, for instance, I'm in the drawing office and happen to say, "What have you done about those ten units?" and they'll say, "Haven't had any instructions." I say, "Well, you go ahead and get the drawings printed and the schedules out." The chap in charge of the drawing office will take my word for it – *not* because he has been instructed that I will give him his instructions but because I've always done so off my own bat and I know that unless somebody tells him he'll stay put.

'That may be the first movement. The lot will go forward to purchasing. Stock control first will run through the schedules, tick off what is in stock, and so forth – there is an automatic passage of the schedule through the various departments. Ultimately somebody, usually it's the stores, will say, "Well, there's a hell of a lot of stuff in for the job. When are you going to start it?" Then everybody will think, 'When are we going to start it?" Because, at the time when I said to Charlie in the drawing office, "It's time you got your schedules out, boy", nobody said to the planning office, "How are we going to fit this job in?" People here are not pushing their jobs through but trying to drag them out the other end, like a surgeon with a pair of forceps trying to drag the baby out . . .

'And our own production manager has no direct control over machining facilities. Whatever he gets done in other shops he has to try to ease in or bolster his way round to try to get them in because there is nothing laid down. I mean, he would go and see the works manager and the planning people but the situation changes so fast, he wouldn't be in the picture all the time. They wouldn't keep him informed; they'd say, "All right, we can put so and so in the machine shop on – you can have them." And twenty minutes later maybe something else comes up, they take his job off and put the new thing on, and nobody would tell him. So two days later he'd come back and ask how the job was getting on. They might be sorry, they might not, but it wasn't their affair really . . .'

The harassed executive saw his firm's troubles as stemming from the lack of a proper line of command. But what his account shows is that his firm had to deal with tasks which could not be handled in this way. The 'functional contact' whose absence he deplored could not possibly, given the sort of work that the firm was doing, be satisfactory if it was a merely or even mainly up-and-down or 'vertical' kind, a matter of clear-cut authority and limited powers.

Yet no other way was thought feasible. When the command system showed signs of strain, a progress committee had been formed as a first move towards another kind of system which would allow for a bigger, less specified contribution from the executives concerned. Even during the meetings, however, the management group had reverted to the command system. They had looked to the managing director for decisions – 'Yes, Sir, that's a jolly good idea' – and for the allocation of a specific job to each of them.

The case of the process production firm

This firm produced rayon filament yarn, using processes which had once been scientifically advanced, but were now thoroughly assimilated into routine production.

Production started with the intake of raw materials (cellulose, carbon bisulphide, sulphuric acid, etc) and the first stage was the arrangement of the stored cellulose sheets into batches of uniform weight. From the weighing machine the cellulose was hand-carted to a vat of caustic solution in which it was steeped for a certain time; after steeping, it was pressed between plates by a hydraulic ram, then carted and fed into the mechanical kneaders. The shredded cellulose was then stored for two or three days in mercerizing rooms, to ensure a homogeneous moisture content, before the next process, where it was mixed with carbon bisulphide in mechanical churns. The resulting product, cellulose xanthate, was dropped through chutes into mixers, in which it was dissolved in a solution of caustic soda and mixed into a homogeneous fluid – viscose. This viscose was then stored under vacuum to remove bubbles; then filtered; and stored again in charge tanks.

This completed the preparatory phase. The next, central, stage consisted in pumping the viscose through a multiple jet into a bath of sulphuric acid, from which it emerged as solid fibres. These were drawn up over a wheel, twisted into thread, and passed down into a spinning pot in which the thread was built up into cylindrical cakes. The cakes were then washed with neutralizing solutions and water dried in heated lockers, inspected, weighed and despatched.

This sequence was a matter of mechanical and muscular efforts and of chemical action, each transforming or 'translating' the raw material a stage further. Alongside it, there took place a set of other actions, mostly a matter of human judgement though some were automatic, designed to keep the sequence running properly and smoothly. The spinning machine was automatic, but was tended by workers who stopped and started it in

237

order to renew broken threads, remove completed cakes and replace empty pots. Thermostatic apparatus controlled heat and humidity in the mercerizing rooms and kept a record; workers were employed to inspect these and other records and report fluctuations outside a certain latitude. Samples were taken every hour from the baths of sulphuric acid; these were analysed in the laboratory, and any fluctuations beyond certain limits were noted and resulted in instructions to the foreman in charge to vary appropriately the input of sulphuric acid. At all stages these controls aimed at keeping the processing changes, and the conditions affecting these changes, within a range of permitted tolerances and as close as possible to a set of ideal constants.

These constants and tolerances were set down in a book (known as the 'Factory Bible') which was in the hands of every department head. It enshrined the norm to which it was everyone's duty to make that part of the process for which he was responsible conform. The process of correcting deviations might be extremely simple; the simplest corrections of all were automatic (thermostatic control). Almost as simple were the actions of a single worker replacing a clogged jet. The laboratory tests were rather more complex, and certain adjustments designed to reconcile technical variations with the production programme involved an elaborate system whose operation took up most of the works manager's time. At the top, the general manager in turn reconciled variations in the operation of production – by means of his control over the various sections within the works – with the requirements of the sales and costing departments and the board of directors.

The whole concern, in fact, can be seen as a three-sided pyramid of power, technical expertise, and knowledge of circumstances. At every step down from the top there was less authority, less technical expertise and less information. Each person's task was clearly laid down and defined by his superior. He knew just what he could do in normal circumstances without consulting anyone else; just what point of deviation from the norm he should regard as the limit of his competence; and just what he should do when this limit was reached – ie report to his superior. The whole system was devised to preserve normality and stability. The downward flow of instructions and orders, and the upward flow of reports and requests for such instructions and orders, were precisely and clearly channelled; it had the characteristics of a smoothly working automatic machine. Since everyone knew both his job and its limits, there was little consultation; contacts ran up and down, from subordinates to superior and vice versa, and the great majority of those contacts resulted in the giving of definite orders. The outstanding characteristics of the structure were that it was mechanical and authoritarian. And it worked very well.

Chapter 37
Performance management

A manager, it is said, is someone who gets things done through people. If you have people working for you, your results will depend largely on how well they do. You need to do whatever you can to improve their performance. You will do this if you:

1. Clarify responsibilities
2. Define and agree targets and standards of performance
3. Improve motivation by increasing understanding of goals, the means of attaining those goals and the rewards associated with their achievement
4. Provide guidance and help which will develop strengths and overcome weaknesses
5. Detect problems and difficulties and agree how to overcome them
6. Plan whatever training and development are needed.

Performance management is about getting results through people. It consists of a range of activities, the primary aim of which is to help managers to increase the effectiveness of their staff, who will be rewarded accordingly.

The four main performance management activities are:

1. Formal performance reviews.
2. Continuous appraisal.
3. Performance improvement programmes.
4. Reward review.

Performance review

The purpose of a performance review is to analyse what a person has done and is doing in his job in order to help him to do better, by developing strengths or overcoming weaknesses. It is a stocktaking exercise which provides a useful way of summing up assessments and agreeing on action to improve performance. Most important, it also provides a setting for the agreement of targets and standards of performance which are an essential starting point for motivating people to achieve the results you expect from them.

However, although a strong case can be made for this periodical 'stocktaking' assessment, appraisal should be a continuous process. Formal procedures are all very well, but they cannot replace the day-to-day guidance (continuous appraisal, as discussed on page 242) that is a key part of your managerial responsibilities.

Results-orientated appraisal

There are a number of methods of reviewing performance, but the best approach is results-orientated appraisal. This involves:

1. The manager and the subordinate agreeing on quantitative, measurable and specific targets covering each of the key result areas of the job. Where it is not possible to define a quantifiable target, a standard of performance is agreed for the task which defines when it can be regarded as having been well done. The processes of setting targets and standards of performance are described opposite.
2. Performance is reviewed jointly against the agreed targets or standards.
3. Agreement is reached on the extent to which targets and standards have been achieved.
4. The reasons for any shortfalls are discussed.
5. In the light of this analysis and discussion, agreement is reached on the individual's strengths and any areas where performance needs to be improved. This may be summarized under headings such as the following (for managers):

   - professional and technical knowledge in relation to job requirements;
   - level of competence in terms of the skills needed to perform the job effectively;
   - judgement – problem-solving, decision-making, deciding priorities;
   - initiative – resourcefulness, enterprise, energy;
   - contribution to team effort;
   - leadership – motivation and development of staff.
6. Action is agreed on the development of strengths and any remedial action which needs to be taken in defined improvement areas.

240

7. Where necessary, revised targets or standards are agreed for the next review period.

The emphasis throughout this process is on agreement and discussion. The essential purpose is developmental – and real and lasting improvement will not be achieved unless the individual has participated fully at each stage and finally 'owns' any actions to be taken because he has been fully involved in planning them.

Target-setting

The essential requirements of an effective target-setting process are that:

1. The individual target should support the achievement of a higher level target.
2. Wherever possible, individual targets should be agreed between the parties directly concerned. Individuals should be given the maximum opportunity to develop their own targets (a bottom-up process) but these must be congruent with the overall target, as long as that is realistic.
3. While targets must be attainable, they do not have to be attainable too easily. In other words, it is perfectly legitimate for management to insist that the targets should 'stretch' the managers who have to meet them. The setting of 'stretch targets', however, implies that managers will be rewarded appropriately if they achieve them.
4. Performance indicators or measures should be available for each target which will enable progress towards them to be monitored and the final result to be evaluated. The performance indicators can include a number of different sorts of measures of effectiveness. For instance:

   - positive, ie a hoped-for event, result or other outcome should occur;
   - negative, ie an undesirable event or other outcome should not occur;
   - measurements in terms of quantity, cost or time.

Standards of performance

A standard of performance provides a qualitative basis for judgement where a quantified target or a set date for completing a task cannot be established. When determining a standard of performance you should always ask yourself: 'How will I and any other people involved know when this task has been well done?' It is hard work defining good standards. You have to visualize a performance review session when you and your boss are looking at a particular work area. You will both need to think of examples and ask yourselves: 'How can we judge that the job has been done well?' For example, a financial director and a newly appointed management accountant get together. One of the latter's responsibilities is to produce for the monthly board meeting a set of management accounts which provides details of performance against budget and highlights any variances. Thinking of examples where things have gone wrong in the past, the financial director suggests the following performance standards or criteria. Performance is up to standard when:

1. A complete set of management accounts is in the hands of board members at least two working days before the board meeting.
2. The accounts are complete and contain no inaccuracies.
3. Key variances are highlighted.
4. Valid explanations are provided as to why variations have taken place.

The new management accountant should agree these standards but can seek further explanation as to what is involved. He might, for example, ask how much authority he has to require explanations for variances from operational managers, and what he must do if he thinks that the explanation is unsatisfactory. In this way, the process of standard-setting becomes a useful method of clarifying responsibilities and authorities, thus reducing ambiguity.

Continuous appraisal

Overall approach

Every time anyone does anything for you, an impression will be formed in your mind of how well or how badly it has been done. The accumulation of these impressions provides you with your overall view of the individual's performance and potential. Your appraisal of staff will therefore be a continuous, although probably an intuitive, process. You may think this is enough, but is it? Challenge your assumption by answering the following questions:

- Am I certain that I do not place too much emphasis on recent evidence of good or indifferent performance, thus ignoring, or at least underestimating, the accumulated evidence of past performance?
- Do I really know the circumstances under which the work has been done, ie the extent to which it has been influenced by luck rather than management, or by factors beyond the individual's control?

- Can I really be sure that my judgements are not affected by my prejudices concerning personality or physical characteristics? Do I, for example, favour the showy extrovert and underestimate the quiet plodder who still gets things done?
- Am I confident that I have not contributed to the failure by not clearly defining what I expected or by not giving the individual the scope, support, guidance and resources he needed?

It is a rare person who can honestly answer all those questions satisfactorily. For those who are less confident, a continuous but systematic approach to appraisal should be considered. This should not involve elaborate and time-consuming techniques with a lot of paperwork. As in all other techniques of management, the motto is 'keep it simple'.

The continuous appraisal approach relates to what the individual is actually doing and how he does it. It takes from results-orientated appraisal the concept of agreed targets, but it rejects the idea of formal periodical review as the only means of helping people to learn how to improve their performance. In McGregor's words in an article in the *Harvard Business Review* (35):

> The semi-annual or annual appraisal is not a particularly efficient stimulus to learning. It provides feedback about behaviour at a time remote from the behaviour itself. People do learn and change from feedback. In fact, it is the only way they learn. However, the most effective feedback occurs immediately after the behaviour. The subordinate can learn a great deal from a mistake, or a particular failure in performance, provided it is analysed while all the evidence is immediately at hand.

Continuous appraisal technique

You should therefore appraise your staff by carrying out continuing reviews of how well agreed tasks have been completed. Provide guidance on where and how to improve as and when required. Encourage your subordinate to think for himself what should be done. Don't impose things on him unless you have to.

Avoid personality assessments. Concentrate on the task and how the task has been done. Sit back now and again and carry out a stocktaking exercise, reflecting on your own how well each of your subordinates is doing. Summarize your conclusions if you like – but on one side of one sheet of blank paper, not on a form. If the personnel department compels you to complete their pet form, do so. Sent it to them and forget about it. They will.

Don't carry out a formal interview after this stocktaking exercise. Most people do it badly and you are likely to do more harm than good. But in the normal course of work, when the opportunity arises, discuss briefly and informally with your subordinate any points you wish to make. Give praise where praise is due, but also get your subordinate to agree on any things he needs to do to improve.

Performance appraisal then becomes a natural part of the process of management, not a technique foisted on you by someone else. It is a way of motivating, training and developing staff rather than an artificial rigmarole which too often produces the opposite effect to that which was intended.

A case study

To appraise people properly you need to know what you are appraising and convey that knowledge to your subordinate. In the *Harvard Business Review*, Harry Levinson told the story of a corporate president who put a senior executive in charge of a failing operation.

His only directive was 'Get it in the black'. Within two years of that injunction, the new executive moved the operation from a deficit position to one that showed a profit of several million. Fresh from his triumph the executive announced himself as a candidate for a higher-level position, and indicated that he was already receiving offers from other companies.

The corporate president, however, did not share the executive's positive opinions of his behaviour. In fact, the president was not at all pleased with the way the executive had handled things. Naturally, the executive was dismayed and, when he asked what he had done wrong, the corporate president told him that he had indeed accomplished what he had been asked to do, but he had done it singlehandedly, by the sheer force of his own personality. Furthermore, the executive was told, he had replaced people whom the company thought to be good employees with those it regarded as compliant. In effect, by demonstrating his own strength, he had made the organization weaker. Until the executive changed his authoritarian manner, his boss said, it was unlikely that he would be promoted further.

Implicit in this vignette is the common major fault in performance appraisal and management by objectives – namely, a fundamental misconception of what is to be appraised.

Performance improvement programmes

Performance improvement programmes are largely in the hands of the manager, whose key roles are to:

1. Motivate and team build, as described in Chapters 32 and 48;
2. Coach, as described in Chapter 17;
3. Recommend or conduct training programmes, as described in Chapter 17;
4. Counsel, as described in Chapter 13.

Performance management means deciding on the rewards employees should receive as a means of recognizing achievement and of encouraging them to achieve even better results. Michael Beer (6) suggests that the conditions necessary for a reward system to improve performance are first, that employees should understand the relationship between performance and reward and second, that they must feel that the rewards are worthwhile.

Reward review

Note that rewards can be financial or non-financial. For many people additional responsibility, the opportunity to achieve and recognition for achievement by praise or gaining the esteem of superiors and colleagues, can be just as effective as money, if not more so.

Chapter 38
Persuading

A manager's job is 60 per cent getting it right and 40 per cent putting it across. Managers spend a lot of time persuading other people to accept their ideas and suggestions.

Persuasion is just another word for selling. You may feel that good ideas should sell themselves, but life is not like that. Everyone resists change and anything new is certain to be treated with suspicion. So it's worth learning a few simple rules that will help you to sell your ideas more effectively.

Six rules for effective persuasion

1. *Define your objective and get the facts.* Decide what you want to achieve and why. Assemble all the facts you need to support your case. Eliminate emotional arguments so that you and others can judge the proposition on the facts alone.

2. *Find out what 'he' wants.* Never underestimate a person's natural resistance to change. But bear in mind that such resistance is proportional, not to the total extent of the change, but to the extent to which it affects him personally. When asked to accept a proposition, the first questions people ask themselves are: 'How does this affect me?' 'What do I stand to lose?' 'What do I stand to gain?' These questions must be answered before persuasion can start.

   The key to all persuasion and selling is to see your proposition from the other person's point of view. If you can really put yourself into the other person's shoes you will be able to foresee objections and present your ideas in the way most attractive to him.

   You must find out how he looks at things – what he wants. Listen to what he has to say. Don't talk too much. Ask questions. If he asks you a question reply with another question. Find out what he is after.

Then present your case in a way that highlights its benefits to him, or at least reduces his objections or fears.

3. *Prepare a simple and attractive presentation.* Your presentation should be as simple and straightforward as possible. Emphasize the benefits. Don't bury the selling points. Lead him in gently so there are no surprises. Anticipate objections.

4. *Make him a party to your ideas.* Get him to contribute, if at all possible. Find some common ground in order to start off with agreement. Don't antagonize him. Avoid defeating him in arguments. Help him to preserve his self-esteem. Always leave him a way out.

5. *Positively sell the benefits.* Show conviction. You are not going to sell anything if you don't believe in it and communicate that belief. To persuade effectively you have to sell yourself. You must spell out the benefits. *What* you are proposing is of less interest to the individual concerned than the effects of that proposal on him.

6. *Clinch and take action.* Choose the right moment to clinch the proposal and get out. Make sure that you are not pushing too hard, but when you reach your objective don't stay and risk losing it. Take prompt follow-up action. There is no point in going to all the trouble of getting agreement if you let things slide afterwards.

Chapter 39
Policies

What are policies?

Anything which indicates what you can or cannot do in certain situations is a policy. It does not have to be written. It may not even have been stated explicitly. But if there is an understanding 'that this is the way we do things round here' then there is a policy.

For example, one business may lay down that 'company salary levels should be at the upper quartile of the range of salaries paid for comparable jobs elsewhere'. This is quite clear, although salary administrators can get bogged down in defining what is comparable and what is not.

Another business may have a salary structure which has developed in a more haphazard way. There may have been a general understanding that the company is prepared to pay above the going rate to get and to keep good quality staff, but nothing so precise as the upper quartile has been defined and nothing has been written down.

Both these companies have salary policies. Which of them has the best policy? There is only one answer to this question. The one that works. A clearly defined, almost rigid policy, quoting the upper quartile is fine if people find out what the upper quartile is and try their best to match it. Otherwise it is useless. A policy of paying above the going rate is great if that is what happens, and as long as the application of the policy is consistent between different jobs and different parts of the company.

Inconsistency is, of course, the danger of ill-defined policies, just as undue restraint of judgement and initiative is the danger of a policy which is too rigid.

Why have policies?

When faced with a crisis or difficult decision it is helpful to have a guide.

When running a business or a department it is essential to let people know what they can and cannot do.

A direct selling business will tell its agents in the field what they can do – they are to sell direct to housewives who are broadly in the middle income group. It will also tell them what they must not do – it is not the firm's policy to go in for high-pressure selling.

A retail store will tell its buyers what it wants them to do – to achieve a three times mark-up on the cost of the goods they purchase. It will also tell them what it does not want them to do – to sacrifice the firm's reputation for quality in the pursuit of low-cost merchandise.

What makes a good policy?

A good policy is one that works. But what makes it work? In general, policies will work if they are appropriate – if they clearly take you in the direction you want to go. They need to be understood, which does not mean that they *have* to be written down. Oral tradition can be a more powerful force than an unused and dusty policy manual.

Policies need to be clear, which is easier said than done. If you try to be completely unambiguous you may only achieve a flood of words which defeat your purpose. Or, worse, your policy may become a prison rather than a pathway. There is a limit to how much you can or should spell out. Take this example:

> Divisional general managers may fix prices for the products under their control so long as:
>
> (a) those prices produce gross profit margins in line with agreed budgets
> (b) price reductions do not adversely affect prices in other divisions.

It looks clear enough, but is it? What does 'in line with' really mean? At what point are prices 'adversely affected'? There is scope for different interpretations in this definition. But is it clear enough? Yes. It gives the divisional managers concerned a general guideline sufficient to keep them from going off the rails. Some room for discretion is, however, allowed. And at this level, this is what policies must do. They should not act as strait-jackets.

Policies must have a degree of permanence or they are not really policies at all. If you constantly change them, no one, in or out of the organization, knows what to count on. But they should not become so hard and fast that they stop a company looking ahead.

How to formulate policies

You cannot just sit down and say 'let's formulate a policy'. Policies should either emerge as a result of a series of decisions forced upon you by events or be part of a deliberate planning process which includes setting objectives and the broad strategies required to achieve them.

Policies should be formulated in response to needs: people require guidance on what or what not to do; plans can only be realized if the line to take is defined; points of reference are required in unfamiliar areas of decision-making.

There is a lot to be said for defining policies in writing. But not in a vast policy manual which no one will read. Make your policy statement as clear and succinct as you can. Ensure that it gets to those who have to implement the policy and check that they understand the policy and are taking steps to put it into practice.

How to implement policies

If your policies are inappropriate or ambiguous the implementation will be hard. If not, all you need to do is to ensure that your staff are clearly briefed on what they are to do and how they are expected to do it. If there are areas left to their discretion, point this out. Less experienced staff may need more explicit guidance at this stage on how they should exercise their discretion. Give them an idea of the circumstances in which you would expect them to come to you for further guidance.

For example, a company introducing a 'promotion from within' policy might express it like this:

> Wherever possible, vacancies should be filled by the most effective people available from within the company subject to the right of the company to recruit from outside if there are no suitable internal candidates.

An experienced personnel officer would know what to do if, say, a departmental manager refused to release a member of his staff who had successfully applied for an internal vacancy. He would quote the policy without browbeating the manager with it, and use his powers of persuasion, based on past experience, to convince the manager to release the man. The inexperienced personnel officer, on the other hand, should be warned in advance that this problem might arise. He should be told not to rely too much on the rigid application of the policy. He should be instructed to use his discretion to decide whether he can gently persuade the manager and, if not, he must be prepared to go to the personnel manager for advice on how to handle the situation.

Once you have briefed staff, all you need to do is to follow up and make sure that the policy is being applied properly and is appropriate. This gives you an opportunity for training your staff, or, if the policy is not working, for recommending amendments to it. You can only find out if a policy works by checking on how it works, and this means talking to the people who have to implement it.

Chapter 40
Power and politics

Power and politics in an organization go together. You may feel, like
Nietzsche, that 'power has crooked legs'. But things don't get done
without the exercise of authority, and authority requires the use of power.
Furthermore, one way of getting authority and power is to indulge in
company politics. You may deplore it, and many chief executives deny that
it happens in their organizations. It does take place, however, because
people seek power and often use political means to attain it.

Power – good or bad?

In his analysis of power in British industry, Antony Jay commented:
'Power lies in the acceptance of your authority by others, their knowledge
that if they try to resist you they will fail and you will succeed. Real power
does not lie in documents etc – it lies in what you can achieve.'

And Mary Parker Follett wrote: 'Our task is not to learn where to plan
power; it is how to develop power. Genuine power can only be grown, it
will slip from every arbitrary hand.'

Power is legitimate if it is used to pursue legitimate ends and is wielded
in a responsible way by responsible people. But it can be employed in a
harsh way.

David McClelland's studies of power in action involving over 500
managers from 25 different US corporations led him to conclude:

> [Managers] must possess a high need for power, that is, a concern for
> influencing people. However, this need must be disciplined and controlled
> so that it is directed towards the benefit of the institution as a whole and
> not towards the manager's personal aggrandizement ... [Managers
> motivated by a need for power] are able to create a greater sense of
> responsibility in their divisions and, above all, a greater team spirit.

Here are two cases of power being used effectively:

Case 1: One of the best managers we have in the company has lots of power based on one thing or another over most people. But he seldom if ever just tells or asks someone to do something. He almost always takes a few minutes to try to persuade them. The power he has over people generally induces them to listen carefully and certainly disposes them to be influenced. That, of course, makes the persuasion process go quickly and easily. And he never risks getting the other person upset by making what that person thinks is an unfair request or command.

Case 2: Product manager Stein needed plant manager Billings to 'sign off' on a new product idea (Product X) which Billings thought was terrible. Stein decided there was no way he could logically persuade Billings because Billings just would not listen to him. With time, Stein felt, he could have broken through that barrier. But he did not have that time. Stein also realized that Billings would never, just because of some deal or favour, sign off on a product he did not believe in. Stein also felt it not worth the risk of trying to force Billings to sign off, so here is what he did:

On Monday, Stein got Reynolds, a person Billings respected, to send Billings two market research studies that were very favourable to Product X, with a note attached saying, 'Have you seem this? I found them rather surprising. I am not sure if I entirely believe them, but still . . .'

On Tuesday, Stein got a representative of one of the company's biggest customers to mention casually to Billings on the phone that he had heard a rumour about Product X being introduced soon and was 'glad to see you guys are on your toes as usual'.

On Wednesday, Stein had two industrial engineers stand about three feet away from Billings as they were waiting for a meeting to begin and talk about the favourable test results on Product X.

On Thursday, Stein set up a meeting to talk about Product X with Billings and invited only people whom Billings liked or respected and who also felt favourably about Product X.

On Friday, Stein went to see Billings and asked him if he was willing to sign off on Product X. He was.

Sources of power

Power is clearly linked to position and rank. But to a certain degree it has to be earned. You can give orders to your subordinates but you are going to get more out of them if you obtain their willing cooperation rather than their grudging submission. Power is bestowed upon you as a manager but you have to justify your use of it.

There are, however, other sources of power, namely:

- *Access to other people with power.* Proximity or a direct line obviously gives you more scope to exert influence, actual or perceived. That is why secretaries are important.

- *Control over information.* 'Knowledge is power' or, alternatively, 'authority goes to the one who knows'. If you are in the know, you are in a better position to control events or, if you want to play politics, to put spokes in other people's wheels.
- *Control over resources.* If you have control over resources such as money, manpower, equipment or services that you or anyone else needs, you have power.
- *Control over rewards and punishments.* You also have power if you can give rewards or punishments or influence others who control them.
- *Expertise.* You gain and keep power if you can convince others that you are the expert.
- *Identification.* You can achieve power over others if you persuade them to identify with what you are doing or with you personally. This is what charismatic leaders do by enthusiasm, dedication, getting people involved and by sheer force of personality.
- *Sense of obligation.* If you develop a sense of obligation by doing favours for people you can reasonably expect that they will feel an obligation to return those favours.

Using power

John Kotter interviewed over 250 managers who were in a position to use power. He found that the successful ones had the following characteristics:

- They use their power openly and legitimately. They are seen as genuine experts in their field and consistently live up to the leadership image they build for themselves.
- They are sensitive to what types of power are most effective with different types of people. For example, experts respect expertise.
- They develop all their sources of power and do not rely too much on any particular technique.
- They seek jobs and tasks which will give them the opportunity to acquire and use power. They constantly seek ways to invest the power they already have to secure an even higher positive return.
- They use their power in a mature and self-controlled way. They seldom if ever use power impulsively or for their own aggrandizement.
- They get satisfaction from influencing others.

Politics – good or bad?

To be politic, according to the *Oxford English Dictionary*, you can be sagacious, prudent, judicious, expedient, scheming or crafty. So political behaviour in an organization could be desirable or undesirable.

Organizations consist of individuals who, while they are ostensibly there to achieve a common purpose, will, at the same time, be driven by their own needs to achieve their own goals. Effective management is the process of harmonizing individual endeavour and ambition to the common good. Some individuals will genuinely believe that using political means to achieve their goals will benefit the organization as well as themselves. Others will rationalize this belief. Yet others will unashamedly pursue their own ends. They may use all their powers of persuasion to legitimize these ends to their colleagues, but self-interest remains the primary drive. These are the corporate politicians whom the *Oxford English Dictionay* describes as 'shrewd schemers, crafty plotters or intriguers'. Politicians within organizations can be like this. They manoeuvre behind people's backs, blocking proposals they do not like. They advance their own reputation and career at the expense of other people's. They can be envious and jealous and act accordingly. They are bad news.

But it can also be argued that a political approach to management is inevitable and even desirable in any organization where the clarity of goals is not absolute, where the decision-making process is not clear-cut and where the authority to make decisions is not evenly or appropriately distributed. And there can be few organizations where one or more of these conditions do not apply.

Andrew Kakabadse (26) recognizes this point when he says in *The Politics of Management*: 'Politics is a process, that of influencing individuals and groups of people to your point of view, where you cannot rely on authority.' In this sense, a political approach can be legitimate as long as the ends are justifiable from the viewpoint of the organization.

Political approaches

Kakabadse identifies seven approaches that organizational politicians adopt:

1. Identify the stakeholders, those who have a commitment to act in a particular way.
2. Keep the stakeholders comfortable, concentrating on behaviour,

values, attitudes, fears and drives that the individuals will accept, tolerate and manage (comfort zones).

3. Fit the image – work on the comfort zones and align their image to that of the people with power.
4. Use the network – identify the interest groups and people of influence.
5. Enter the network – identify the gatekeepers, adhere to the norms.
6. Make deals – agree to support other people where this is of mutual benefit.
7. Withhold and withdraw – withhold information as appropriate and withdraw judiciously when the going gets rough.

Some of these precepts are more legitimate than others. Organizational life requires managers to identify the key decision-makers when they are involved in developing new approaches and getting things done. Before coming to a final conclusion and launching a fully fledged proposal at a committee or in a memorandum, it makes good sense to test opinion and find out how other people may react. This testing process enables managers to anticipate counter-arguments and modify their proposals either to meet legitimate objections or, when there is no alternative, to accommodate other people's requirements.

Making deals may not appear to be particularly desirable, but it does happen, and managers can always rationalize this type of behaviour by reference to the end result. Withholding information is not legitimate behaviour, but people do indulge in it in recognition of the fact that knowledge is power. Judicious withdrawal may also seem to be questionable, but most managers prefer to live to fight another day rather than launch a doomed crusade.

Dangers

The danger of politics, however, is that they can be carried to excess, and they can then seriously harm the effectiveness of an organization. The signs of excessive indulgence in political behaviour include:

- Back-biting
- Buck-passing
- Secret meetings and hidden decisions
- Feuds between people and departments
- Paper wars between armed camps – arguing by memoranda, always a sign of distrust
- A multiplicity of snide comments and criticisms
- Excessive and counter-productive lobbying

● The formation of cabals – cliques which spend their time intriguing.

Dealing with organizational politicians

One way to deal with this sort of behaviour is to find out who is going in for it and openly confront them with the damage they are doing. They will, of course, deny that they are behaving politically (they wouldn't be politicians if they didn't) but the fact that they have been identified might lead them to modify their approach. It could, of course, only serve to drive them further underground, in which case their behaviour will have to be observed even more closely and corrective action taken as necessary.

A more positive approach to keeping politics operating at an acceptable level is for the organization to manage its operations as openly as possible. The aims should be to ensure that issues are debated fully, that differences of opinion are dealt with frankly and that disagreements are de-personalized, so far as this is possible. Political processes can then be seen as a way of maintaining the momentum of the organization as a complex decision-making and problem-solving entity.

Use of politics

There are occasions when a subtle appeal rather than a direct attack will pay dividends; and sometimes you have to exercise your powers of persuasion indirectly on those whose support you need. The following case study illustrates the legitimate use of politics:

James Hale was the personnel director of a large divisionalized group in the food industry. The rate of growth by expansion and acquisitions had been very rapid. There was a shortage of really good managers and a lack of coordination between the divisions in the group and between those divisions and head office. Hale believed that setting up a group management training centre would be a good way of helping to overcome these problems. He knew, however, that he would have to get agreement to this plan not only from the managing director, who would be broadly sympathetic, but also from his co-directors. The MD would not act without the support of a majority on his board.

In any case Hale genuinely felt that there was no point in developing a facility of this sort for people who were not interested in it. He therefore sat back and deliberately worked out a strategy for getting agreement to his proposal. He knew that a frontal attack might fail. Management development was perceived by his colleagues as a somewhat airy-fairy idea which had little relevance to their real concerns as directors. He therefore had to adopt a more subtle approach. He did not call it a political campaign, but that is what it was. He was setting out to influence people indirectly.

The basis of his plan was an individual approach to each of his colleagues, adjusted to their particular interests and concerns. In the case of the marketing director, he got the general sales manager to advocate the need for training in sales management for divisional sales staff. He ran several pilot courses in hotels and invited the marketing director to the winding-up session. He made sure that the marketing director was impressed, not only by what the divisional sales staff had learned from the course, but also by the new spirit of identification with group aims and policies engendered by the training. Casually, the personnel director let slip the thought that if the group had its own training centre this feeling of commitment could be developed even more strongly.

The same basic technique was used with the production director. In addition he was helped to come to the view that a centre owned by the group could speed up the introduction of new ideas and provide a facility for communicating directly with key staff which was not available at present.

The finance director was a more difficult person to convince. He could easily assess the costs but found it difficult to accept largely subjective views of the potential benefits. In this case James Hale did not try too hard to persuade him against his will. He knew that the majority of the board was now in favour of the plan, including the managing director. Hale felt safe in leaving his financial colleague in an isolated and ultimately untenable position. The qualitative arguments, as absorbed by the other members of the board, including the managing director, had the ring of truth about them which no purely quantitative arguments could overcome.

Hale was content that he had enough support. To clinch the argument he played his last political card by warning the marketing and production directors that there might be some financial opposition. He then got them to agree with the thesis that they wouldn't allow 'Mr Money Bags' to adopt a narrow financial view and thus dictate the destiny of the firm.

James Hale had no difficulty in getting his proposal accepted at the next board meeting.

The non-legitimate use of politics

The following is an example of non-legitimate use of politics. Unfortunately, it is a fairly common one. In most organizations there are people who want to get on, and do not have too many scruples about how they do it. If it involves treading on other people's faces, then so be it.

Two directors of a company both aspired to be the next managing director. Mr Black, the finance director, had the ear of the MD. Mr White, the technical director, was more remote.

Mr White had a number of ideas for introducing new technology and had proved, to his own satisfaction at least, that the pay-off was considerable. Unfortunately, he jumped the gun in order to anticipate comments from Black, and presented a paper to the managing director which was not as well argued as it might be. Black carefully lobbied the MD and convinced him that the proposal was full of holes – he also hinted that this was yet another example of White's inability to understand the wider commercial issues.

The MD accepted this view more or less completely and agreed with Black's suggestion that the whole proposal should be off-loaded on to a board sub-committee – a well-known device to delay if not to stifle new ideas. This was done, and the introduction of new technology was unnecessarily delayed by 18 months. But Black had made his point as the practical man of affairs who would not allow the company to get involved in expensive and unrewarding projects.

Chapter 41
Presentations and effective speaking

A manager's job usually includes giving formal or informal presentations at meetings, and addressing groups of people at conferences or training sessions. To be able to speak well in public is therefore a necessary management skill which you should acquire and develop.

The three keys to effective speaking are:

- Overcoming nervousness
- Thorough preparation
- Good delivery.

Overcoming nervousness

Some nervousness is a good thing. It makes you prepare, makes you think and makes the adrenalin flow, thus raising performance. But excessive nervousness ruins your effectiveness and must be controlled.

The common reasons for excessive nervousness are: fear of failure, fear of looking foolish, fear of breakdown, a sense of inferiority and dread of the isolation of the speaker. To overcome it there are three things to remember and six things to do.

Three things to remember about nervousness

- Everyone is nervous. It is natural and, for the reasons mentioned earlier, a good thing.
- Speaking standards are generally low. You can do better than the other fellow.
- You have something to contribute. Otherwise why should you have been asked to speak?

Six things to do about nervousness

- *Practise.* Take every opportunity you can get to speak in public. The more you do it, the more confident you will become. Solicit constructive criticism and act on it.
- *Know your subject.* Get the facts, examples and illustrations which you need to put across.
- *Know your audience.* Who is going to be there? What are they expecting to hear? What will they want to get out of listening to you?
- *Know your objective.* Make sure that you know what you want to achieve. Visualize, if you can, each member of your audience going away having learned something new which he is going to put into practical use.
- *Prepare.*
- *Rehearse.*

Preparation

Allow yourself ample time for preparation in two ways. First, leave yourself plenty of low-pressure time; start thinking early – in your bath, on the way to work, mowing your lawn, any place where you can freely develop new ideas on the subject. Second, you should leave yourself lots of time actually to prepare the talk. There are eight stages of preparation.

1. Agreeing to talk

Do not agree to talk unless you know you have something to contribute to *this audience* on *this subject*.

2. Getting informed

Collect facts and arguments for your talk by: brainstorming and writing down all the points as they occur; reading up the subject; talking to colleagues and friends and keeping cuttings and files on subjects you may have to speak on.

3. Deciding what to say

Start by defining your objective. Is it to persuade, inform, interest or inspire? Then decide the main message you want to get across. Adopt the 'rule of three'. Few people can absorb more than three new ideas at a time. Simplify your presentation to ensure that the three main points you want to get across come over loud and clear. Finally, select the facts and arguments which best support your message.

Never try to do too much. The most fatal mistake any speaker can make is to tell everything he knows. Select and simplify using the rule of three.

4. Structuring your talk

Good structure is vital. It provides for continuity, makes your thoughts easy to follow, gives the talk perspective and balance and, above all, enables you to ram your message home.

The classic method of structuring a talk is to 'tell them what you are going to say – say it – tell them what you have said'. This is the rule of three in action again, as applied to attention span. Your audience will probably only listen to one-third of what you say. If you say it three times in three different ways they will at least hear you once.

You were no doubt told at school that an essay should have a beginning, a middle and an end. Exactly the same principle applies to a talk.

Tackle the middle of your talk first and:

● Write the main messages on separate postcards
● List the points you want to make against each main message
● Illustrate the points with facts, evidence, examples and introduce local colour
● Arrange the cards in different sequences to help you to decide on the best way to achieve impact and a logical flow of ideas.

Then turn to the opening of your talk. Your objectives should be to create attention, arouse interest and inspire confidence. Give your audience a trailer to what you are going to say. Underline the objective of your presentation – what *they* will get out of it.

Finally, think about how you are going to close your talk. First and last impressions are very important. End on a high note.

Think carefully about length, reinforcement and continuity. Never talk for more than 40 minutes at a time. Twenty or 30 minutes is better. Very few speakers can keep people's attention for long. An audience is usually very interested to begin with (unless you make a mess of your opening) but interest declines steadily until people realize that you are approaching the end. Then they perk up. Hence the importance of your conclusion.

To keep their attention throughout, give interim summaries which reinforce what you are saying and, above all, hammer home your key points at intervals throughout your talk.

Continuity is equally important. You should build your argument progressively until you come to a positive and overwhelming conclusion.

Provide signposts, interim summaries and bridging sections which lead your audience naturally from one point to the next.

5. Prepare your notes

The best sort of notes are the postcards used in preparing the talk. Each card should cover one section and include the main headings. Avoid using too many words on each; they will only confuse you.

Cards of this type can easily be referred to during your talk and should not distract your audience. It is quite a good idea, however, to write out your opening and closing remarks, in full, on separate cards. You can then learn these by heart, ensuring a confident start and a positive end to your presentation.

6. Prepare visual aids

As your audience will only absorb one-third of what you say, if that, reinforce your message with visual aids. Appeal to more than one sense at a time. Flip charts, slides and so on all provide good back-up, but don't overdo them and keep them simple. Too many visuals can be distracting, and too many words, or an over-elaborate presentation, will distract, bore and confuse your audience.

7. Rehearse

Rehearsal is vital. It instils confidence, helps you to get your timing right, enables you to polish your opening and closing remarks and to coordinate your talk and visual aids.

Rehearse the talk to yourself several times and note how long each section takes. Get used to expanding your notes without waffling. Never write down your talk in full and read it during rehearsal. This will guarantee a stilted and lifeless presentation.

Practise giving your talk out loud – standing up, if that is the way you are going to present it. Some people like to tape record themselves but that can be off-putting. It is better to get someone to hear you and provide constructive criticism. It may be hard to take but it could do you a world of good.

Finally, try to rehearse in the actual room in which you are going to speak, using your visual aids and with someone listening at the back to make sure you are audible.

8. Check and prepare arrangements on site

Check the visibility of your visual aids. Make sure that you know how to use them. Test and focus the overhead or slide projector. Brief your film projector operator and get him to run through the film to ensure that there are no snags.

If you are using slides in a carousel go through the lot to check that the sequence is right and none is upside down.

Be prepared for something to go wrong with your equipment. You may have to do without it at short notice. That is why you should not rely too much on visual aids.

Before you start your talk, check that your notes and visual aids are in the right order and to hand. There is nothing worse than a speaker who mixes up his speech and fumbles helplessly for his next slide.

Delivery

With thorough preparation you will not fail. You will not break down. But the way you deliver the talk will affect the impact you make. Good delivery depends on technique and manner.

Technique

Your *voice* should reach the people at the back. If you don't know that you can be heard, ask. It is distracting if someone shouts 'speak up'. Vary the pace, pitch and emphasis of your delivery. Pause before making a key point, to highlight it, and again afterwards to allow it to sink in. Try to be conversational. Avoid a stilted delivery. This is one reason why you should *never* read your talk. If you are your natural self the audience is more likely to be on your side.

Light relief is a good thing if it comes naturally. People are easily bored if they feel they are being lectured, but you should never tell jokes unless you are good at telling jokes. Don't drag them in because you feel you must. Many effective and enjoyable speakers never use them.

Your *words* and *sentences* should be simple and short.

Your *eyes* are an important link with your audience. Look at them, measure their reaction and adjust to it. Don't fret if people look at their watches; it's when they start shaking them to see if they've stopped that you should start to worry.

Use *hands* for gesture and emphasis only. Avoid fidgeting. Don't put your hands in your pockets.

Stand naturally and upright. Do not stand casually. Be and look like someone in command. If you pace up and down like a caged tiger you will distract your audience. They will be waiting for you to trip over some equipment or fall off the edge of the platform.

Manner

Relax and show that you are relaxed. Convey an air of quiet confidence. Relaxation and confidence will come with thorough preparation and practice.

Don't preach or pontificate to your audience. They will resent it and turn against you.

Show sincerity and conviction. Obvious sincerity, belief in your message, positive conviction and enthusiasm in putting your message across count more than any technique.

Conclusion

- You can learn to become an effective speaker with practice. Seize every opportunity to develop your skills.
- Nervousness can be controlled by preparation and knowledge of technique.
- Good preparation is more than half the battle.
- Technique is there to help you to exploit your personality and style to the full, not to obliterate them.

Chapter 42
Problem-solving and decision-making

Problems and opportunities

It is often said that 'there are no problems, only opportunities'. This is not universally true, of course, but it does emphasize the point that a problem should lead to positive thinking about what is to be done now, rather than to recriminations. If a mistake has been made, the reasons for it should be analysed, to ensure that it does not happen again. But it is then water under the bridge.

Faced with a continuous flow of problems and decisions you may occasionally feel utterly confused. We all feel like that sometimes.

Improving your skills

How can you improve your ability to solve problems and make decisions? There are a few basic approaches you should use:

Improve your analytical ability

A complicated situation can often be resolved by separating the whole into its component parts. Such an analysis should relate to facts, although, as Peter Drucker points out, when trying to understand the root causes of a problem you may have to start with an opinion. Even if you ask people to search for the facts first, they will probably look for those facts that fit the conclusion they have already reached.

Opinions are a perfectly good starting point as long as they are brought out into the open at once and then tested against reality. Analyse each hypothesis and pick out the parts which need to be studied and tested.

Mary Parker Follett's (18) 'law of the situation' – the logic of facts and events – should rule in the end. And although you may start out with a hypothesis, when testing it, use Rudyard Kipling's six honest serving men:

I keep six honest serving men
(They taught me all I knew)
Their names are What and Why and When
and How and Where and Who.

Adopt a systematic approach

Use the methods discussed in Chapter 6: analysing the situation, identifying possible courses of action, weighing them up and deciding what to do.

But do not expect the system to produce a black and white solution. Remember that Drucker (15) says in *The Effective Executive*:

A decision is a judgement. It is a choice between alternatives. It is rarely a choice between right and wrong. It is at best a choice between almost right and probably wrong – but much more often a choice between two courses of action neither of which is probably more nearly right than the other.

You should not expect, or even welcome, a bland consensus view. The best decisions emerge from a clash of conflicting points of view. This is Drucker's first law of decision-making – 'one does not make a decision without disagreements'. You need a clash of opinion to prevent people falling into the trap of starting with the conclusion and then looking for the facts that support it.

Alfred P Sloan of General Motors knew this. At a meeting of one of his top committees he said: 'Gentlemen, I take it we are all in complete agreement on the decision here.' Everyone round the table nodded assent. 'Then,' continued Mr Sloan, 'I propose we postpone further discussion of this matter until our next meeting to give ourselves time to develop disagreement and perhaps gain some understanding of what the decision is all about.'

Use your imagination

A strictly logical answer to the problem may not be the best one. Use lateral thinking, analogies and brainstorming, as described in Chapter 14, to get off your tramlines and dream up an entirely new approach.

Keep it simple

One of the first principles of logic is known as Occam's razor. It states that 'entities are not to be multiplied without necessity'. That is, always believe the simplest of several explanations.

Implementation

A problem has not been solved until the decision has been implemented. Think carefully not only about how a thing is to be done (by whom, with what resources and by when) but also about its impact on the people concerned and the extent to which they will cooperate. You will get less cooperation if you impose a solution. The best method is to arrange things so that everyone arrives jointly at a solution freely agreed to be the one best suited to the situation (the law of the situation again).

Problem-solving and decision-making techniques

Effective problem-solving and decision-making require the following steps:

1. *Define the situation.* Establish what has gone wrong or is about to go wrong.
2. *Specify objectives.* Define what you are setting out to achieve now or in the future as you deal with an actual or potential problem or a change in circumstances.
3. *Develop hypotheses.* If you have a problem, develop hypotheses about the cause.
4. *Get the facts.* In order to provide a basis for testing hypotheses and developing possible courses of action, find out what is happening now and/or what is likely to happen in the future. If different people are involved, get both sides of the story and, where possible, check with a third party. Obtain written evidence wherever relevant. Do not rely on hearsay.

   Define what is supposed to be happening in terms of policies, procedures or results and contrast this with what is actually happening. Try to understand the attitudes and motivation of those concerned. Remember that people will see what has happened or is happening, in terms of their own position. Obtain information about internal or external constraints that affect the situation.
5. *Analyse the facts.* Determine what is relevant and what is irrelevant. Establish the cause or causes of the problem. Do not be tempted to concentrate on symptoms rather than causes. Dig into what lies behind the problem. When analysing future events, try to make a realistic assessment in terms of existing trends both within and outside the organization. But be careful not to indulge in crude extrapolations. Consider the various internal and external organizational and environmental factors which may affect future developments.

6. *Consider possible courses of action.* List the possible courses of action in the light of the factual analysis. Where appropriate, use brainstorming and creative-thinking techniques to identify courses of action which may not be immediately evident.

7. *Evaluate possible courses of action.* Consider the possibilities, listing pros and cons and comparing anticipated results with your specified objectives. Evaluate the immediate and future consequences both inside and outside the organization. Compare costs with benefits. Assess how far the needs of those involved will be met and the extent to which your decisions will be acceptable. Consider the risk of creating dangerous precedents. Consider also the implications of any internal or external constraints that might exist. Ensure that all concerned participate in the evaluating and decision-making process. Note, however, that the degree of participation will depend on the nature of the problem and the participation procedures and management style of the organization.

8. *Decide and implement.* Decide which, on balance, is the preferred course of action, and discuss it with those concerned. Consider carefully how the decision is likely to affect them. Decide on the method of presentation, giving the reasons for the decision and, so far as possible, allaying any fears. Before implementing the decision ensure that everyone who needs it gets the relevant information.

9. *Monitor implementation.* Check on how effectively the decision is being implemented. Obtain the reactions of those affected. Take corrective action where necessary.

Chapter 43
Productivity improvement

The benefits of improved productivity

Work measurement programmes usually show that staff not on an incentive scheme perform at about 50 to 60 per cent of the standard that can reasonably be expected from an average worker.

It has been established that productivity audits of manufacturing and distribution activities consistently pinpoint opportunities of improving output by from 25 to 40 per cent with much the same plant and human resources. Similarly, clerical work measurement programmes can almost always save more than 15 per cent of staff without affecting output or quality. The scope for improvement is tremendous and so is the pay-off, as the following analysis shows.

Payroll as a percentage of sales	Percentage increase in profit before tax* from improvement in productivity of:			
	5%	10%	20%	40%
20	20	40	80	160
30	30	60	120	240
40	40	80	160	320
50	50	100	200	500
* Assumes a return on sales of 5 per cent.				

The pay-off from improving productivity is high, but how can you achieve it?

The first thing to do is to overcome apathy. Both managers and workforce must be persuaded somehow that they have a common interest in increasing output per head. This is a difficult exercise. It requires considerable powers of leadership from the top and this means positive programmes for motivating and involving all concerned to obtain their commitment to improvement.

A continuous drive for productivity is required and a productivity improvement programme based on a productivity audit should be the instrument.

Productivity improvement programme

The objective of a productivity improvement programme should be to achieve a significant change for the better in the relationship between outputs and inputs or, to put it another way, an improvement in the following ratio:

$$\frac{\text{Performance achieved}}{\text{Resources consumed}}$$

What are the factors for success?

A successful productivity improvement campaign depends on:

- A well-planned programme based on a productivity audit, with positive objectives and a clearly defined timetable
- A commitment on the part of management and supervisors to the programme
- The involvement of employees in the programme so that they are prepared, with suitable safeguards concerning their future, to participate in implementing it
- A recognition that the benefits resulting from the programme should be shared among everyone concerned: the organization, management and all other employees.

These are demanding criteria and they are not easily achieved. Things can go wrong. Managers, supervisors and other employees with all be suspicious of the programme. They will see it either as a device for exposing their inadequacies, an instrument for producing unacceptable change or a threat to their livelihood. These are emotional reactions and, once emotion comes in at the door, reason goes out of the window. So communication, education, involvement and persuasion are essential aspects of the programme.

Even if your powers of persuasion are great and you manage to involve employees in the programme sufficiently to overcome their natural resistance to change, there are a number of mistakes to be avoided in implementing productivity improvements. These include:

- Making recommendations based on inaccurate information or conclusions
- Making recommendations on new equipment, methods or procedures without properly evaluating the cost-effectiveness of the proposals
- Making recommendations without properly evaluating the impact of changes on other departments
- Proposing changes without giving sufficient consideration to the reactions of those involved.

These are common, but avoidable, errors. Those responsible for productivity improvement programmes will be much less likely to commit them if they are made aware of the dangers in advance. This is why it is important to be quite clear about who runs the programme and how it should be conducted.

Who runs the programme?

The programme for improving productivity must be run by top management. They should set the objectives, define terms of reference, appoint the executive responsible for the programme, provide him with the resources he needs and monitor the results achieved.

A senior manager responsible directly to the chief executive should be in charge of the programme. Never use a committee. It will spend its time talking, not doing. The productivity executive will need help – from organization and methods, work study, personnel and accounts departments – and he should get his aides involved directly, rather than sitting them round a table to talk to one another. It may be necessary to set up small project teams comprising members of different departments to carry out tasks, but they should be given specific things to do.

The employment of outside consultants will have to be considered. You should normally only use them as an 'extra pair of hands' providing expertise and resources not necessarily available within the organization. But they should be kept under control. They are there to work under the direction of the productivity executive, not to pursue their own line.

Consultants are often used as hatchet men to put forward the unpleasant recommendations that no one else wants to make. This is a pity. If you believe in productivity, you should realize that its achievement may not always be a comfortable process. You ought to be prepared to take justified action yourself and not rely on others to do it for you.

When you have decided who runs the programme, make sure that they know what you want them to achieve and that they adopt a systematic approach along the lines of the following productivity audit checklist.

Productivity audit checklist

What to look for

When you conduct a productivity audit you should look first at performance:

1. Actual compared with company standards and trends
2. Actual compared with other organizations
3. Reasons for unsatisfactory performance, which should be listed under the following headings:

   - Poor planning, budgeting and control procedures
   - Inefficient methods or systems of work
   - Inadequate use of work measurement
   - Insufficient mechanization or inadequate plant and machinery
   - Poor management
   - Poorly motivated employees
   - Badly paid employees
   - Too many restrictive practices
   - Inadequate training
   - Excessive waste.

The audit should then examine the following areas. Each one should be checked to discover what *should* be done, to what extent it *is* being done; and comment on any remedial action required.

1. Planning, budgeting and control – check that:

(a) Productivity performance tasks and standards are clearly defined, attainable, accurate and measurable
(b) Individuals are fully aware of the targets and standards they are expected to achieve
(c) Manpower plans and budgets are specifically concerned with setting and achieving realistic productivity targets
(d) Control reports clearly identify variances and deviations from the plan
(e) Individuals are fully accountable for failures to achieve targets or standards
(f) Prompt corrective action is taken by management to deal with adverse variances or results.

273

2. Work methods – check that:

(a) A continuous programme of reviewing and improving work methods in all parts of the organization is in existence
(b) The method improvement programme has the support of management, trade unions and employees
(c) The programme is producing real improvements in productivity.

3. Work measurement – check that:

(a) Work measurement is used, wherever feasible, to develop standards, give better controlled information and improve methods and procedures
(b) Work measurement is used to provide the basis for effective incentive schemes.

4. Technology – check that:

(a) There is a constant search by management for ways of improving productivity by the use of new technology – mechanization, computerization and automation
(b) Investment in equipment or machinery is justified on a cost-benefit basis
(c) Use of existing equipment is managed to achieve maximum productivity.

5. Management – check that:

(a) Management is fully conscious of the need for productivity
(b) Management and supervisors take active and successful steps to improve the productivity consciousness of their staff
(c) Productivity performance is treated as a key criterion in assessing the capabilities and rewards of management and supervisors
(d) The organization of work ensures that decisions on key aspects of productivity are taken at the point where work is carried out and the impact is greatest
(e) Research into methods of improving productivity is an important function in the organization.

6. Motivation and involvement – check that:

(a) Employees are motivated by management and supervisors to achieve greater productivity
(b) A continuous review is carried out by management into ways of improving motivation for productivity

(c) Employees are involved in seeking ways of improving productivity

(d) Employees appreciate that improvements in productivity benefit themselves as well as the company.

7. **Pay** – check that:

(a) Payment-by-results schemes are used wherever possible to boost productivity

(b) Payment-by-results schemes are kept under close review to ensure that they are cost effective

(c) Rewards to those not on payment-by-results schemes are related to achievement

(d) Schemes for sharing the rewards from increased productivity among employees are used to promote further gains in productivity.

8. **Restrictive practices** – check that:

(a) Productivity agreements are negotiated with trade unions to buy out restrictive practices

(b) The agreements are cost effective; that is, that the value of improvements in productivity resulting from the elimination of restrictive practices outweighs the cost of buying them out.

9. **Training** – check that:

(a) Analyses of training needs concentrate on ways of improving productivity

(b) Training programmes are derived from such analyses

(c) All those who can benefit from training to improve their productivity, especially new employees, are given such training

(d) The impact of training is followed up to ensure that it is cost effective; that is, that gains on productivity resulting from training outweigh the cost of training.

10. **Elimination of waste** – check that:

(a) There is a continuous attack led by top management on all forms of excessive manpower costs and wasteful use of manpower

(b) Work and method study is used to improve the use of manpower by introducing more efficient techniques, systems and procedures

(c) Increases of staff, enlargement of support departments and the engagement of indirect workers is rigidly controlled

(d) Managers and supervisors are held strictly accountable for wasteful practices.

Implementing improvements

It will be much easier to implement improvements in productivity if the objectives of your programme are understood and accepted by all concerned. Clear direction from the top and a systematic approach to conducting investigations are also important. But you will fail to achieve the results you want if you cannot get your workforce involved in the programme.

If you can get your staff involved they will identify themselves with the results. This will reduce their natural resistance to change and ensure their cooperation. It will become *their* programme rather than something imposed upon them.

Chapter 44
Profit improvement

Robert Heller wrote that 'businesses and managers don't earn profits, they earn money. Profit is an abstraction from the true, underlying movement of cash in and cash out.' It can be argued that profit is the result, not the objective, of efficient management.

On its own, profit, as shown on the balance sheet, is not necessarily an accurate measure of success in business. Profit figures can be 'influenced' by factors quite distinct from the trading performance of the company. These include how research and development is treated in the accounts, how stocks and work in progress are valued and how the flow of funds resulting from investments and realization of investments is dealt with. Rolls Royce is the classic example of a company whose profit figures proved to be misleading because of the way research and development expenditure was treated.

The president of International Harvester once said: 'All you have to do in business is to make some stuff and sell it to someone else for more than you paid for it.' And the controller of Bethlehem Steel stated: 'We're not in business to make steel, we're not in business to build ships, we're not in business to erect buildings. We're in business to make money.'

Both these statements are, of course, gross over-simplifications, but at least they emphasize the importance of the flow of money. Profit improvement is about increasing the flow of money into the business and reducing the flow of money out. It is not about maximizing an abstraction called 'profit' which is subject to so many extraneous influences. Perhaps we should think of it as performance improvement measured in financial terms rather than profit improvement. But profit improvement is what most people call it, and this is the term used here, with the reservations expressed above.

Factors affecting profit improvement

The three key factors are sales, costs and effectiveness.

Sales

The maximization of sales revenue depends first on good marketing. There are two approaches to marketing.

One is to assess the market in terms of what existing and potential customers will buy. This means an analysis of existing wants and buying patterns along with possible future needs. The other is to assess the scope for creating wants which do not exist at the moment, by developing and offering new products or services.

A company can maximize its market penetration by moving into market development (new markets for existing products), product development (improved or new products for existing markets) and diversification (new products for new markets).

Good marketing ensures that the company and its products are presented to customers by advertising, merchandizing and public relations in a way which will best promote sales.

Finally, good marketing ensures that prices match what customers can be persuaded to pay, with the objective of maximizing contribution to profits and direct overheads. Maximizing profit means getting the right balance between high margins and high sales volume.

Sales depend on good marketing but do not necessarily follow from it. A well-trained, well-motivated and well-controlled sales force is an essential ingredient.

The final, but often neglected, ingredient is distribution. Effective marketing and selling will go for nought if order processing is inefficient, if the turn round of customer orders takes too long, if the wrong distribution channels are used from the point of view of speed, reliability and cost, or if customer queries and complaints are not dealt with properly.

Costs

One of the many wise things Peter Drucker has said (15) is that: 'Cost, after all, does not exist by itself. It is always incurred – in intent at least – for the sake of a result. What matters therefore is not the absolute cost level but the rates between efforts and their results.'

The approach to cost reduction should therefore be to distinguish between those costs which are producing results and those which are not. Indiscriminate attacks on all costs – the 10 per cent slash approach – are counter-productive. On a selective basis, it may be better to cut something out altogether than to try and make a series of marginal cost reductions. As Drucker says: 'There is little point in trying to do cheaply what should not be done at all.'

Effectiveness

The objective should be effectiveness rather than just efficiency: to do the right things rather than merely to do things right.

Effectiveness should be aimed for in the areas of:

- *Productivity* – getting more for less, whether it is manpower (output per head), capital (return on investment) or equipment (output per unit)
- *Finance* – tightening credit policies, cracking down on bad debts, controlling quantity and settlement discounts, optimizing cash holdings while gaining maximum interest on surplus cash and reducing interest payments on bank overdrafts to a minimum
- *Inventory* – keeping the amount tied up in working capital to the minimum consistent with the need to satisfy customer demand
- *Buying* – using supplier's warehouse space by 'calling off' at specified intervals, ensuring that competitive bids are obtained for all new or renewed contracts, specifying to buyers how they should use 'clout' to get good terms, resisting the temptation to over-order, having clearly laid down policies on mark-ups.

Approach to profit improvement

Profit improvement should be a continuous exercise. It should not be left until a crisis forces you to think about it. Start with an analysis of your current situation, using the checklist at the end of this chapter. Look at the whole product range for each market and assess the relative profitability and potential of all products and markets. Try to spot those which are fading and the up-and-coming ones. For fading products or markets, consider whether remedial or surgical treatment is appropriate. For up-and-coming products or markets work out how their progress can be assured and, possibly, accelerated.

Use the 80/20 rule (Pareto's Law) to suggest the 20 per cent of your products/markets which generate 80 per cent of your profits. Concentrate on maximizing the effectiveness of the 20 per cent of areas where the impact will be greatest.

Identify those factors within the business which are restraining its potential and, in Drucker's words, 'convert into opportunity what everybody else considers dangers'. Build on strengths rather than weaknesses.

Then look ahead. Project trends, anticipate problems and, where appropriate, innovate so that you can challenge the future rather than being overwhelmed by it.

Above all, bear in mind the results of the following highly pertinent research carried out by William Hall (22). Hall looked at 64 companies in depth to determine which had the best hopes of surviving in a hostile environment. Writing in the *Harvard Business Review* he identified two key factors. The best business survivors are, first, those which can deliver their products at the lowest cost, and/or second, those which have the 'highest differentiated position'. This means having the product which the customers perceive most clearly as being different and, in important respects, rather better than the competition.

Profit improvement checklist

Corporate analysis

1. Analyse result areas (divisions, markets, products) according to the revenue contribution they make and the costs they generate.
2. Assess for each product line or product in each market:

   (a) The extent to which it is thriving, static or retracting
   (b) Its potential for the future on the basis of different assumptions about the level of investment or cost necessary for development or survival.

3. Analyse corporate sales performance against plan and explain variances.
4. Analyse direct and overhead costs against plan and explain variances.
5. Assess development achievements (product and market) against plan and explain deviations.
6. Analyse key financial ratios (current and trends) and establish reasons for variations from the norm.
7. Conduct a zero- or priority-based budgeting exercise to assess the justification for all major expenditure.
8. Find the answers to three key questions:

   (a) What business are we in?
   (b) What business should we be in?
   (c) What are we good at doing?

9. Assess corporate strengths and weaknesses in the fields of organization, management ability, calibre of staff, industrial relations, planning, development, marketing, selling, distribution, buying, inventory, financial base, productivity, production methods and facilities, use of new technology, including computers, management information and financial control.
10. Assess threats and opportunities:

    (a) External, eg competition, government policies and interventions, market and product developments, inflation, exchange rates
    (b) Internal, eg staff, innovation, systems, financial resources (including cash flow).

Strategic plans

11. Prepare strategic plans which:

    (a) Exploit opportunities and strengths revealed by the corporate analysis
    (b) Are based on realistic assumptions and projections of future trends
    (c) Take into account the cash required to finance expansion and product or market development.

Marketing

12. Find out everything possible about existing customers: buying habits, likes and dislikes, desire for changes or improvements to products or services.
13. Identify potential for getting new customers: what the company can do to meet existing needs or to create new wants.
14. Segment the market where this will reach different customers and can be profitable.
15. Penetrate new markets if this can be done profitably.
16. Check on cost effectiveness of advertising and promotional expenditure. Re-jib and expand advertising campaigns where it is confidently believed that this will improve results.
17. Pay more attention to merchandizing, eg advising retailers/agents on selling, holding special promotions, providing better point-of-sale material.

Product mix and development

18. Redistribute resources (finance, people, production and distribu-

tion) between products, as required, to optimize returns on investment.

19. Maximize product profitability by:

    (a) Cutting high-risk, high-capital projects
    (b) Developing low-cost, low-risk products
    (c) Cutting costs – advertising, promotion, packaging material, servicing or selling
    (d) Reducing stockholding
    (e) Reducing discounts
    (f) Increasing prices.

20. Develop new products or services to meet defined market needs or to create new wants.
21. Eliminate unprofitable products or markets.

Sales

22. Improve the order-to-call ratio of sales representatives by better field supervision and training and more effective incentives.
23. Concentrate upon key accounts.
24. Eliminate unprofitable accounts.
25. Develop more high-volume accounts.
26. Improve discount structure.
27. Provide incentives for customers to place larger orders or to remain loyal to the company's products.
28. Provide better support to sales representatives in the form of advertising, sales literature, merchandizing and direct mail shots.
29. Speed response to customer enquiries.

Distribution

30. Analyse transport costs and switch to more economic methods.
31. Rationalize depot structure to speed deliveries and cut distribution and storage costs.
32. Use fewer, larger capacity vehicles and lengthen their life.
33. Introduce automatic handling methods wherever justified by the return on investment.
34. Make better use of storage space.

Production

35. Use quick sharp doses of method study to identify areas where output can be improved, eg eliminating bottlenecks, illogical work flows, inefficient work scheduling.

36. Use value analysis techniques to reduce material costs.
37. Use group technology techniques to group associated processes into self-contained and easily controlled work units.
38. Rationalize product design so that more parts are interchangeable.
39. Ensure that procedures exist to relate customer orders and priorities to shop-floor capacity.
40. Improve shop loading and production control techniques in order to smooth work flow, rationalize distribution of work, and eliminate delays because of shortages in materials, parts or tools.
41. Revise design standards and tolerances to match production facilities.
42. Reduce waste and scrap rates.
43. Increase machine utilization.
44. Introduce automation (mechanization) where justified by return on investment.

Buying

45. Use 'clout' to get better terms (but beware of placing orders which are too large).
46. Find alternative, cheaper or more reliable sources of supply.
47. Reserve capacity if there is a genuine and predictable need.
48. Place guaranteed orders in exchange for bulk prices.
49. Analyse for over-specification and reduce specifications to the minimum safe level.
50. Use 'call-off system for regular supplies to cut storage costs.
51. Alter product design to allow for standard parts purchasing.

Inventory

52. Use economic order-quantity techniques to establish order points, taking into account inventory carrying charges, order preparation costs and demand for the item.
53. Use material requirements planning (MRP) techniques to ensure that the exact quantity of material wanted is on hand or is delivered not too long before it is required in accordance with sales demands.
54. Use computer modelling techniques to determine optimum stock levels, balancing the need to reduce working capital with the need to avoid being out of stock.
55. Improve information on inventory so that action can be taken in good time to reduce stock to optimum levels.

Cost reduction

56. Look at the scope for cutting costs in all the major areas where expenses are incurred:

    (a) Labour costs – look for overmanning, especially in indirect, service and staff departments
    (b) Manufacturing costs – streamline production methods, reduce material costs
    (c) Selling costs – advertising, promotions, public relations, packaging and display material
    (d) Inventory – stock levels too high
    (e) Operating – space, computers, services, plant and equipment.

57. Use zero or priority-based budgeting and organization and methods techniques to analyse every activity not directly concerned with production. Establish the extent to which each is essential and the degree to which costs could be cut without making a significant impact on the productivity and efficiency of the business.

58. Reduce waste created by the company by eliminating:

    (a) Unnecessary forms
    (b) Over-complicated paperwork procedures
    (c) Too many levels of management
    (d) Delays in decision-making because authority is not delegated down the line
    (e) Bottlenecks and inefficient work flows.

59. Reduce waste created by staff, eg time wasting, absenteeism, extravagant use of the company's facilities and equipment.

Productivity

60. Extend or introduce a comprehensive method improvement programme.
61. Use work measurement to develop standards, give better control information and improve methods and procedures.
62. Introduce new technology, when justified, on a cost/benefit basis.
63. Set productivity performance targets.
64. Buy out restrictive practices by productivity bargaining.

People

65. Identify effective managers and promote them.
66. Identify ineffective managers and remove them.

67. Introduce payment schemes which have a significant effect on motivation.
68. Encourage and train managers and supervisors to motivate their staff better.
69. Achieve better motivation by improving organization (more direct and immediate management) and the quality of working life. Get employees involved in productivity and quality improvement programmes.

Finance

70. Tighten credit policies.
71. Set priorities for capital expenditures.
72. Take steps to reduce bad debts.
73. Delay payments for as long as creditors will stand.
74. Analyse key ratios (eg profits as a percentage of sales and cash flow to current liabilities) and ensure that steps are taken to remedy adverse trends.
75. Ensure that management information, which allows proper control to be maintained over all aspects of the business, is available promptly.

Chapter 45
Report writing

The ability to express oneself clearly on paper and to write effective reports is one of a manager's most important skills. As often as not, it is through the medium of reports that you will convey your ideas and recommendations to your superiors and colleagues and inform them of the progress you are making.

What makes a good report?

The purpose of a report is to analyse and explain a situation, to propose and gain agreement to a plan. It should be logical, practical, persuasive and succinct.

To be an effective report writer you start by having something worthwhile to say. Clear thinking (Chapter 6), creative thinking (Chapter 14), problem-solving (Chapter 42) and trouble-shooting (Chapter 50) techniques will all help. Your analysis of opinions and facts and your evaluation of options should provide a base for positive conclusions and recommendations.

There are three fundamental rules for report writing:

- Give your report a logical structure
- Use plain words to convey your meaning
- Remember the importance of good, clear presentation of material.

Structure

A report should have a beginning, a middle and an end. If the report is lengthy or complex it will also need a summary of conclusions and recommendations. There may also be appendices containing detailed data and statistics.

Beginning

Your introduction should explain: why the report has been written, its aims, its terms of reference, and why it should be read. It should then state the sources of information upon which the report was based. Finally, if the report is divided into various sections, the arrangement and labelling of these sections should be explained.

Middle

The middle of the report should contain the facts you have assembled and your analysis of those facts. The analysis should lead logically to the conclusions and recommendations included in the final section. One of the most common weaknesses in reports is for the facts not to lead on naturally to the conclusions; the other is for the conclusions not to be supported by the facts.

Summarize the facts and your observations. If you have identified alternative courses of action, set out the pros and cons of each one, but make it quite clear which one you favour. Don't leave your readers in mid-air.

A typical trouble-shooting report would start by describing the present situation; it would then list any problems or weaknesses in that situation, and proceed to explain why these have occurred.

End

The final section of the report should set out your recommendations, stating how each of them will help to achieve the stated aims of the report or overcome any weaknesses revealed by the analytical studies.

The benefits and costs of implementing the recommendations should then be explained. The next stage is to propose a method of proceeding – the programme of work, complete with deadlines and the names of people who would carry it out. Finally, tell the recipient(s) of the report what action, such as approval of plans or authorization of expenditure, you would like them to take.

Summary

In a long or complex report it is very helpful to provide a summary of conclusions and recommendations. It concentrates the reader's mind and can be used as an agenda in presenting and discussing the report. It is useful to cross-reference the items to the relevant paragraphs or sections of the report.

Plain words

'If language is not correct, then what is said is not what is meant; if what is said is not what is meant, then what ought to be done remains undone.' (Confucius)

The heading of this section is taken from Sir Ernest Gowers' *The Complete Plain Words* (21). This book is required reading for anyone interested in report writing. Gowers' recommendations on how best to convey meaning without ambiguity, and without giving unnecessary trouble to the reader, are:

1. Use no more words than are necessary to express your meaning, for if you use more you are likely to obscure it and to tire your reader. In particular do not use superfluous adjectives and adverbs, and do not use roundabout phrases where single words would serve.
2. Use familiar words rather than the far-fetched if they express your meaning equally well; for the familiar are more likely to be understood.
3. Use words with a precise meaning rather than those that are vague, for they will obviously serve better to make your meaning clear; and in particular, prefer concrete words to abstract for they are more likely to have a precise meaning.

You will not go far wrong if you follow these precepts.

Presentation

The way in which you present your report affects its impact and value. The reader should be able to follow your argument easily and not get bogged down in too much detail.

Paragraphs should be short and each one should be restricted to a single topic. If you want a list or highlight a series of points, tabulate them. For example:

Salary reviews
Control should be maintained over increments by issuing guidelines to managers on:

(a) the maximum percentage increase to their pay roll allowable for increments to individual salaries;

(b) the maximum percentage increase that should be paid to a member of staff.

Paragraphs should be numbered for ease of reference. Some people prefer the system which numbers main sections 1, 2, etc, sub-sections 1.1, 1.2, etc, and sub-sub-sections 1.1.1, 1.1.2, etc. However, this can be clumsy and distracting. A simpler system, which eases cross-referencing, is to number each paragraph, *not* the headings, 1, 2, 3, etc; sub-paragraphs or tabulations are identified as 1(a), 1(b), 1(c), etc and sub-sub-paragraphs if required as 1(a)(i), (ii), (iii), etc.

Use headings to guide people on what they are about to read and to help them to find their way about the report. Main headings should be in capitals and sub-headings in lower case.

A long report should have an index listing the main and sub-headings and their paragraph numbers like this:

	Paragraphs
SALARY ADMINISTRATION	83–92
Salary structure	84–88
Job evaluation	89–90
Salary reviews	91–92

In a shorter report it is often helpful to include a list of headings and paragraph numbers in the introduction.

Your report will make most impact if it is brief and to the point. Read and re-read your draft to cut out any superfluous material or flabby writing.

Do not clutter up the main pages of the report with masses of indigestible figures or other data. Summarize key statistics in compact, easy-to-follow tables with clear headings. Relegate supporting material to an appendix.

Chapter 46
Strategic management

What is strategic management?

To think strategically is deliberately and consciously to articulate the direction in which you want to go.

Strategic management is therefore the process by which an organization and its managers determine:

- Where they are going in the medium and longer term – the strategic intent
- How they are going to get there – strategic or long-range planning, which may be expressed in the form of a corporate plan
- What they are going to do to ensure that they will arrive where they want to be – the direction of the organization and their own functions and departments so that they move constantly towards the achievement of the strategic plan.

Benefits of strategic management

The benefits of adopting a strategic approach to management are that:

- A sense of direction is provided for the organization as a whole and its individual managers and staff
- A longer-term view is adopted which avoids over-preoccupation with transient issues
- The process of management becomes more coherent within the defined framework of the strategic plan
- Cohesiveness within the organization is increased against the background of established goals which, ideally, will have been discussed and agreed with key people

- A basis is provided for the definition of targets, critical success factors and performance measures.

Organizations and managers who think strategically are looking ahead at what they need to achieve in the middle or relatively distant future. Although they are aware of the fact that businesses, like managers, must perform well in the present to succeed in the future, they are concerned with the broader issues they are facing and the general directions in which they must go to deal with these issues to achieve longer-term objectives. They do not take a narrow or restricted view.

Strategic management is concerned with both ends and means. As an end it describes a vision of what something will look like in a few years' time. As means, it shows how it is expected that the vision will be realized. Strategic management is therefore visionary management, concerned with creating and conceptualizing ideas of where the organization should be going. But it is also empirical management which decides how in practice it is going to get there.

The focus is on identifying the organization's mission and strategies but attention is also given to the resource base required to make it succeed. It is always necessary to remember that strategy is the means to create value. Managers who think strategically will have a broad and long-term view of where they are going. But they will also be aware that they are responsible for planning how to allocate resources to opportunities which contribute to the implementation of strategy, and then managing these opportunities in ways which will significantly add value to the results achieved by the firm.

This chapter first examines the concept of strategy and then describes the process of strategic planning.

Strategy

Definition

Perhaps it is best to start off negatively by stating that a strategy is *not*:

- A plan
- Objectives
- Financial projections
- Critical success factors.

These are simply expressions of a strategy.

A strategy should be defined more specifically as a means of addressing critical longer-term issues at the level of the business as a whole or an aspect of it (for example, a business unit or function).

291

It is a statement of where the organization as a whole, or a significant part of it, is going. It is therefore a declaration of intent which provides the basis for defining the organization's mission, goals and specific objectives, and leads to the preparation of strategic and action plans for their accomplishment.

Levels of strategy

There are two levels of strategy:

Corporate:

- Corporate portfolio
- Portfolio cohesiveness
- Mergers, acquisitions and divestments
- Image/imagination of the company
- Ethos of how to control the business.

Business unit (competitive):

- Definition of the business
- Value of the business
- Economics
- Competitive position – 'sustainable competitive advantage'.

Formulating strategies – key concepts

The following are the key concepts used in formulating strategies:

1. *Distinctive competence* – working out what the organization is best at and what its special or unique capabilities or attributes are, and planning to do these things.
2. *Competitive advantage* – selecting markets where the organization can excel and where its distinctive competences give it a competitive edge. Markets are selected where the business can either beat competitors or avoid them. Without competitive edge there is no ability to earn a true economic profit.
3. *Synergy* – developing a product–market posture with a combined performance that is greater than the sum of its parts (ie 2 + 2 = 5). Synergy in sales takes place when products use common distribution channels, common sales forces and administration or common warehousing. In operational terms, synergy occurs when there is higher utilization of facilities and personnel, spreading of overheads and bulk purchasing. Management synergy happens if the abilities and skills of individual managers can be used to solve problems and

develop strategies better or more comprehensively than they would have been able to do on their own.

4. *Environmental scanning* – strategic thinking and management involve scanning the internal and external environment of the firm to ensure that full awareness is gained of strengths and weaknesses, opportunities and threats.

5. *Resource allocation* – understanding the resource requirements of the strategy (human, financial, plant and equipment) and ensuring that the resources are made available and that their use is optimized.

Ingredients of a business strategy

The ingredients of a business strategy will be:

1. Analytical:

   - customer needs
   - supply costs
   - competitive economics
   - segmentation
   - profitability.

2. Visionary.
3. Clear.
4. Achievable.
5. Flexible.

The outcomes will be:

1. A mission statement.
2. Financial projections.
3. Company positioning:

   - pricing
   - costs
   - market share.

4. Functional outcomes (strategies)

   - *Corporate*: long-term growth; increased profitability; product-market development; diversification; acquisition; investment and disinvestment.
   - *Marketing*: target markets, the market segments on which the company will concentrate and the marketing position it proposes to adopt in each segment; the marketing mix, ie the blend of controllable marketing variables which will produce the required response in the target markets and will include new products,

293

prices, promotion, and the placing of sales and distribution activities.

- *Manufacturing*: the resources required in terms of plant, equipment and any form of new technology to meet market requirements and improve quality and productivity.
- *Research and development*: the thrust of basic and applied research in the light of assessed market needs; the direction in which development activities should go to support marketing and manufacturing strategies.
- *Personnel*: human resource management – the acquisition, motivation and development of the human resources required by the organization; organization development – the steps necessary to manage change and create a more effective organization; employee relations – creating constructive and cooperative relationships with employees.
- *Finance*: the acquisition and utilization of the financial resources required by the firm to its best advantage.
- *Data processing*: planning the information technology, hardware and software requirements of the firm to meet growth and improve effectiveness.

Formulating strategies

The following is a model of the process of strategy formulation:

1. Analyse existing strategies.
2. Evaluate strategies in the light of an analysis of the existing situation (environmental scanning) and projections of future trends.
3. Generate alternative strategies.
4. Evaluate alternatives.
5. Select strategy.

But this model, although theoretically correct, implies that strategy formulation is a rational and continuous process, which it is not, as was pointed out by Henry Mintzberg (37) in *The Nature of Managerial Work*. He believes that, rather than being consciously and systematically developed, strategy re-orientations happen in brief quantum leaps which may be forced upon the organization by the pressure of external events, or emerge in response to an evolving situation.

Strategic planning

Purpose

The purpose of strategic planning is to relate the company to its external environment – to match the company's internal strengths, weaknesses and basic values with the opportunities and threats present in the external environment in the pursuit of sustainable competitive advantage.

Aims

The aims of strategic planning are to:

1. Define and plan the long-term future of the business.
2. Increase the rate of growth of the enterprise in the long run.
3. Ensure that the organization can meet the challenge of change and can profit from new opportunities.

Rosabeth Moss Kanter believes that strategic plans 'elicit the present actions for the future' and become 'action vehicles – integrating and institutionalizing mechanisms for change'.

The process of strategic planning

Strategic planning consists of the following stages:

Stage 1. Define the business you are in
You may think you are in publishing, but you could really be in the leisure or entertainment business. An analysis of the business you are in helps you to understand the existing market and to reappraise its potential accordingly. If a book club says that it is in the leisure business it is recognizing that it is competing against other suppliers of leisure products for the disposable income of customers and not simply satisfying the needs of book buyers.

Stage 2. Define the mission of the organization
The mission statement of an organization expresses its sense of purpose – the business it is in and the broad direction in which it is going. The preparation of mission statements is dealt with in Chapter 31.

Stage 3. Define corporate values
A value statement expresses the beliefs of the organization on the behaviour which is considered to be good for it and the things which it thinks are important. It provides a reference point for the formulation of

295

strategic plans. The preparation of value statements is also considered in Chapter 31.

Stage 4. Environmental scanning

Environmental scanning involves conducting a SWOT analyis – an internal appraisal of the strengths and weaknesses of the company and an external appraisal of the opportunities and threats facing it.

- *Internal appraisal.* This involves analysing the organization's strengths (expertise, resources and achievements) and weaknesses, deciding how the strengths could be exploited and the weaknesses could be overcome and assessing the effects of proposed actions on profitability. The analysis should cover:

  - Product quality
  - Product maturity
  - Product availability
  - Cost structure
  - Market share
  - Brand strength
  - Customer loyalty
  - Management
  - Organization
  - Human resources
  - Employee relations
  - Financial reserves and cash flow
  - Innovative ability
  - Flexibility
  - Quality
  - Customer service.

- *External appraisal.* This involves analysing the environment in which the company operates: the economy, competition, government policies and market trends. The aim is to identify the key factors for success in present markets and the opportunities for profitably entering new markets or introducing new products. You should provide answers to Peter Drucker's two key questions:

  1. What are the restraints and limitations that make the business vulnerable, impede its full effectiveness and hold down its economic results?
  2. What are we afraid of, what do we see as a threat to this business, and how can we use it as an opportunity?

An external analysis of opportunities and threats should cover:

- Economic factors: exchange rates, interest rates, growth rates
- Government influences: regulation, de-regulation, privatization
- Market trends: consumer behaviour
- Competitors' behaviour: new products, new processes, mergers
- Technological change
- Social factors: ecology, health and safety, consumer movements, etc
- Supply factors: costs, availability of energy and new materials.

In a building society this review might cover, among other things:

- Prospects for the economy, especially in interest rates
- The possible effects of government action
- Trends in the availability of disposable income and in savings
- Population movements
- Changes in the wants and needs of purchasers
- An appraisal of competitors, especially banks and insurance companies.

Stage 5. Analyse existing strategies
The aim is to establish their relevance in the light of the external and internal appraisal. This will include gap analysis which will determine the extent to which environmental factors might lead to differences between what could be achieved if no changes were made and what needs to be achieved if objectives are to be reached.

Stage 6. Define strategic issues
The strategic issues will be the key factors which the organization has to address in developing its corporate plan. They are defined by reference to the SWOT and gap analyses and may include such questions as:

- How are we going to maintain growth in a declining market for our most important, ie profitable, product?
- In the face of aggressive competition, how are we going to maintain our competitive advantage and market leadership?
- To what extent do we need to diversify into new products or markets?
- What proportion of our resources should be allocated to research and development?
- What are we going to do about our ageing machine tool resources?
- What are we going to do about our overheads?
- How are we going to get our stock levels down?
- How are we going to finance our growth?
- What do we do about improving quality?

- How do we improve levels of customer service?
- How are we going to find and develop the well-qualified and highly motivated people we need in the future?

Stage 7. Identify and evaluate alternative strategies

The next stage is to identify and evaluate alternative strategies. The important thing is to let every possible idea come to the surface. The potentially most rewarding and practical ideas can then be selected. These will provide the basis for drawing up an overall statement of strategy (a declaration of strategic intent) and for developing objectives and action plans which will also define time-scales and the resources required.

When assessing alternatives you need to take three factors into account:

1. *Uncertainty.* This is in the nature of things. Dr Johnson said: 'He is no wise man who will quit a certainty for an uncertainty.' Unfortunately, you have to do this in business all the time. Strategic plans can do no more (or less) than give you a general outline of the way ahead. They enable you to be prepared for eventualities and they provide a point of reference against which you can measure progress and deviations and take action accordingly. But uncertainty remains. To deal with it you may have to prepare contingency plans. You will definitely have to ensure that your plans are flexible and are updated regularly or whenever conditions change.

2. *Risk.* This arises from uncertainty, but risks need to be assessed and classified. Drucker (15) has suggested that there are essentially four kinds of risk:

   (a) the risk one must accept – the risk that is built into the business;
   (b) the risk one can afford to take;
   (c) the risk one cannot afford to take;
   (d) the risk one cannot afford not to take.

3. *Resources.* The availability of financial and human resources will have to be assessed. This could be a limiting factor. Strategic planning is concerned with the optimum use of resources as well as with determining the course of events.

Stage 8. Prioritize

The priority to be given to each strategy should be assessed in the light of its relative importance and the availability of resources, as determined at stage 7. A further resource, time, will have to be taken into account.

Stage 9. Produce a statement of strategy

The statement of strategy defines in broad terms the intentions of the enterprise. It will address the strategic issues in accordance with the evaluation of alternative strategies carried out in stage 7 and the priorities established at stage 8. The statement need not elaborate on the detailed plans required to implement the strategies; these will be set out in the corporate plan (stage 11). A declaration of strategic intent can and, if possible, should be expressed on the classic one side of a sheet of paper as in the following example.

Here is a statement of business strategy which is reproduced with the permission of Roger Cooke of Coopers & Lybrand Deloitte. It is based on an actual statement but, for obvious reasons, has been disguised.

A strategic mission has been developed for Division A to provide a clear direction for the business into the 1990s.

1. The chosen strategy recognizes that Division A is uncompetitive in three of its product groups and that a major restructuring of the manufacturing base and product support is necessary.
2. The strategic mission for Division A is to lead a business integrating product groups B and C to become the leading worldwide competitor in specialist automatic gearbox systems for heavy duty off-road vehicles. The principle applications will be:
   - wheeled military vehicles
   - construction vehicles
   - agricultural vehicles.
3. A major investment programme in alloy and other non-ferrous castings and a minor reinvestment in oil seal technology are to be adopted. It is not intended to be involved in the realization of new basic designs.
4. Facilities for components presently located at factory X will be relocated at Y and future assembly will be located at Z. Factory X will be closed before the expiry of the lease.
5. The product support business is to be reorganized to form a separate profit centre located in Z No 2 building.
6. The cellular manufacturing strategy will be continued and this, together with the overall reduction in business complexity and improved control, will remain the basis for the necessary improvements in operating performance.
7. In order to refund this reinvestment programme, P and Q business will be divested. It is proposed, however, to expand the profitable R business as a hedge against declining turnover.
8. Finally, to establish Division A as a leading supplier in specialist automatic gearbox systems markets, this strategy envisages integrating the relevant activities of Divisions B and C to establish a formidable competitor on a worldwide scale.

Stage 10. Define objectives and critical success factors

Objectives can be defined in terms of outputs (what the strategies are required to produce) and outcomes (the impact of the outputs on the results achieved by the organization).

In a profit-making company the overall objective may be to maximize the return to the shareholders in the form of capital growth. But this primary aim needs to be expanded.

You could usefully follow the example of Owen Green, the chairman of BTR, a conglomerate which over a decade increased sales from £50 million to £510 million and net profit from £1.5 million to £43 million. His 'ethic' is:

- Growth is the objective
- Profit is the measure
- Security is the result.

But you need to be more precise than that. Corporate economic objectives in a trading company could be too:

- Increase the return on capital employed from 15 per cent to 20 per cent by 19–
- Achieve a minimum annual increase in turnover of 10 per cent in real terms.

In an insurance company a broad statement of objectives might read:

To achieve and maintain an optimum return on increasing capital employed; the return must be such as:

(a) to give shareholders an increasing return on their investments which compares favourably with the return available by investing elsewhere;
(b) to be consistent with the company's obligations to its policy holders.

When setting objectives it is important to define the critical success factors or success criteria which will indicate when they have been achieved. Where objectives are quantified in the form of targets this is easy, but where they are related to task achievement it is even more necessary to take care to spell out the factors that will contribute to successful performance and the standards to be met.

At IBM, the definition of critical success factors is part of the strategic planning programme with a consensus approach including groups of senior managers. This takes place in seven steps, as follows:

Step 1. Understand the mission
- The team collectively agrees a mission statement.
- The statement should not be longer than three or four short sentences and should clearly define the circumstances when the mission will have been successfully accomplished.

Step 2. Identify issues which will impact on mission
- The team focuses on the mission and identifies dominant issues by listing one-word descriptions of everything they think will impact on the mission's achievement.
- The normal brainstorming rules apply, ie

  - everyone should contribute
  - everything is fair game, no matter how crazy or outrageous
  - nobody is permitted to challenge any suggestion
  - the facilitator writes everything down on a flip chart so that the team can see the whole list.

Step 3. Identify the critical success factors
- By reference to the list of issues which it is believed will impact on the mission the team identifies the critical success factors (CSFs). The characteristics of a CSF statement are that it:

  - defines what the team believes *needs* to be done to achieve the mission
  - is not only *necessary* to the mission but also, together with the other CSFs, *sufficient* to achieve the mission (the necessary and sufficient rule).

- The list of CSFs should:

  - not exceed eight
  - include a mix of strategic and tactical factors.
- Absolute consensus must be achieved on what is included in the list.

Step 4. Define business processes
- Identify and list what has to be done to meet the critical success factors.
- Define the business processes (actions) needed to meet CSF requirements.
- The rules for defining business processes are:

  - the selection should be rigorous in accordance with the necessary and sufficient role
  - each description should follow an active verb plus object sequence
  - each business process should have an owner, the person responsible for carrying out the process
  - the owner should be a member of the management team that agreed to the CSFs
  - no owner should have more than three or four processes to manage.

301

Step 5. Draw up CSFs and business processes matrix
- The team draws up a matrix which lists the critical success factors and the business processes relevant to each CSF.

Step 6. Review CSFs and processes
- The team reviews each CSF to ensure that it is supported by necessary processes which together are sufficient to achieve the results required.

Step 7. Confirm action plan
- The team proceeds to confirm the action plan associated with the processes and sets up the implementation programme.
- Monitoring and follow-up arrangements are also made.

Stage 11. Prepare corporate plan

The corporate plan summarizes the conclusions reached by the strategic planning process. It may be set out under the following main headings:

- The mission statement
- The values statement
- The SWOT analysis
- The strategic issues
- The statement of strategic intent
- The objectives and critical success factors
- Business development plans – to cover expansion and withdrawals in markets and products, diversifications and technical development
- Organization plans – to decide what activities have to be carried out and outline a structure which will cater for them
- Resource plans – the finance, manpower and facilities required
- Operational plans – the detailed operating targets and budgets for each activity and department.

Stage 12. Action planning

Action plans implement strategies and the corporate plan, having taken into account the critical success factors and the resources available. They can be grouped under three main headings:

1. Operational plans for the major operating functions such as marketing and manufacturing.
2. Resource plans which programme the acquisition or development of human, financial and material resources.
3. Project plans which programme projects for launching new products, introducing new technology, developing new markets, etc.

Techniques of managerial planning are discussed in Chapter 28.

Implementing the strategic plan

If it has been formulated properly, a strategic plan will spell out objectives, targets, critical success factors, action plans and budgets.

The implementation of the plan is then achieved by ensuring that everyone knows about those aspects of the plan which affect them and what they have to do to contribute to its achievement. This is the normal management process of organizing and programming work, designating responsibilities, delegating authority, monitoring performance and taking corrective action on the basis of feedback information.

A good strategic plan will not replace the need to manage the task effectively as part of the day-to-day process of management. But it does provide everyone concerned with a much clearer sense of direction and a means of monitoring and measuring performance.

When planning goes wrong

Winston Churchill summed up the problems of strategic planning when he said that: 'It is wise to plan ahead but difficult to look further than you can see.' And Robert Heller has said that what often goes wrong with long-range planning 'is that sensible anticipation gets converted into foolish numbers and their validity hinges on large loose assumptions'.

Planning goes wrong either because people are over-confident about their ability to predict and shape the future or are over-ambitious. Robert Heller in *The Business of Success* (24) has six prescriptions for a company suffering from either of these diseases.

- Stick to a basic theme
- Concentrate short-term activity on improving basic efficiencies
- Couple short-term emphasis on efficiency with plans for medium- and long-term defence and improvement of market positions
- Use acquisition sparingly, either to strengthen the above tactics and strategies or to add *immediately* to the return on assets
- Make stability, in management and in business development, a prime aim
- Last, but not least, never succumb to the notion that you're a genius: even if (which is unlikely) you are.

Conclusion

The future is always obscure but that does not obviate the need to think strategically. It just means that you must be cautious about committing yourself too heavily to any course of action which relies on unreliable assumptions about what is going to happen.

The main advantages of strategic planning, even when it has to be based on somewhat fallible assumptions, are that it gives you a sense of direction, a purpose in life and an idea of the resources you will need in the future. Unrealistic planning can be avoided if you limit your planning to a period over which you can forecast trends with reasonable accuracy, and regularly update your plans when conditions change.

Chapter 47
Stress management

The activities of most managers are characterized by brevity, variety and fragmentation. They are constantly exposed to change – indeed chaos. They are frequently working under pressure which within reason is normal, perhaps desirable, as a motivating force. It can make the adrenalin flow and concentrates the mind wonderfully. It is only when the pressure becomes excessive that it can turn into stress, which will then have a demotivating effect. Because some degree of stress is almost inevitable in these turbulent times, it is desirable to understand something about the varieties of stress, its causes and how to cope with it.

Varieties of stress

Emotionally induced stress can be classified into four general categories:

1. *Time stress.* This is an anxiety reaction, either to the feeling that something, or a number of things, must be done before a deadline, or to the general feeling that time is running out and something terrible will happen when it does.
2. *Anticipatory stress.* This is commonly known as 'worry'. This is a feeling of anxiety about an impending event. It is often a generalized anxiety, with little or no specific basis.
3. *Situational stress.* This is anxiety as a result of finding oneself excessively pressurized by events or people. It occurs in situations which are threatening and wholly or partially beyond one's control. It can also happen when there is conflict or distrust between people
4. *Encounter stress.* This is anxiety about dealing with individuals or groups of people who are perceived as potentially unpleasant or unpredictable.

Causes of stress

The main causes of stress are:

- *Working conditions* – unpleasant working conditions, such as the need to work fast or expend a lot of physical effort or excessive or inconvenient hours, can affect both physical and mental health.
- *Work overload* – either having too much work to do, or carrying out work that is beyond one's capacity.
- *Role ambiguity* – when individuals are unclear about the scope and responsibilities of their jobs or the authority they have to make decisions.
- *Role conflict* – where individuals have conflicting job demands, are doing things they do not want to do, or are having to do things which are outside the specification of their jobs.
- *Responsibility* – increased responsibility for people means being involved more in interacting with others, attending meetings and meeting deadline pressures and schedules. Such people may also worry about 'carrying the can' for the mistakes or inadequacies of their staff.
- *Accountability* – accountability for results can increase stress because of the pressure on meeting targets and improving standards of performance, especially in conditions where the future is uncertain.
- *Change* – coping with rapid technological change, the acquisition of new skills, different responsibilities in the job and the variety of tasks to be undertaken in turbulent conditions.
- *Relationships with subordinates* – inability to delegate, critical or uncooperative staff, difficulties in exercising authority.
- *Relationships with colleagues* – office politics, rivalry, competitiveness, lack of support, difficulties in achieving cooperation on joint projects.
- *Job security* – fears of redundancy, obsolescence or early retirement.
- *Lack of status* – actual or perceived.
- *Feelings about job or career* – frustration at reaching career ceiling, lack of prospects, under- or over-promotion.
- *Impact of the organization* – pressurized or tense climate, autocratic management style, restrictions on behaviour, lack of information and involvement.
- *External pressures* – clash between demands made by the organization and those made by the family or other external interests; problems at home created by excessive hours at work; priority being given to work rather than partner and family; travelling away from home, company transfers.

STRESS MANAGEMENT

These causes can combine in many ways. They are probably most acute for middle managers who are pressurized from above and from below, are busy making their mark and advancing their career, are having to travel and move with the company, yet who may be married with growing responsibilities at home. But older managers may also be subject to stress either because of the extra weight of responsibility or because their career has 'plateaued' and their ambitions are not being realized.

Coping with stress

How people deal with stress will depend on their personality, tolerance for ambiguity and ability to live with change. Motivation also comes into it. Motivation is a form of pressure. People can be too highly motivated and pressure becomes stress when they cannot achieve what they set out, or are expected, to do.

Stress can be managed by adaptive behaviour. An overworked manager may adapt successfully by delegating more work and spending more time in managing time (see Chapter 49). But someone else may accept the overload, with the result that pressure and stress increase and performance deteriorates.

The following are various ways in which you can manage stress:

1. Build rewarding, pleasant, supportive relationships with your boss, colleagues and subordinates.
2. If in any doubt about your role, seek clarification from your boss.
3. If there are problems between you and other managers, bring the issues out into the open and discuss them in a frank but friendly way.
4. Take steps to clarify your objectives and have them agreed by your boss.
5. However much you may wish to present yourself as the willing horse, don't take on extra work and make promises you will have great difficulty in keeping. Don't refuse outright or you will get the reputation of being uncooperative. Don't plead overwork or you may be regarded as a shirker. Simply say that you have a set of priorities which you have to keep to and that, while you will be glad to help, you will have to give this job a lower priority, unless your other priorities can be changed. If the task is completely beyond your capabilities, say so, but offer to help in finding someone who has the required skills and knowledge.
6. Appraise your own strengths and weaknesses. If your problems are

307

because of an identifiable weakness, do something about it or seek help.

7. Determine a goal in your career which is realistic in relation to your own self-appraisal. Check on the competences and qualifications required to move to where you want to be. If you are confident that you have them, pursue your ambition vigorously. If you do not have the qualities required, decide whether or not you can build them. If so, go ahead. If not, think of an alternative goal and career path which is within your capabilities.
8. If you are under pressure to meet deadlines or have too many balls in the air at once, plan your priorities to fit the time available, and delegate as much work as possible.
9. If you are facing a crisis, take time to decide how to tackle it. Don't run in all directions at once like a headless chicken.
10. If under extreme pressure, deliberately allow yourself time to relax for a few minutes.
11. Use time management techniques as described in Chapter 49 to plan your working day, always allowing some time – even if only ten minutes – for complete privacy and freedom from pressure.
12. Try to make sure that you are placed in a job suitable to your characteristics and talents.
13. Face up realistically to what you can do and achieve.
14. Do whatever you can to achieve an acceptable balance between yourself, your work and your family.
15. Foster relationships which help you to cope with work pressure, and enable you to admit, and take steps to remedy, work-related stress.

Chapter 48
Team building

A manager spends much of his time leading teams and dealing with people in groups. Getting people to work well together is as important as motivating individuals.

Team building is a matter of establishing mutual confidence and trust among any group of people working for you. Your aim is to create a feeling of interdependence. A good team feels shared responsibility for getting results.

People do not necessarily work well together. Personal and inter-departmental rivalries exist in all organizations. Look out for them; they can ruin the most brilliant schemes.

Take the example of a bright and brash young marketing executive imported by a British company to develop and market a new product. He had lots of ideas and all the qualities of initiative and drive that anyone could want in a development job. But he tended to ride rough-shod over the production, distribution and customer service departments. So far as he was concerned they were there to do as they were told. He dealt with them separately and never bothered to find out if there were any problems of coordination between them on matters relating to his product. As a result, the managers of these departments in more or less subtle ways sabotaged his efforts. They failed to get together on inter-departmental matters – partly because no one gave them a lead, and partly because there were rivalries and misunderstandings between them. Eventually, although the marketing concept was brilliant, the project failed, owing to the refusal of the bright young executive to appreciate the importance of team building.

The company learnt its lesson. The next time an outsider was brought in to launch a new product, time was spent before he arrived to get a team together in the production, distribution and servicing divisions. They did the preliminary work setting up the project at their end, and were encouraged to feel that this was *their* project. As a result, when the new executive arrived, an atmosphere of enthusiasm and commitment existed.

There was no problem in getting the team to work well together, especially as the new man was well aware of the need to build up a cohesive team.

Good teamwork is essential, but the existence of other highly cohesive groups is not necessarily a good thing for an organization. To become an effective team builder it is useful to know something about group behaviour and what makes an effective group.

How groups behave

Formal and informal groups

In the late 1920s Elton Mayo conducted his first studies in group behaviour in the General Electric Hawthorne plant. He defined the two types of group that can exist within organizations:

- *Formal groups* set up by the organization to achieve a defined purpose which satisfies the organizational needs
- *Informal groups* set up by members of the organization because they have some affinity for one another. This type of group exists primarily to satisfy the needs of its members.

Informal groups may work for the organization, but they may work against it. For example, employees may get together to restrict output so that management will not tighten up a bonus scheme. In such a case the members of the group gang up against any 'ratebuster'.

Numerous investigations since Mayo's time have confirmed his observations. And you will find the same things happening today wherever people work together.

From management's point of view the advantages of well-established informal groups are that they provide important extra channels of communication, promote teamwork and satisfy social needs that the organization or team leader cannot.

The disadvantages are that they may cut across the normal organizational channels and can develop norms or behaviour patterns in conflict with the aims of the leader.

The ideal situation is for formal and informal groupings to coincide, thus satsifying the needs of both the organization and the individuals in it.

Characteristics of established groups

The main characteristics of a well-established group (formal or informal) are as follows:

1. It is cohesive – the members of the group put up a united front to outsiders (who may include their boss or the management).
2. The members are interdependent – they rely upon each other for support in achieving both work and social goals.
3. It establishes its own norms of the group to act in ways which are not in accordance with their own needs, or those of the organization, or those of the group leader.
4. The members of the group will tend to share beliefs and values (the group develops its own ideology) which may or may not be in accord with those of the organization or their boss.
5. The whole is greater than the sum of the parts, ie a well-knit group may exert greater influence when working as a whole than the total influence of each of its members if they were working separately.

One of the important things to look for in groups is the status system that may exist within them. If you understand the informal as well as the formal pecking order you will be better equipped to deal with problems within the team.

An interesting piece of research on status was carried out by William Whyte in the restaurant industry. Whyte points out that every work group has a status system. The various jobs into which the work of the group is subdivided have different prestige values in the eyes of the workers. The supervisor must know the status system of his group to cope effectively with problems of human relations.

Whyte's description of work groups in the kitchen of the Mammoth Restaurant illustrates the complex factors which determine an organized status system.

First, he observed that the work situations in the kitchen were socially ranked. At the top was the range where all the cooking was done. The most highly paid and most skilled positions were found at the range. Next came the salad station, which also dealt in finished foods of high prestige. Next in order of status were the chicken-preparation and meat-preparation stations. Towards the bottom of the hierarchy were the chicken-cooking and vegetable-preparation stations. At the very bottom was the fish station.

The larger stations had a status system of their own. For instance, the vegetable-preparation station consisted of eight women. The tasks of the women in order of status were as follows: One and Two were the vegetable cooks; Three divided her time between cooking and preparing vegetables; Four was in charge of preparation under the direction of One and occasionally did some cooking; Five, Six, Seven and Eight did no cooking. This status pattern had developed as a result of the formally specified division of labour (eg cooking duties versus non-cooking duties) and personal factors. (Seven and Eight were older women who worked sitting down, thus giving the younger workers the opportunity to organize and direct the work.)

Status influenced the assignment of different vegetables to the women; for vegetables, it seems, differ markedly in social standing. Such decorative or luxury vegetables as parsley, chives and celery are at the top. Green beans head the regular vegetables, followed by spinach and carrots. Next to the bottom are potatoes. Onions are considered the most undesirable of all because of their odour.

Higher-status workers tended to work on higher-status vegetables. When all the women were working on the same vegetable, the higher-status workers handled later stages in the process of preparation (eg dicing carrots instead of scraping them). This brought them closer to the social pinnacle of the kitchen – the range – and put them in a position to criticize the work of the earlier stages.

The working supervisor of the fish station was one of the most skilled and valuable workers in the kitchen. Yet her station stood at the bottom of the status hierarchy because the other workers considered the fish station a smelly, dirty and unpleasant place to work.

Effective teams

An effective team is cohesive, self-supportive and knows where it is going. Douglas McGregor (36) described the main features which indicate such a team:

1. The atmosphere tends to be informal, comfortable, relaxed.
2. There is a lot of discussion in which initially everyone participates, but it remains pertinent to the task of the group.
3. The task or objective of the group is well understood and accepted by the members. There will have been free discussion of the objective at some point until it was formulated in such a way that the members of the group could commit themselves to it.
4. The members listen to each other. Every idea is given a hearing. People do not appear to be afraid of looking foolish by putting forward a creative thought, even if it seems fairly extreme.
5. There is disagreement. Disagreements are not suppressed or overriden by premature group action. The reasons are carefully examined, and the group seeks to resolve them rather than to dominate the dissenter.
6. Most decisions are reached by a kind of consensus in which it is

clear that everybody is in general agreement and willing to go
along.

7. Criticism is frequent, frank and relatively comfortable. There is
little evidence of personal attack, either openly or in a hidden
fashion.

8. People are free in expressing their feelings as well as their ideas both
on the problem and on the group's operation.

9. When action is taken, clear assignments are made and accepted.

10. The leader of the group does not dominate it, nor does the group
defer unduly to him.

These characteristics present an ideal which you might strive for but will
seldom attain. There will be times when you have to do away with some
of the more time-consuming ones, such as 2, 6 and 8, and concentrate on
3 and 9: 'The task or objective of the group is well understood and
accepted by the members . . . when action is taken, clear assignments are
made and accepted.'

Leadership

As the team leader you are responsible for seeing that it displays as many
of the above characteristics as are appropriate to the situation. The role of
the leader is critical, especially in times of crisis, when the group must get
into action fast. Robert Hamblin of the University of Michigan carried
out an interesting laboratory investigation into the effects of a crisis on
team leaders.

In his experiment college students, divided into 24 groups of three, were
asked to play a modified shuffleboard game for about 30 minutes. They
were told to learn the special rules of the game by trying out different
procedures. A red light would flash every time a rule was violated; a green
light every time a score was made.

The game was presented to the students as a test of their ability to
analyse a rather complex situation. The groups were told they were in
competition with high school students who had earlier participated in a
similar experiment and that comparative cumulative scores would be
posted at the end of each of the game's six five-minute playing periods.

Each time a player suggested a procedure for testing a rule or suggested
a possible rule, he was given an 'influence-attempt score'. If the attempted
suggestion was adopted by the group, he was given an 'accepted influence
score'. Two measures were then calculated for each player for each playing
period: the influence ratio and an acceptance rate. The influence ratio was
the number of influence-attempt scores of each divided by the average
influence-attempt scores of the other two group members. The acceptance

rate was the proportion of a subject's influence attempts which were accepted.

By the end of the first three playing periods, the average group had learned most of the rules of the game and was enjoying a comfortable, albeit fictitious, lead over the high school competitors. In the fourth playing period, twelve of the groups were exposed to a 'crisis' – an unannounced change in the rules was made. Procedures that had been legal were now made illegal and vice versa. As soon as the players learned a new rule, it was again changed. The members of the crisis groups were unable to make a single score during the last three periods. The remaining 12 groups (control groups) continued to play under the original rules.

The results indicated two things. First, leaders have more influence at a time of crisis. The members of a group accept leadership when faced with a crisis. Second, a group rejects its old leader and replaces him if the old leader does not quickly and decisively meet the crisis. Whereas nine of the twelve crisis groups replaced their original leaders, only three of the control groups did so.

Getting cooperation

The members of an effective team cooperate equally well with one another and with their team leader.

Elton Mayo and many other investigators of teamwork have demonstrated that the manager can exert considerable, if indirect, influence by simply showing interest in how the team operates and getting involved with its members. In his Hawthorne studies Mayo showed that the output of some of the teams of girls he was studying increased just because the investigators were taking an interest in them:

> By asking for their help and cooperation the investigators had made the girls feel important. Their whole attitude had changed from that of separate cogs in a machine to that of a congenial group trying to help the company solve a problem. They had found stability, a place where they belonged and work whose purpose they could clearly see. And so they worked faster and better than they ever had in their lives.

Team building methods

To build an effective team, exercise your leadership skills. It is particularly important for you to demonstrate to your team that:

- You know where you want them to go
- You know how they are going to get there

- You know what you expect each member of the team to achieve
- You know what you are doing.

Such an approach to leadership provides firm base which will allow you to concentrate on doing the following things:

1. Encourage participation in agreeing objectives and targets.
2. Group related tasks together so that group members know that they can make their jobs easier by cooperating with others.
3. Rotate jobs within groups so that group members identify with the team as a whole rather than with their own jobs.
4. Ensure that communications flow freely within and between groups.
5. Encourage informal meetings between groups to resolve problems.

How best to work in a team

To work effectively in a team you need to:

1. Understand the purpose of the team.
2. Find out what you are expected to contribute.
3. Analyse the other members of the team, especially the leader, to decide who plays which role.
4. Observe the behaviour of the team to identify group norms so that you can conform or consciously deviate from them if necessary.
5. Analyse your own skills and competences to establish how you might best contribute, referring to the lists of roles for guidance on how you might use your talents most effectively.
6. Prepare yourself well before meetings – get your facts and arguments at your fingertips.
7. Don't talk too much. It is often best to 'keep your powder dry' and not rush in too quickly. The art of being a good team member is to know when and how to intervene.
8. Assess your own performance as a team member. Ask yourself what you are good and not so good at doing by reference to your successes and failures, and take appropriate action.

Chapter 49
Time management

I wasted time, now doth time waste me (*Richard II*).

If you were told by your chairman that he wanted you for a special assignment which would mean working directly under him, give you the opportunity to deal with strategic issues, broaden your experience and provide you with excellent promotion prospects, would you take it? The answer would, of course, be yes. If, however, you were told that you would spend one day a week on this assignment and carry out your present duties in the remaining four days, would you still accept the job? Of course you would. But you would be admitting that you could, if you organized yourself better, do your existing work in four-fifths of the time you spend at the moment.

To recover that one-fifth or more, you need to think systematically about how you use your time. You can then take steps to organize yourself better and to get other people to help or at least not to hinder you.

Analysis

The first thing to do is to find out where there is scope for improving your use of time.

Your job

Start with your job – the tasks you have to carry out and the objectives you are there to achieve. Try to establish an order of priority between your tasks and among your objectives.

It is more difficult to do this if you have a number of potentially conflicting areas of responsibility. A good example of this was a director of administration who had a ragbag of responsibilities including property, office services and staff. He had perpetual problems with conflicting priorities and, all too frequently, at the end of the day he would say to himself: 'I have wasted my time, I have achieved next to nothing.'

He took a day off to think things through and realized that he had to take a broad view before getting into detail. He felt that if he could sort out the relative importance of his objectives he would be in a better position to attach priorities to his tasks. He quickly realized that, as an administrator, his first objective was to set up and maintain systems which would run smoothly. Having done this, he could rely on preventive maintenance to reduce problems. But when a crisis did occur – which was inevitable in his area – he could concentrate on fire-fighting in one place without having to worry about what was going on elsewhere.

His second objective, therefore, was to give himself sufficient free time to concentrate on major problems so that he could react swiftly to them. He then classified the sort of issues that could arise and decided which could safely be delegated to others and which he should deal with himself. He was thus prepared to allocate priorities as the problems landed on his desk and to select the serious ones to deal with himself, knowing that the administrative system would go on without interruption.

How you spend your time

Having sorted out your main priorities you should analyse in more detail how you spend your time. This will identify time-consuming activities and indicate where there are problems as well as possible solutions to them.

The best way to analyse time is to keep a diary. Do this for a week, or preferably two or three, as one week may not provide a typical picture. Divide the day into 15-minute sections and note down what you did in each period. Against each space, summarize how effectively you spent your time by writing V for valuable, D for doubtful and U for useless. If you want to make more refined judgements give your ratings plusses or minuses. For example:

Time	Task	Rating
9.00– 9.15	Dealt with incoming mail	V
9.15– 9.30	Dealt with incoming mail	V
9.30– 9.45	Discussed admin problem	D
9.45–10.00	Discussed admin problem	D
10.00–10.15	Deputized at meeting	U
10.15–10.30	Deputized at meeting	U
10.30–10.45	Deputized at meeting	U
10.45–11.00	Deputized at meeting	U

At the end of the week analyse your time under the following headings:

- Reading

- Writing
- Dictating
- Telephoning
- Dealing with people (individuals or groups)
- Attending meetings
- Travelling
- Other (specify).

Analyse also the VDU ratings of the worth of each activity under each heading.

This analysis will provide you with the information you need to spot any weaknesses in the way in which you manage time. Use the time-consumer's checklist at the end of this chapter to identify problems and possible remedies.

Organizing yourself

Such an analysis will usually throw up weaknesses in the way you plan your work and establish your priorities. You have to fit the tasks you must complete into the time available to complete them, and get them done in order of importance.

Some people find it difficult, if not impossible, to plan their work ahead. They find that they work best if they have to achieve almost impossible deadlines. Working under pressure concentrates the mind wonderfully, they say. Journalists are a case in point.

But ordinary mortals, who work under a variety of conflicting pressures, cannot rely upon crisis action to get them out of log-jams of work. For most of us it is better to try to minimize the need for working under exceptional pressure by a little attention to the organization of our week or day. At the very least you should use your diary for long-range planning, organize your weekly activities in broad outline and plan each day in some details.

Use the diary

Attempt to leave at least one day a week free of meetings and avoid filling any day with appointments. In other words leave blocks of unallocated time for planning, thinking, reading, writing and dealing with the unexpected.

Weekly organizer

Sit down at the beginning of each week with your diary and plan how you are going to spend your time. Assess each of your projects or tasks and work out priorities. Leave blocks of time for dealing with correspondence and seeing people. Try to preserve one free day, or at least half a day, if it is at all possible.

If it helps you to put everything down on paper, draw up a simple weekly organizer form and record what you intend to do each morning, afternoon and, if it's work, evening.

Daily organizer

At the beginning of each day, consult your diary to check on your plans and commitments. Refer to the previous day's organizer to find out what is outstanding. Inspect your pending tray and in-tray to check on what remains and what has just arrived.

Then write down the things to do:

1. Meetings or interviews
2. Telephone calls
3. Tasks in order of priority:

   A – must be done today
   B – ideally should be done today but could be left till tomorrow
   C – can be dealt with later.

Plan broadly when you are going to fit your A and B priority tasks into the day. Tick off your tasks as they have been completed. Retain the list to consult next day.

You do not need an elaborate form for this purpose. Many successful time managers use a blank sheet of paper, but a simple form which you can use is shown below.

DAILY ORGANIZER   Date ....

Meetings and appointments

Committee/person	Where	When

To telephone

Person	About what	When

To do

Tasks *(in order of priority)*	Priority rating* A, B or C	Approximate timing

* A = must be done today. B = ideally done today. C = later.

Organizing other people

Your first task is to organize yourself, but other people can help, if you can guide and encourage them. They include your secretary, boss, colleagues, subordinates and outside contacts.

Your secretary

A secretary can be a great help: sorting incoming mail into what needs immediate attention and what can be looked at later; management appointments within your guidelines; keeping unwanted callers at bay; intercepting telephone calls; dealing with routine or even semi-routine correspondence; sorting and arranging your papers and the filing system for easy accessibility; getting people on the telephone for you, and so on. The list is almost endless. Every efficient boss will recognize that he depends a lot on an efficient secretary.

Your boss

Your boss can waste your time with over-long meetings, needless interruptions, trivial requests and general nitpicking. Maybe there is nothing you can do about him. But you can learn how to avoid doing the same to your own staff.

On your own behalf you can cultivate the polite art of cutting short tedious discussions. Such formulas as 'I hope you feel we have cleared up this problem – I'll get out of your hair now and get things moving' are useful. And you might be able, subtly, to indicate that he is going to get better performance from you if he leaves you alone. It's difficult but it's worth trying.

Your colleagues

Try to educate them to avoid unnecessary interruptions. Don't anger them by shutting them out when they have something urgent to discuss. But if it can wait, get them to agree to meet you later at a fixed time. Try to avoid indulging in too many pleasantries over the telephone. Be brisk but not brusque.

Your subordinates

You will save a lot of time with your subordinates if you systematically decide what work you can delegate to them. You save even more time if you delegate clearly and spell out how and when you want them to report back.

An 'open door' policy is fine in theory but time wasting in practice. Learn to say no to subordinates who want to see you when you are engaged on more important business. But always give them a time when they can see you and stick to it.

Talking generally to your staff about their job and outside interests can be time well spent if it helps to increase mutual understanding and respect. Allow for this in your schedule and be prepared to extend business discussions into broader matters when the opportunity arises. But don't overdo it.

Outside contacts

The same rules apply to outside contacts. Prevent them from seeing you without an appointment. Ask your secretary to block unwanted telephone calls. Brief your contacts on what you expect from them and when meetings should be arranged.

Time-consumer's checklist

Problem	Possible remedies
TASKS	
1. Work piling up	• Set priorities • Set deadlines • Make realistic time estimates – most people underestimate – add 20 per cent to your first guess.
2. Trying to do too much at once	• Set priorities • Do one thing at a time • Learn to say no to yourself as well as other people
3. Getting involved in too much detail	• Delegate more.

Problem	*Possible remedies*
4. Postponing unpleasant tasks	● Set a timetable and stick to it ● Get unpleasant tasks over with quickly – you will feel better afterwards.
5. Insufficient time to think	● Reserve blocks of time – part of a day or week – for thinking. No paperwork, no interruptions.

PEOPLE

6. Constant interruptions from people calling into your office	● Use secretary to keep unwanted visitors out ● Make appointments and see that people stick to them ● Reserve block times when you are not to be interrupted.
7. Constant telephone interruptions	● Get your secretary to intercept and, where appropriate, divert calls ● State firmly that you will call back when convenient.
8. Too much time spent in conversation	● Decide in advance what you want to achieve when you meet someone, and keep pleasantries to a minimum at the beginning and end ● Concentrate on keeping yourself and the other person to the point – it is too easy to divert or be diverted ● Learn how to end meetings quickly but not too brusquely.

PAPERWORK

9. Flooded with incoming paper	● Get your secretary to sort it into three folders: action now, action later, information ● Take yourself off the circulation list of useless information ● Only ask for written memos and reports when you really need them ● Encourage people to present information and reports clearly and succinctly ● Ask for summaries rather than the whole report ● Take a course in rapid reading.

Problem	Possible remedies
10. Too many letters/memos to write or dictate	• Use the telephone more • Avoid individually typed acknowledgements • Practise writing a succinct 'yes/no/let's talk' on the memos you receive and return them to the sender.
11. Paperwork piling up	• Do it now • Set aside the first half hour or so in the day to deal with urgent correspondence • Leave a period at the end of the day for less urgent reading • Aim to clear at least 90 per cent of the paper on your desk every day.
12. Lost or mislaid papers	• Arrange, or get your secretary to organize, papers on current projects in separate easily accessible folders • Don't hang on to papers in your pending tray – clear it daily • Set up a filing and retrieval system which will enable you to get at papers easily • Ensure that your secretary keeps a day book of correspondence as a last resort method of turning up papers • Keep a tidy desk.
MEETINGS 13. Too much time spent in meetings	• If you set up the meeting: avoid regular meetings when there is nothing that needs saying regularly, review all the meetings you hold and eliminate as many as you can • Get yourself taken off committees if your presence is not essential or if someone else is more appropriate • As chairman: set limits for the duration of meetings and keep to them, cut out waffle and repetition, allow discussion but insist on making progress, have a logical agenda and stick to it

Problem	Possible remedies
	• As a member: don't waffle, don't talk for the sake of talking, don't waste time scoring points or boosting your ego.
TRAVELLING 14. Too much time spent on travelling	• Use the phone or post • Send someone else • Ask yourself, every time you plan to go anywhere, 'is my journey really necessary?' • Plan the quickest way – air, rail or car.

Chapter 50
Trouble shooting

No matter what you do, things will sometimes go wrong. As a manager, you will often be called upon to put them right, or to employ other people to do it for you.

Trouble shooting requires diagnostic ability, to size up the difficulties; know-how, to select the required solution and decide how to implement it; and managerial skill, to put the solution into effect. It can be divided into three main parts:

- Planning the campaign
- Diagnosis
- Cure.

Planning the campaign

Even if you decide to do it yourself without using management consultants, you can still take a leaf out of the consultant's book. A good management consultant will go through the following stages:

- Analysis of the present situation – what has happened and why
- Development of alternative solutions to the problem
- Decision as to the preferred solution, stating the costs and benefits of implementing it
- Defining a method of proceeding – how and over what time-scale should the solution be implemented, who does it and with what resources. If a staged implementation is preferred, the stages will be defined and a programme worked out.

The most important thing to do at the planning stage is to define the problem, clarify objectives and terms of reference. A problem defined is a problem half solved. And it is the difficult half. The rest should follow quite naturally if an analytical approach is adopted.

Once you know what the problem is you can define what you want done and prepare terms of reference for those who are conducting the investigation, including yourself. These should set out the problem, how and by whom it is to be tackled, what is to be achieved and by when. All those concerned in the exercise should know what these terms of reference are.

The next step is to programme the trouble-shooting assignment. Four things need to be decided: the information you need, where you get it from, how you obtain it and who gets it. Draw up lists of facts required and the people who can supply them. Remember you will have to deal with opinion as well as fact; all data are subject to interpretation. List those who are likely to understand what has happened and why; those who might have good ideas about what to do next.

Then draw up your programme. Give notice that you require information. Warn people in plenty of time that you want to discuss particular points with them and that you expect them to have thought about the subject *and* have supporting evidence to hand.

Diagnosis

Diagnosis means finding out *what* is happening – the symptom – and then digging to establish *why* it is happening – the cause. There may be a mass of evidence. The skilled diagnostician dissects the facts, sorts out what is relevant to the problem and refines it all down until he reveals the crucial pieces of information which show the cause of the problem and point to its solution.

Analytical ability – being able to sort the wheat from the chaff – is a key element in diagnosis. It is a matter of getting the facts and then submitting each one to a critical examination, in order to determine which is significant.

During the process of diagnosis you must remain open-minded. You should not allow yourself to have preconceptions or to be over-influenced by anyone's opinion. Listen and observe, but suspend judgement until you can arrange all the facts against all the opinions.

At the same time, do whatever you can to enlist the interest and support of those involved. If you can minimize their natural fears and suspicions, those close to the problem will reveal ideas and facts which might otherwise be concealed from you.

Trouble-shooting checklist

Base your diagnosis on an analysis of the factors likely to have contributed to the problem: people, systems, structure and circumstances.

People

1. Have mistakes been made? If so, why? Is it because staff are inadequate in themselves or is it because they have been badly managed or trained?
2. If management is at fault, was the problem one of system, structure or the managers themselves?
3. If the people doing the job are inadequate why were they selected in the first place?

Systems

4. To what extent are poor systems or procedures to blame for the problem?
5. Is the fault in the systems themselves? Are they badly designed or inappropriate?
6. Or is it the fault of the people who operate or manage the systems?

Structure

7. How far has the organization or management structure contributed to the problem?
8. Do people know what is expected of them?
9. Are activities grouped together logically, so that adequate control can be exercised over them?
10. Are managers and supervisors clear about their responsibilities for maintaining control and do they exercise these responsibilities effectively?

Circumstances

11. To what extent, if any, is the problem a result of circumstances beyond the control of those concerned? For example, have external economic pressures or changing government policies had a detrimental effect?
12. If there have been external pressures, has there been a failure to anticipate or to react quickly enough to them?
13. Have adequate resources (people, money and materials) been made available, and if not, why not?

HOW TO BE AN EVEN BETTER MANAGER

Cure

The diagnosis should point the way to the cure. But this may still mean that you have to evaluate different ways of dealing with the problem. There is seldom 'one best way', only a choice between alternatives. You have to narrow them down until you reach the one which, *on balance*, is better than the others.

Your diagnosis should have established the extent to which the problem is one of people, systems, structure or circumstances. Fallible human beings may well be at the bottom of it. If so, remember not to indulge in indiscriminate criticism. Your job is to be constructive; to build people up, not to destroy them.

Avoid being too theoretical. Take account of circumstances – including the ability of the people available now to deal with the problem, or, if you have doubts, the availability of people from elsewhere who can be deployed effectively. Your recommendation should be practical in the sense that it can be made to work with resources which are readily available and within acceptable time-scales.

You must make clear not only what needs to be done but *how* it is to be done. Assess costs as well as benefits and demonstrate that the benefits outweigh the costs. Resources have to be allocated, a time-scale set and, above all, specific responsibility given to people to get the work done. Your recommendations have to be realistic in the sense that they can be phased in without undue disruption and without spending more time and money than is justified by the results.

Take care when you apportion blame to individuals. Some may clearly be inadequate and have to be replaced. Others may be the victims of poor management, poor training or circumstances beyond their control. Their help may be essential in overcoming the trouble. It is unwise to destroy their confidence or their willingness to help.

Using management consultants

A management consultant has been described, or dismissed, as a man with a briefcase 50 miles from home. Robert Townsend (51) has suggested that consultants are people 'who borrow your watch to tell you what time it is and then walk off with it'.

Calling in consultants in desperation can indeed be an expensive and time-wasting exercise. But they have their uses. They bring experience and expertise in diagnosis. They can act as an extra pair of hands when suitable people are not available from within the organization. And, as a third party, they can sometimes see the wood through the trees and unlock ideas within the company which, sadly, are often inhibited by structural or managerial constraints.

There are, however, a number of rules which you should be aware of when contemplating bringing in consultants.

DO

Get tenders from two or three firms and compare, not only their fees, but their understanding of your problem and the practical suggestions they have on how to tackle it.

Check on the experience of the firm and, most important, of the consultant who is going to carry out the assignment.

Brief the firm very carefully on the terms of reference.

Get a clear statement of the proposed programme, total estimated costs (fees *plus* expenses) and who is actually going to carry out the assignment.

Meet and assess the consultant who is going to do the work.

Insist on regular progress meetings.

Ensure that the outcome of the assignment is a practical proposal which you can implement yourself, or with the minimum of further help.

DON'T

Be bamboozled by a smooth principal who is employed mainly as a salesman.

Go for a big firm simply because it has a good reputation. It may not have the particular expertise you want.

Accept any old consultant who comes along. Many redundant executives have set up as consultants without having a clue about how to do it. There is a lot of skill in being an effective consultant. Check that the firm is a member of the Management Consultants Association or that the principal is a member of the Institute of Management Consultants (for UK-based firms). These provide a guarantee of professional status.

Allow the consultant to change programme without prior consultation.

Leave the consultant to his own devices for too long. Keep in touch. Appoint a member of your staff to liaise or even to work with him.

General bibliography

1 Adair, John, *Action Centred Leadership*, London, McGraw-Hill, 1974.
2 Adair, John, *Effective Leadership*, Aldershot, Gower, 1983.
3 Back, Ken and Kate, *Assertiveness at Work*, Maidenhead, McGraw-Hill, 1982.
4 Barnard, Chester, *Functions of the Executive*, Cambridge, MA, Harvard University Press, 1972, new edition.
5 Beckhard, Richard, *Organizational Development*, Reading, MA, Addison-Wesley, 1969.
6 Beer, Michael, 'Reward systems' from *Managing Human Assets*, edited by Michael Beer, Bert Spector, Paul Laurence, D Quinn Mills and Richard Walton, New York, The Free Press, 1984.
7 Bell, Coral, *The Conventions of Crisis*, Oxford, Oxford University Press, 1971.
8 Burns, T and Stalker, G, *The Management of Innovation*, London, Tavistock, 1957.
9 Croome, Honor, *The Human Problems of Innovation*, London, HMSO, 1960.
10 Deal T E and Kennedy A, *Corporate Cultures*, Reading, MA, Addison-Wesley, 1982.
11 De Bono, Edward, *Lateral Thinking for Managers*, London, McGraw-Hill, 1971.
12 Dixon, Norman F, *On the Psychology of Military Incompetence*, London, Futura, 1979.
13 Drucker, Peter, 'The coming of the new organization', *Harvard Business Review*, January–February 1988.
14 Drucker, Peter, *Innovation and Entrepreneurship*, London, Heinemann, 1985.
15 Drucker, Peter, *The Effective Executive*, London, Heinemann, 1967.
16 Drucker, Peter, *The Practice of Management*, London, Heinemann, 1955.
17 Fiedler, F E, *A Theory of Leadership Effectiveness*, New York, McGraw-Hill, 1967.
18 Follett, Mary Parker, *Dynamic Administration*, London, Pitman, 1941.

19 Gilder, George, *The Spirit of Enterprise*, New York, Simon & Schuster, 1984.
20 Goldsmith, Walter and Clutterbuck, David, *The Winning Streak*, London, Weidenfeld and Nicolson, 1984.
21 Gowers, Sir Ernest, *The Complete Plain Words*, London, HMSO, 1986.
22 Hall, William, 'Survival strategies in a hostile environment', *Harvard Business Review*, March–April 1976.
23 Harvey-Jones, John, *Making It Happen*, Glasgow, Collins, 1988.
24 Heller, Robert, *The Business of Success*, London, Sidgwick & Jackson, 1982.
25 Herzberg, Frederick W, *The Motivation to Work*, New York, Wiley, 1957.
26 Kakabadse, Andrew, *The Politics of Management*, Aldershot, Gower, 1983.
27 Kanter, Rosabeth Moss, *The Change Masters*, London, Allen & Unwin, 1984.
28 Kanter, Rosabeth Moss, *When Giants Learn to Dance*, London, Simon & Schuster, 1989.
29 Katz, D and Kahn, R L, *The Social Psychology of Industry*, New York, Wiley, 1964.
30 Koestler, Arthur, *The Act of Creation*, London, Hutchinson, 1964.
31 Lawler, E E and Porter, L W, *Managerial Attitudes and Performance*, Homewood, IL, Irwin-Dorsey, 1968.
32 Lawrence, P R and Lorsch, J W, *Developing Organizations – Diagnosis and Action*, Reading, MA, Addison-Wesley, 1969.
33 Maslow A H, *Motivation and Personality*, New York, Harper, 1954.
34 McClelland, David, *The Achieving Society*, New York, Van Nostrand, 1961.
35 McGregor, Douglas, 'An uneasy look at performance appraisal', *Harvard Business Review*, May–June 1957.
36 McGregor, Douglas, *The Human Side of Enterprise*, New York, McGraw-Hill, 1960.
37 Minzberg, Henry, *The Nature of Managerial Work*, New York, Harper & Row, 1973.
38 Pascale, Richard and Athos, Anthony, *The Art of Japanese Management*, London, Sidgwick & Jackson, 1986.
39 Pedlar, Mike, Burgoyne, John and Boydell, Tom, *A Manager's Guide to Self-Development*, Maidenhead, McGraw-Hill, 1986.
40 Peter, Lawrence J, *The Peter Principle*, London, Allen & Unwin, 1972.
41 Peters, Thomas, J, *Thriving on Chaos*, London, Macmillan, 1988.
42 Peters, Thomas J and Waterman, Robert, *In Search of Excellence*, London, Harper & Row, 1983.
43 Pinchot, Gifford, III, *Intrapreneuring*, New York, Harper & Row, 1985.
44 Reddin, W J, *Managerial Effectiveness*, London, McGraw-Hill, 1970.
45 Schwartz, Howard and Davies, Stanley, 'Matching corporate culture and business strategy', *MAP Concept Paper*, Cambridge, MA, 1983.
46 Secretan, Lance, *Managerial Moxie*, London, Kogan Page, 1986.
47 Stebbing, Susan, *Thinking to Some Purpose*, Harmondsworth, Penguin Books, 1959.
48 Stewart, Rosemary, *Managers and Their Jobs*, London, Macmillan, 1967.

49 Tannenbaum, R and Schmidt, W H, 'How to chose a leadership pattern', *Harvard Business Review*, May–June 1973.
50 Taylor, Frederick, *Principles of Scientific Management*, New York, Harper, 1911.
51 Townsend, Robert, *Up the Organization*, London, Michael Joseph, 1970.
52 Vroom, Victor H, *Work and Motivation*, New York, John Wiley, 1964.
53 Walton, Richard, 'From control to commitment in the workplace', *Harvard Business Review*, March–April 1985.
54 Woodward, Joan, 'Resistance to change', *Management International Review*, Vol 8, 1968.

Bibliography – management texts

Armstrong, Michael, *A Handbook of Management Techniques*, London, Kogan Page, 1986.

Child, John, *Organization: A Gudie to Problems and Practice*, London, Harper & Row, 1984, revised edition.

Drucker, Peter, *The Effective Executive*, London, Heinemann, 1967.

Drucker, Peter, *Managing for Results*, London, Heinemann, 1967.

Drucker, Peter, *The Practice of Management*, London, Heinemann, 1955.

Geneen, Harold, *Managing*, London, Granada, 1985.

Gilder, George, *The Spirit of Enterprise*, New York, Simon & Schuster, 1984.

Handy, Charles, *Understanding Organizations*, Harmondsworth, Penguin Books, 1985.

Harvey-Jones, John, *Making It Happen*, Glasgow, Collins, 1988.

Heller, Robert, *The Naked Manager*, London, Barrie & Jenkins, 1972.

Jay, Antony, *Management and Machiavelli*, London, Hodder & Stoughton, 1967.

Kakabadse, Andrew, *The Politics of Management*, Aldershot, Gower, 1983.

Kanter, Rosabeth Moss, *The Change Masters*, London, Allen & Unwin, 1984.

Kanter, Rosabeth Moss, *When Giants Learn to Dance*, London, Simon & Schuster, 1989.

Lawrence, Peter, *Management in Action*, London, Routledge & Kegan Paul, 1984.

Minzberg, Henry, *The Nature of Managerial Work*, New York, Harper & Row, 1973.

Pascale, Richard and Athos, Anthony, *The Art of Japanese Management*, London, Sidgwick & Jackson, 1986.

Peters, Tom, *Thriving on Chaos*, Excel, 1987.

Peters, Thomas J and Austin, Nancy, *A Passion for Excellence*, London, Collins, 1985.

Peters, Thomas J and Waterman, Robert, *In Search of Excellence*, London, Harper & Row, 1983.

Sloan, Alfred P, *My Years with General Motors*, London, Sidgwick & Jackson, 1986.

Stewart, Rosemary, *The Reality of Management*, London, Heinemann, 1963.
Townsend, Robert, *Up the Organization*, London, Michael Joseph, 1970.

Index

tactics 216–22
trade union 213–14
Norms 78

Objectives 223–6
Organization
    charts 232–4
    design 230–31
    guidelines 231–3
Organization climate 78, 82–3
Organizational effectiveness 223–9
Organizing 73–4

Pascale, Richard 135
Performance management 239
Performance review 239–41
Personal qualities 145–6
Personality 19, 22
Persuading 246–7
Peter principle 147–9
Peters, Tom 11, 12, 17, 135
Planning 73
    managerial 184–8
    strategic 295–300
Policies 248–51
Politics 255–9
Power 252–4
Presentations 260–65
Problem solving 61, 97–8, 266–9
Productivity 66, 176, 270–76
Profit to sales ratio 61
Profits 223, 277–85

Ratio analysis 67–70

Reinforcement 58
Report writing 286–9
Return on capital employed 67–8
Reward system 208
Role ambiguity 14
Role conflict 14

Satisfaction 207
Sloan, A P 37, 267
Speaking 260–65
Standards 241–2
Stewart, Rosemary 17–19
Stock ratios 68–9
Strategic management 290–91
Strategic planning 295–300, 303
Strategy 291–4
Stress management 305–8

Target setting 241
Team building 309–10, 314–15
Teams 312–13
Time management 316–24
Townsend, Robert 25, 135, 234
Training 122–3
Trouble-shooting 325–9

Value analysis 91–2
Values 78, 81–2, 200–203

Woodward, Joan 39

Zero-based budgets 31–2